OXFORD

165701

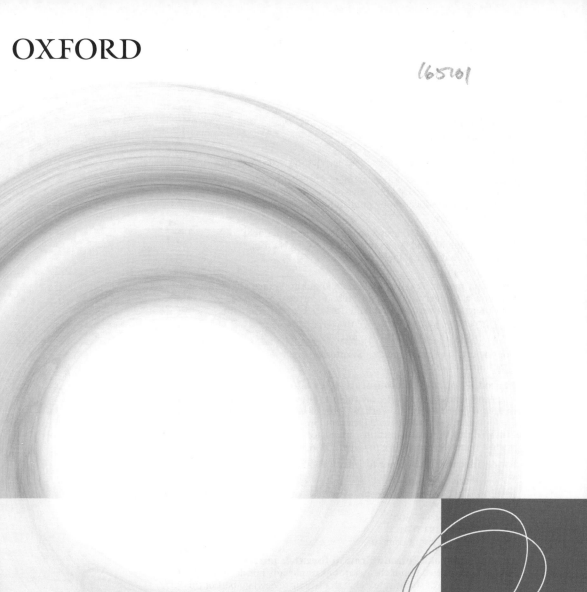

INTERNET AND
E-COMMERCE LAW

D1359995

JAY **FORDER** AND DAN **SVANTESSON**

OXFORD
UNIVERSITY PRESS

253 Normanby Road, South Melbourne, Victoria 3205, Australia

Oxford University Press is a department of the University of Oxford.
It furthers the University's objective of excellence in research,
scholarship, and education by publishing worldwide in

Oxford New York

Auckland Cape Town Dar es Salaam Hong Kong Karachi
Kuala Lumpur Madrid Melbourne Mexico City Nairobi
New Delhi Shanghai Taipei Toronto

With offices in

Argentina Austria Brazil Chile Czech Republic France Greece
Guatemala Hungary Italy Japan Poland Portugal Singapore
South Korea Switzerland Thailand Turkey Ukraine Vietnam

OXFORD is a trademark of Oxford University Press
in the UK and in certain other countries

Copyright © Jay Forder and Dan Svantesson 2008
First published 2008

Reproduction and communication for educational purposes

The Australian *Copyright Act 1968* (the Act) allows a maximum of one chapter
or 10% of the pages of this work, whichever is the greater, to be reproduced
and/or communicated by any educational institution for its educational purposes
provided that the educational institution (or the body that administers it) has
given a remuneration notice to Copyright Agency Limited (CAL) under the Act.

For details of the CAL licence for educational institutions contact:

Copyright Agency Limited
Level 15, 233 Castlereagh Street
Sydney NSW 2000
Telephone: (02) 9394 7600
Facsimile: (02) 9394 7601
E-mail: info@copyright.com.au

Reproduction and communication for other purposes

Except as permitted under the Act (for example, any fair dealing
for the purposes of study, research, criticism or review) no part of this
book may be reproduced, stored in a retrieval system, communicated or
transmitted in any form or by any means without prior written permission.
All enquiries should be made to the publisher at the address above.

National Library of Australia Cataloguing-in-Publication data

Forder, Jay.
Internet and e-commerce law.

Includes index.
ISBN 9780195560534 (pbk.).

1. Internet—Law and legislation—Australia—Textbooks.
2. Electronic commerce—Law and legislation—Australia—
Textbooks. I. Svantesson, Dan Jerker B. II. Title.

343.9409944

Edited by WriteSideUp
Cover and text design by Jo Groud
Typeset by Jo Groud in ITC Stone Serif, 9.5pts/12.5pts
Indexed by Puddingburn
Printed by Ligare Book Printers, Australia

CONTENTS

CHAPTER 06 Consumer Protection 73

CHAPTER 07 Payment Systems 89

TABLE OF CASES

TABLE OF STATUTES/ INTERNATIONAL INSTRUMENTS

COMMONWEALTH

AUSTRALIAN CAPITAL TERRITORY

NEW SOUTH WALES

NORTHERN TERRITORY

QUEENSLAND

SOUTH AUSTRALIA

TASMANIA

VICTORIA

WESTERN AUSTRALIA

ACKNOWLEDGMENTS

One cannot write a book such as this without becoming indebted to many people.

We have enjoyed a wonderfully cooperative relationship with Karen Hildebrandt, Higher Education Publishing Editor at Oxford University Press, and would like to start by thanking her. She has been efficient, enthusiastic and supportive from beginning to end. Trischa Baker's impressive speed and precision as an editor helped keep the project moving quickly. We also thank all the other OUP and associated staff who were involved at various stages. Their experience and efficiency kept the whole project running smoothly.

In researching several chapters, we were aided by some talented research assistants. They were Seamus Byrne, Zachary Kominar, Nicole Murdoch and Kristie O'Brien. We take this opportunity to acknowledge their contribution and thank them for a job well done. Many other students have rewarded and inspired us over the years with their interest and enthusiasm—we thank them also, and we look forward to exploring the issues with many more students in the future.

William Van Caenegem gave us useful feedback on the copyright chapters, and Tim Jay provided valuable comments on the tax chapter, but it would be remiss not to mention the encouragement and support we received from all our colleagues at Bond University.

Finally, we thank Gill Forder and Bianca Svantesson for their support and for patiently reading, commenting on, and re-reading various parts of the book.

The research and writing took place in the first five months of 2007—we have stated the law as we perceived it to be at the end of May 2007.

Jay Forder and Dan Svantesson
July 2007

INTRODUCTION AND SCOPE

OBJECTIVES // BY THE END OF THIS CHAPTER, YOU WILL:

O Understand the structure of this book
and know what topics it covers

O Appreciate the nature of Internet law

O Recognise the recurring themes
in this area of law

WHAT THIS BOOK IS ABOUT

Very few Australians would not have heard of the **Internet** or e-commerce.[1] Many use the Internet regularly,[2] and a large number have bought or sold things on the 'Net'.[3] This book is about legal issues that arise in the course of these activities.

As the title *Internet and E-commerce Law* indicates, the book deals with:

O   legal issues associated with commercial activity on the Internet (e-commerce); and

O   other, non-commercial, legal issues associated with the Internet.

Its focus is on the way Australian law deals with these issues.

Internet
A global network of interconnected computer systems using the suite of protocols known as TCP/IP.

1

Consumer protection
The law that protects the interests of consumers, notably the *Trade Practices Act 1974* (Cth) and similar state legislation such as the various Fair Trading Acts.

Intellectual property rights
A collective term used to describe a number of concepts involving rights closely connected with information, ideas, or other intangibles. Examples include copyright, patents, and trade marks.

Patent
A form of monopoly granted by legislation that gives the owner of the patent the exclusive right to exploit a device, substance, method or process which is new, inventive and useful.

THE RANGE OF TOPICS COVERED

The Internet is remarkable. At the same time, it is remarkably unremarkable because it merely reflects human society. The power of the technology and the range of things we do on the Internet are all attributable to people. Seen from this perspective, it is the human mind and society that are remarkable, not the Internet. However, we still maintain the Internet is itself remarkable. What makes it remarkable is how well it reflects the human mind and society—or, perhaps more accurately, how widely and efficiently it distributes a reflection of the human mind and society.

The Internet's ability to distribute information was well illustrated in 2003 when a boy living with his mother in California found a picture of himself on a 'missing persons' website and thus discovered he had been kidnapped fourteen years earlier.[4] It would be naïve to think the Internet could be purer, or better, than human society in general. We discuss the way the Internet is used to commit crimes, and the way the law responds, in Chapter 16.

The Internet's ability to distribute content has led to its being used for commercial purposes. One can buy an amazing range of things online—from a cure 'for all Diseases, including Cancer and AIDS'[5] to an 'intimate' night with a Swedish supermodel (who in the case in point was not aware she was 'for sale' until a newspaper brought it to her attention).[6]

Commercial issues are dealt with in several different chapters. Chapter 4 deals with formation of online contracts; Chapter 5 deals with authenticating the parties to a transaction; Chapter 6 addresses **consumer protection** issues; Chapter 7 examines Internet payment systems; and Chapter 8 deals with taxation of Internet activity.

---

[1] The Department of Communications, Information Technology and the Arts (DCITA) reports that 77 per cent of Australians over 14 have accessed the Internet at least once: *Online Statistics*, Doc ID 57471, 12 February 2007 (citing Nielsen/Net Ratings), available at <www.dcita.gov.au/communications_for_business/industry_development/statistical_benchmarking/online_statistics> last accessed 24 April 2007.

[2] DCITA reported 70% of Australians over 14 had accessed the Internet in the last month: Ibid.

[3] DCITA reported 64% of Australian Internet users over 14 had bought and sold online: Ibid.

[4] 'Kidnap past learned on Web', *Toronto Sun*, 17 February 2004 <www.canoe.ca/NewsStand/TorontoSun/News/2004/02/17/pf-350646.html> last accessed 20 July 2007.

[5] Dr L Day, *Natural, Alternative Therapies for all Diseases, including Cancer and AIDS* <www.drday.com> last accessed 27 April 2007.

[6] Leif Kasvi, 'Victoria Silvstedt rasar mot sexsajt', *Aftonbladet*, 18 May 2003 <www.aftonbladet.se/vss/nyheter/story/0,2789,308068,00.html> last accessed 27 April 2007.

As far as technology is concerned, commercial interests are often protected by **intellectual property rights** such as copyright, **patents** and **trade marks**. These issues, as well as the **law of confidentiality**, the tort of **passing off** and the regulation of **domain names** are discussed in chapters 11 to 14.

When talking about the way the Internet reflects the human mind and society we cannot avoid concepts of public morality and policy. So far, the most searched event in Internet history has been the Super Bowl during which US singer Janet Jackson's 'wardrobe malfunction' exposed one of her breasts.[7] This raises the difficult line to be drawn between public morality, censorship and free speech. We discuss the way Australian law draws this line in the Internet context in Chapter 15.

Policy raises its head in other areas too. It is ironic that the Internet is often seen as a great tool for anonymity, yet it is increasingly used for surveillance.[8] In a cat-and-mouse game, new ways of tracking Internet activity are circumvented as fast as they are invented. We discuss the way privacy law affects, and is affected by, the Internet and e-commerce in Chapter 9. Another example of the electronic cat-and-mouse game is the ever-growing problem of unsolicited e-mail or **spam**. We deal with this in Chapter 10.

News reports of Internet activities often focus on scandal, but they give an interesting insight into the way the Internet is used. Not only do they give an indication of the extraordinary diversity of Internet activity but they also draw attention to the legal issues that arise. These issues are often described as leading to a new area of law.

IT LAW, CYBERSPACE LAW AND INTERNET LAW

Several terms are used to describe this area of law. We discuss three of them: IT law, cyberspace law and Internet law.

Information technology law (IT law) is the broadest of the three. It covers all legal issues raised by information technology.

Trade mark
A sign or mark used to distinguish one's goods or services from those of another, usually registered under the *Trade Marks Act 1995* (Cth), although the laws of passing off and the *Trade Practices Act 1974* (Cth) may provide some protection for the use of an unregistered mark.

Law of confidentiality
The law relating to breaches of confidentiality having regard to the nature of the sensitive information and any subsequent communication of that information.

Passing off
A cause of action in torts law that involves misrepresenting goods or services as being those of another, or holding out goods or services as having some association or connection with another.

Domain name
A unique name corresponding to one or more IP addresses, used as an Internet address (for example www.svantesson.org).

Spam
Unsolicited e-mail, often sent in bulk.

---

[7] 'Janet's breast makes net history', *BBC NEWS*, 5 February 2004 <http://news.bbc.co.uk/1/hi/technology/3461459.stm> last accessed 27 April 2007.

[8] See for example Michael S Chase and James C Mulvenon, *You've Got Dissent! Chinese Dissident Use of the Internet and Beijing's Counter-Strategies*, RAND Monograph, 2002 <www.rand.org/publications/MR/MR1543> last accessed 20 July 2007.

World Wide Web
A system of making documents and other multimedia resources available to others over the Internet, based on a protocol that supports clickable links between the documents.

IT law includes such diverse technologies as computer software, the **World Wide Web** and EFTPOS (Electronic Funds Transfer at the Point of Sale). It is also increasingly difficult to distinguish communications technology; modern communications technology is arguably just a branch of information technology. IT law would thus also cover satellite communications and digital broadcasting. We conclude that the label IT law is too inexact for our use, as this book is restricted to issues that relate to the Internet.

The terms 'cyberspace law' and 'Internet law' are both more specific than 'IT law'. The word 'cyberspace' comes from the novel *Neuromancer* (1984), written by William Gibson. It referred to a direct brain-to-computer link that gave the user an illusion of moving around in a data 'matrix'—an unreal world.[9] The analogy with being 'on the Net' was appealing.

Although the name 'cyberspace law' gives this field an exciting and mysterious character, 'Internet law' is preferred for our purposes. The reason is that the Internet is a relatively fixed concept, defined by network technology. The concept of cyberspace, on the other hand, is rather abstract and flexible. It might well change with developments in technology, and might mean different things to different people. The term 'Internet' is more limited in scope[10] and more static than cyberspace, and is therefore better suited to our purpose.

Is Internet law a new area of law?

We noted earlier that Internet law is sometimes described as a new area of law. This is an oversimplification. Expressed more accurately, the study of Internet law consists of an examination of:

O   the application of general, non-Internet-specific law to the Internet environment in a non-contentious manner;
O   problem areas where the application of general, non-Internet specific law to the Internet environment does not work well;
O   the development and application of new, Internet-specific laws; and
O   legal gaps where the Internet has raised issues not covered by any law.

The first category is illustrated by situations where privacy law is applied to online publications (see Chapter 9). An example of the second category is where tax laws focusing on the place of consumption are applied to online sales of digitised products such as music or movie files (see Chapter 8). The third category includes laws specifically created to address online issues; we deal with several examples, such as the *Electronic Transactions Act 1999* (Cth) (chapters 4 and 5) and the *Spam Act 2003* (Cth)

---

9   Tim Hiller, *Sourcebook on Public International Law*, London, Cavendish Publishing Ltd, 1998, p 256.
10   A view shared by other commentators, such as Darrel Menthe in 'Jurisdiction in Cyberspace: A Theory of International Spaces' (1998) 4 *Mich Telecomm & Tech L Rev* 69.

(Chapter 10). The final category covers areas where law has not yet caught up with technology. An example is the question whether software can appropriately be classed as goods (Chapter 6).

The recurring themes of Internet law

Certain themes recur throughout this book—we have already hinted at some of them. Having an understanding, or at least an awareness, of these themes will assist the reader's comprehension of the issues being discussed.

First, law struggles to keep up with technological development. This has undesirable consequences where for example particular behaviour is lawful simply because the legislators have not had time to make it unlawful. At the same time, the law cannot be expected to predict technology's development path. Consequently, it is understandable that law is to a degree reactive, rather than proactive.

Second, many lawyers struggle to understand the technology. While the fact that law cannot keep up may be something we simply have to live with, this should not be an excuse for the legal profession. The unfortunate truth is that many, including judges, academics, solicitors and barristers, simply do not have sufficient understanding to deal with the legal challenges in an informed way. There is a lot of truth in the following observation:

> Judges and legislators faced with adapting existing legal standards to the novel environment of cyberspace struggle with terms and concepts that the average [...] five-year-old tosses about with breezy familiarity.[11]

A third theme is that our society is increasingly globalised—our thinking is no longer focused on our immediate surroundings to the exclusion of the bigger picture. In the Internet context, when deciding what newspaper to read, or where to buy CDs, we consider sources from all over the world. Globalisation might have occurred to some degree even without the Internet, but there is little doubt that the Internet encourages a global outlook in ways that were not previously possible. The Internet is an international medium, and this has implications for the way a country can regulate Internet activity. If Australia were to ban certain online activity, this would have little impact if the activity continued to take place outside Australia, and Australians could continue to access and participate in it over the Internet. In many areas of Internet and e-commerce law, international cooperation is the only truly effective way forward. These issues are discussed in Chapter 3.

A fourth theme is that the Internet and e-commerce have had dramatic growth patterns. However, neither the Internet generally, nor e-commerce in particular, has reached its growth potential. The main reason is that many businesses as well as **consumers** fear the risks involved. Their concerns may relate

Consumer
For the purposes of the *Trade Practices Act* in Commonwealth law and Fair Trading legislation in state law, someone who purchases goods or services for personal, domestic or household use, or costing less than $40 000.

---

[11]   *American Libraries Association v Pataki*, 969 F Supp 160, 170 (SDNY, 1997) (Preska J).

to fraud, privacy, validity of e-contracts and issues that arise from the international nature of Internet interactions. The question for the law is how it can help inspire confidence in the Internet so it achieves its potential.

CONCLUDING REMARKS

We sincerely hope you will find this book interesting and accessible. It is written in plain English, and avoids legal and technical jargon. Terms that may require explanation are defined in the margin notes, and also in the glossary at the end of the book.

In writing the book we have aimed to create a resource that is suitable regardless of the reader's background. We have assumed no prior technical or legal knowledge, so it should be useful to students in business, information technology, law or any other field of study. To that end, Chapter 2 provides an introduction both to the legal system and to relevant technology.

We anticipate that some students—particularly law students at an advanced stage of their studies—might require more depth than the analysis we provide. For them, our treatment should be a useful and easy-to-read starting point, to be supplemented by journal articles or other readings. This has the added advantage that supplementary reading can be used to highlight new developments or changes in the law. Our tips for further reading at the end of each chapter should be helpful here. We start with a tip at the end of this chapter about accessing law online.

We wish you good luck with your study of Internet and e-commerce law.

Accessing law online

We have chosen not to include copies of legislation and cases in appendices at the end of this book. This is not because we wish to discourage you from reading them. It is rather that we wish to encourage you to use online sources. Besides being appropriate when studying Internet law, online sources are also easy to access; easy to search; easy to copy when you want to quote the exact words used; and likely to be up-to-date with new material or amendments.

Here are some good places to start:

○   Australasian Legal Information Institute (AustLII): <www.austlii.edu.au> for access to cases, legislation and other information, including links to similar resources in other countries;

○   Australian Parliamentary Library site, with information and links to other relevant sites: <www.aph.gov.au/library/intguide/law/auslaw.htm>

○   The access point for all Australian government sites: <www.gov.au>

Review questions for this chapter can be found on the book's Online Resource Centre at www.oup.com.au/orc/fordersvantesson.

THE INTERNET AND THE LEGAL SYSTEM

OBJECTIVES // BY THE END OF THIS CHAPTER, YOU WILL:

○ Be able to explain the development of the Internet and the way it works

○ Understand why the Internet is not managed by a single organisation, and be able to describe the two main worldwide organisations that look after its technical operations

○ Be able to describe early use of the Internet, and the development of e-commerce

○ Have an overview of the nature and development of civil and common law legal systems

○ Have a basic understanding of the Australian legal system and its main features

WHAT THIS CHAPTER IS ABOUT

As we noted in the previous chapter, the Internet has become so pervasive that most readers will be familiar with it. Descriptions of its development abound, not least on the Internet itself. It will be useful, however, to give a brief description of its development here so we can assume a basic understanding in the remainder of this book. We provide an overview of how the Internet developed, how it is managed, and what it is used for.

In the remainder of the book we will also need to assume a basic understanding of what law is and the way legal systems operate. We cover this background knowledge in the second part of this chapter, describing different types of legal system, and introducing the Australian system.

TCP/IP protocol
Technically a suite of
protocols that implement a
packet switched network
and have become the
standard for data trans-
missions over the Internet.
The main protocols are the
Transmission Control
Protocol (TCP) and the
Internet Protocol (IP).

DARPA
Defense Advanced Research
Projects Agency (originally
ARPA, renamed twice, now
DARPA again), a research
body set up by the US
Department of Defense in
1957. See also *ARPANET*.

ARPANET
Advanced Research Projects
Agency Network (see also
DARPA). In 1969 DARPA
launched the wide-area
network from which the
Internet evolved.

Packet switching
A communication system
that divides messages into
packets of data and sends
each packet separately, to
be reassembled at their
destination.

Internet Protocol (IP)
The protocol that ensures
that packets of data arrive
at the correct network
destination.

THE INTERNET

Background

The word 'internet' is a contraction of 'inter-network'. It means a network of computer networks, or a number of networks joined to each other, enabling each computer to communicate with other computers on the network. In this book we follow the convention of using internet with a lowercase 'i' to refer to the general concept of a network of networks, and with a capital 'I' to refer to the specific worldwide network operating under the **TCP/IP protocol**—which we explain shortly.

Origin and design

The origin of the Internet is usually traced to a network developed by the Defense Advanced Research Projects Agency (**DARPA**—at the time called ARPA) in 1969. Known as **ARPANET**, it connected the US Government's military defence computers and networks across the country. It was deliberately designed to be decentralised and self-maintaining, so that communications could get through without human intervention even if part of the network was damaged during war.

Two central ideas made this possible. The first was reasonably obvious—multiple links were encouraged between networks, with routers controlling and directing traffic at each major network juncture or access point (node). The second was an innovative idea that was not so obvious. Unlike a telephone network, which requires an electronic circuit to be maintained for the duration of the call, ARPANET depended on '**packet switching**'. All communications are divided into small packets of data and sent independently to their destination. Each packet carries its destination address in a header. When the packets reach their destination, they are reassembled in the correct order to reconstitute the message. While all packets often travel along the same route, this is not a requirement. If one part of the network becomes overloaded or damaged, the packets can easily be directed along different routes to the same destination. If any packets are delayed or corrupted in transit, a request is sent back asking for them to be retransmitted. All this happens in seconds or fractions of a second. The standard that handles the breaking-up and reassembly of packets is known as the Transmission Control Protocol (TCP); and the one that ensures the packets arrive at their destination is known as the **Internet Protocol (IP)**. This TCP/IP protocol, updated and improved over the years, still stands behind the Internet as we know it.

It is ironic that, despite initially being developed by the military, the network was not designed to protect the security of messages or packets. Traffic passes through any number of routers under the control of unknown strangers, and each inspects the header of the packet to determine where to send it next. This is why the Internet is described as an open network. It raises interesting **authentication** and security issues, which we discuss in Chapter 5.

Development

Several academics involved in research for the US military had access to ARPANET. They found the sharing of files and ease of communication extremely useful, and word began to spread. ARPANET itself eventually split into a purely military network (MILNET) and a more general network that was gradually absorbed into the US National Science Foundation network, **NSFNET**. During the 1970s and early 1980s other similar networks were formed around the world, such as JANET (the Joint Academic Network in the United Kingdom) and AARNET (the Australian Academic and Research Network).

Non-academic usage also began to develop in the 1980s with the formation of free community networks such as the Cleveland Free-Net Community Computer System in 1986. Commercial networks such as America Online, CompuServe and Prodigy attracted subscribers by offering their own network services and information. Other networks were established to serve particular methods of communicating, such as USENET (in which e-mail-like messages are distributed to newsgroups for open discussion) and FIDONET (a bulletin board system popular with computer hobbyists for accessing messages and sharing files). While some of these networks did not originally use the TCP/IP protocol, during the 1980s and 1990s they began to adopt it and link to each other. This network of networks grew rapidly and developed into the Internet.

One development that made the Internet easier to use was the domain name system, introduced in 1984. While **IP numbers** are still the basis of each computer's unique address on the Internet, humans tend to find it easier to remember and deal with addresses in the form of words. The Domain Name System (DNS) allows names to be registered for host computers. The names are recorded in a large **database** hosted at several duplicate sites around the world. When a user requests information from a computer by specifying a domain name, the request looks up the name in a copy of the database, and finds the relevant IP number. The speed with which this is

Authentication
A process by which you verify whether someone or something is genuine or valid.

NSFNET
A network established in 1986 by the US National Science Foundation (NSF) that replaced ARPANET as the foundation of the Internet.

IP number
The address used by the Internet protocol to identify a computer or other network destination.

Database
A structured collection of records or data, stored in a way that makes it easy to access the information.

accomplished means it is virtually unnoticeable to the user. We discuss the domain name system and the legal issues it raises in Chapter 13.

Management

Given our interest in Internet law, it would be useful to know who controls or manages the Internet, and whether they have authority to make Internet-wide regulations. The answer is negative—there is no single entity with the necessary degree of control or authority. Local computers and networks are owned and controlled by individuals and organisations. The telephone lines, cables and satellites that connect these networks are also owned by identifiable organisations, businesses or governments. If some of these important players withdrew and removed their networks or cables, the Internet might not be as large, quick or useful as it would otherwise be. But as long as a sufficient number of networks continue to connect to each other using the standard **protocol**, the Internet will continue to exist. It is an inspiring example of cooperation on a global scale.

While no single entity controls or manages the Internet, some important organisations play crucial roles in making the Internet work the way it does. The two most important are **ICANN** and **ISOC**. The Internet Corporation for Assigned Names and Numbers (ICANN) was formed in 1998 with specific responsibility for administering the Internet's system of unique identifiers—both the IP number system and the domain name system (DNS).[1] The Internet Society (ISOC) is an umbrella organisation, formed in 1992, to coordinate the work of the technical committees responsible for the protocols underlying the Internet.[2] These technical committees include the Internet Architecture Board (IAB) and the Internet Engineering Task Force (IETF), which operate the well-known RFC (referred for comment) system that publicises any proposed changes and invites comment. Both ICANN and ISOC are international democratic organisations, with participation from hundreds of countries; decisions are made only after a consensus is reached. Neither organisation has authority to make or enforce legal rules.

One further comment about the role of technology as a regulator of human activity deserves mention. In 1999 Lawrence Lessig, a professor of law at Stanford University, suggested that at least in the early stages of development, the design of Internet technology itself would largely govern how people could or would use it—and in a sense this was a means of control.[3] He

Protocol
A standard or agreed way of doing something.

ICANN
Internet Corporation for Assigned Names and Numbers. An international, non-profit organisation established in 1998 to organise the domain name and IP number systems (including the accreditation of domain name registrars).

ISOC
The Internet Society, formed in 1992 by Internet experts and enthusiasts to oversee administration of the Internet.

---

[1]   See *ICANN Information*, 2007, ICANN <www.icann.org/general> last accessed 20 July 2007.
[2]   See *All About the Internet Society*, 2006, ISOC <www.isoc.org/isoc> last accessed 30 January 2007.

illustrated this argument by showing how the ease of copying on the Internet changes the power of law to protect against copyright infringement. On the other hand, he suggested that if every aspect of copying could be controlled by technology, there would no longer be a need for the concept of 'fair use' in copyright law.[4] The value of Lessig's writing is that it forces us to recognise the interesting interrelationship between technology and law. While technology affects what needs to be regulated and how it can be regulated, law might also shape the way technology develops.

INTERNET USAGE

We mentioned that one of the first uses of the network was as a method of communication between academics working on projects for the US military. What else is the Internet used for?

Early protocols

Use of any network requires an agreed way of doing things, so the remote devices can understand each other (known as a protocol). We offer a brief description of some of the early protocols to illustrate the range of activities that soon developed:

○   The file transfer protocol (FTP) handles the transfer of files between devices.

○   The simple mail transfer protocol (SMTP) ensures the proper recognition and display of text messages (such as e-mail).

○   Telnet allows a user to log on and enter commands on a machine from a remote computer or terminal. Before the Web developed, many library catalogues were searchable using Telnet.

○   USENET (from 'User's Network') established newsgroups—public discussion forums, categorised by interest group. Users 'post' messages, which are displayed for all to see, and others reply, creating a 'thread' of discussion on a given topic. To read messages, users access the newsgroup of their choice.

○   Listserv is an automated manager of mailing lists that allows a user to subscribe to a particular list. Any messages sent to the list are automatically distributed to all subscribers.

○   IRC (Internet Relay Chat) enables real-time interaction. When a user types a message, it is immediately copied to all others participating in the 'chat', allowing them to reply in a simulated live discussion.

---

[3]   L Lessig, *Code and Other Laws of Cyberspace*, Basic Books, New York, 1999: see <http://code-is-law.org> last accessed 20 July 2007. Lessig actually argues that four factors regulate the Internet: law, norms, market, and architecture.

[4]   He developed these ideas further in L Lessig, *The Future of Ideas: The Fate of the Commons in a Connected World*, Vintage Books, New York, 2002. He also invited free comment on the ideas in his first book (see <http://codebook.jot.com/WikiHome>) and incorporated these in a new edition, *Code: Version 2.0*, Basic Books, New York, 2006.

The Web and electronic commerce

The catalyst for the biggest leap in Internet use occurred in 1991. The US National Science Foundation withdrew its prohibition on using its network (NSFNET) for commercial purposes; in the same year the European Council for Nuclear Research (CERN) released specifications for the World Wide Web (the Web). Until 1991 the Internet was a bland, text-dominated environment inhabited mostly by 'computer geeks'. The Web changed it into a non-threatening, easy-to-use, point-and-click environment suited to the average person. The web protocol[5] supports graphics, audio, video and animation, thus allowing a rich interactive environment. The suitability of this environment for commercial purposes was fairly obvious. Information about one's products or services could be presented attractively; it was available 24 hours a day, was accessible from anywhere in the world, and could be updated quickly and easily.

The client/server model—which is the basis of the web protocol—deserves further mention because of its relevance to several legal issues we discuss in later chapters. Someone wishing to make information available creates a website (a collection of pages or other resources, such as audio or video clips) and places it on a computer that acts as a 'server'. This is known as 'uploading' the information. Other users—the 'clients'—then access this information (download it) using browser software. Every resource on a website has a unique address (known as a Uniform Resource Locator or **URL**)—but it is generally not necessary for users to know the address, because resources can be connected to each other, or to other resources anywhere else on the Web, by clickable **hyperlinks**. By clicking on a link or typing a URL the user causes the browser software to send a request to the relevant host server for a copy of the resource identified by the link or URL. The server sends a copy back; the copy is then displayed or otherwise activated on the user's machine. The process is often described as 'reactive'—the web server reacts to the actions of the web browser.

This simple description of the client/server model used to disseminate information does not begin to describe the more advanced ways the Web is used. Servers can be set up to run programs in response to a user's click.[6] Web pages can also contain small programs (scripts or applets) that will run on the *client's* machine when downloaded. Both these techniques increase the sophistication and interactivity possible on the Internet. For example in an e-commerce environment a program on the host server might analyse the user's request for a product, query the product database, verify that sufficient quantities are in stock, generate a message confirming receipt of the order and initiate dispatch of the product.

URL
A uniform resource locator identifies an Internet resource and provides a method of locating it; often also used in the sense of a web address.

Hyperlink
An electronic reference to another document or web page that can be activated by clicking on it with a pointing device such as a mouse.

---

[5] The Hypertext Transfer Protocol (http—an abbreviation often seen as part of a web address).

[6] Known as a common gateway interface (cgi).

The size of the Internet

It is difficult to work out the size of the Internet. Most estimates involve counting the number of host servers (computers with registered IP addresses), but we could equally try to measure the number of registered domain names, the number of actual users, or the volume of data being transferred. Whichever way we measure, the growth has been impressive. Four hosts were operating in 1969; this grew to 188 hosts in 1979, and 159 000 hosts by 1989. Once restrictions on commercial use were lifted in 1991 and the Web developed, it grew even more quickly. There were 56 210 000 hosts in 1999; by July 2006 there were 439 286 364.[7]

As for e-commerce, the growth appears to have been steady rather than exceptional. The Australian Bureau of Statistics puts the value of orders received over the Internet by Australian businesses during 2004–05 at $40 billion.[8] In 2001–02 it was $11 billion, representing a growth of 263 per cent over three years.

The growth of the Internet and its technologies, combined with increasing commercial use, will continue to raise many legal issues. You will get a sense of the breadth of these issues by glancing through the table of contents of this book. To engage with these issues, a basic understanding of the nature of legal systems, and the Australian legal system in particular, is necessary.

LAW AND LEGAL SYSTEMS

This section provides an overview of the different types of legal system, with an emphasis on the development of the Australian legal system. It will be helpful for those without prior legal knowledge.

Legal systems

Modern societies are complex. They require rules if they are to operate efficiently. A set of rules on its own, however, would not suffice—the rules need to be enforced. The combination of a set of rules with a method of enforcing them is what we mean by a 'legal system'.

Legal systems, like the societies they serve, have always operated within recognised geographic boundaries. This gives rise to the concept of **jurisdiction**.[9] A legal system is therefore

Jurisdiction
A geographical area within which certain laws operate (for example a country). See the glossary for other meanings.

---

[7] For these figures and other interesting charts showing the growth of the Internet, see Robert H Zakon, *Hobbes' Internet Timeline* <www.zakon.org/robert/internet/timeline/Growth> last accessed 30 January 2007.

[8] Australian Bureau of Statistics, 2004–2005 Business Use of Information Technology, Ref 8129.0 available at <www.ausstats.abs.gov.au> last accessed 30 January 2007.

[9] The term is discussed in more detail in the next chapter.

Common law
In the context of a legal system, refers to a system strongly based on the doctrine of precedent (like the English system), as opposed to systems based on the interpretation of statutory codes (like the civil law systems of Europe). See the glossary for other meanings.

Civil law
In the context of a legal system, refers to a system based primarily on the interpretation of statutory codes (like the legal systems of much of Europe) as opposed to systems based on the doctrine of precedent (like the English common law system). See the glossary for other meanings.

an instrument of social regulation, consisting of laws—and methods of enforcing them—that operate within recognised boundaries.

The more complex the society, the more detailed and developed the rules need to be. Legal systems develop as a result of changes in society. For example road traffic rules needed to be made more sophisticated when motor vehicles became common. This resulted in more orderly road use, which in turn encouraged more people to use the roads. We are witnessing the same growth in the rules that apply to the Internet, and part of the debate is whether they will encourage or discourage further development and use. To comprehend Australia's approach in developing these rules, and the weight or significance of similar laws in other countries, you will need some understanding of Australia's background and place in the world's legal systems.

Common law and civil law systems

When the term '**common law**' is used to describe a legal system (as in 'Australia has a common law system') it is usually to differentiate it from **civil law** systems.[10] The difference is best understood with some historical background. When French-speaking Normans conquered England in 1066, they developed a unified and strong administrative system in which royal judges travelled to all areas of the kingdom. While the judges did not totally abandon local customs and laws, they began to assimilate them with their own ideas of justice and with the best customs and laws from around the country—a common set of laws for everyone. In a deliberate attempt to unify this law and achieve certainty, judges would draw on, and follow, decisions made by their colleagues. This developed into what we now call the doctrine of precedent—judges are bound to follow a decision made by a more senior court on similar facts. In a sense, this means judges themselves *make* law—or at least senior judges do—since judges in lower courts are bound to follow a senior court's decision.

The same is not true of other European legal systems. This is because many European countries developed written laws. The most influential, the *Code Napoléon*, was introduced in 1804 after Napoléon Bonaparte conquered most of continental Europe. He felt the laws needed to be tidied up and unified, so he introduced codes—collections and restatements of the law—that replaced the previous law.

---

[10]   The term is also used in a slightly different sense to differentiate between the law that developed in the King's courts ('common law') and the Chancellor's courts ('equity') in England. The difference between common law (in this sense) and equity is not of great concern to us here.

When the law is authoritatively stated in a single written document the role of judges inevitably changes. Since the code contains the single ultimate statement of the law, judges merely have to interpret what is written—they do not make law as such. Therefore, in civil law systems, while judges might be persuaded by the interpretation of a fellow judge, they are not bound by an interpretation with which they disagree.

In the modern world the influence of both civil and common law approaches is felt far beyond Europe, due to the colonisation of poorer nations by European powers during the eighteenth and nineteenth centuries. Countries settled or influenced by the British tend to have a common law system based on English law; countries settled or influenced by other major European nations tend to have civil law systems. For this reason, decisions of courts in other British Commonwealth countries, like New Zealand and Canada, tend to have more persuasive weight in Australia than decisions of courts in European countries like Germany or France. As for the USA, its laws are of British origin, and do carry some weight in Australia. But US law has also been shaped by a fiercely independent Congress and Supreme Court, and guided by a strong and enforceable constitution. As a result, its English common law character is no longer as recognisable as it might once have been. On the other hand, the USA's dominant role in the development of the Internet means its laws in this area are better known (and perhaps more likely to be persuasive) than the law of other countries.

Other legal systems

Before leaving our discussion of legal systems we should dispel any notion that common and civil law systems are the only legal systems in the world. There are several different approaches to classifying legal systems, but the topic goes beyond the scope of this book. For our purposes it will suffice to note that other legal systems include those of the Far East (such as Chinese and Japanese law, both of which are influenced to some extent by European civil law), and those based on religious law (such as Islamic and Hindu systems). For want of a better label, we will refer to these as Eastern systems.

Like all legal systems, the Eastern systems reflect the values of their own communities. In this respect, there is sometimes a discernible difference between them and the values shared by civil and common law systems. Examples of values that are not always as strongly reflected in the Eastern systems include:

○ An assumption that there is a democratically elected sovereign power (usually known as a parliament), which can make or change the law, but is answerable to its citizens.

○ A belief in the rule of law—the principle that everyone (including government and public authorities) is equally subject to law, and that the law should be publicly administered in independent courts.

○ A conviction that anyone should be free to practise any religion they wish, but that religious rules of behaviour should be kept separate from national law.

Criminal law
The branch of law that relates to wrongful actions that are prosecuted and punished by the state.

○ A sharp distinction between **criminal law** (action taken on behalf of the state to punish transgressors) and civil law (action taken by private entities to gain compensation or redress from those who have caused them harm).

The borderless nature of the Internet means the rules of the various systems, and the values that underlie them, will come into conflict—the topic of the next chapter.

The Australian legal system

As a result of its colonisation by the United Kingdom in the eighteenth century Australia has a common law system based on English law. The original colony of New South Wales, which had ill-defined borders but comprised most of the eastern half of the continent, was gradually split into five separate colonies.[11] In keeping with English constitutional theory, each acquired English law as it existed at the time the colony was established. Each colony was eventually given its own constitution with wide law-making powers and control over its own affairs through an elected parliament.

In 1901 these states formed a federation known as the Commonwealth of Australia. The federal government was also given control of a number of territories that did not have their own governments. There are now ten such territories, although three of them (the Northern Territory, the Australian Capital Territory and Norfolk Island) have limited self-government arrangements.[12]

Under the federal constitution, control of certain specified topics (known as heads of power) is given exclusively to the federal parliament. Examples include defence, foreign relations, postal services and (notably for our purposes) telecommunications. In other areas, the federal parliament and the state parliaments have power to pass laws (known as concurrent power), but if there is a conflict the federal laws take precedence. In these limited areas, the federal parliament is more powerful than the state parliaments. In all other areas, the states retain their wide powers and the federal parliament has no power at all.

The states and territories still have their own courts, which interpret and apply their laws. There are three tiers:

o   Magistrates' Courts, which deal with the most common criminal offences (traffic infringements, minor assaults, etc) and smaller civil claims between private entities (for example to recover debts).

o   Intermediate courts (District Court or County Court),[13] which hear the majority of serious criminal offences, often with a jury. They also deal with more serious civil claims up to certain monetary limits.

o   Supreme Courts, which deal with the most serious criminal cases and the most important civil claims. Trials are heard by single Supreme Court judges, although the court also sits as a 'bench' of three judges (known as a Full or Appeal Court) to hear appeals from decisions made by lower courts or single judges.

---

[11]   Tasmania (1825), South Australia (1836), Victoria (1850) and Queensland (1856), leaving the remainder as New South Wales. The colony of Western Australia was established separately in 1829.

[12]   The remaining seven territories are Ashmore and Cartier Islands, Australian Antarctic Territory, Christmas Island, Cocos (Keeling) Islands, Coral Sea Islands, Jervis Bay Territory, and the Territory of Heard Island and McDonald Islands.

[13]   Tasmania has no intermediate court.

Laws passed by the federal parliament are interpreted and applied in different courts and tribunals. Tribunals—such as the Administrative Appeals Tribunal and the Copyright Tribunal—hear specialised issues. Other minor matters are heard by the Federal Magistrates' Court. More serious issues are heard by the Federal Court, which is seen as the equivalent of the state Supreme Courts. The Federal Court would, for example, hear cases involving the *Trade Practices Act 1974* (Cth) or intellectual property law. Like the Supreme Courts, it also sits as a bench of three judges to hear appeals.[14]

The most senior court in Australia, the High Court, was created by the Constitution.[15] Its two key roles are to decide cases of special federal significance, such as constitutional challenges to the validity of laws, and to hear appeals from other federal, state and territory courts. It is the most significant court, since under the doctrine of precedent, its decisions will be binding on all other Australian courts. Decisions of the state and territory Supreme Courts will be binding on lower courts within their own jurisdiction; Federal Court decisions will bind lower courts exercising federal jurisdiction.

CONCLUDING REMARKS AND FURTHER READING

In this chapter we have covered basic concepts regarding the Internet, e-commerce and the legal system. We have tried to ensure that all students, no matter what their background, will have the necessary building blocks to understand the discussion in the rest of this book. We recommend further reading to supplement our necessarily brief treatment.

On the history and development of the Internet

The Internet Society's collection of links at <www.isoc.org/internet/history>

Descriptions of the Internet and WWW adopted by the US District Court in *American Civil Liberties Union, et al v Janet Reno, AG of the USA*, 929 F Supp 824 (1996), US District Court for the Eastern District of Pennsylvania, Civil Action No 96–963, 11 June 1996 (usefully reproduced in Yee Fen Lim, *Cyberspace Law: Commentaries and Materials*, 2nd edn, Oxford University Press, Melbourne, 2007)

R Clarke, *Origins and Nature of the Internet in Australia*, Xamax Consultancy Ltd <www.anu.edu.au/people/Roger.Clarke/II/OzI04.html>

R Clarke, *A Primer on Internet Technology*, Xamax Consultancy Ltd <www.anu.edu.au/people/Roger.Clarke/II/IPrimer.html>

On the Australian legal system

R Chisholm and G Nettheim, *Understanding Law*, 6th edn, LexisNexis–Butterworths, Sydney, 2002

---

[14]   For a description of the various Federal courts and tribunals, see the Federal Government website at <www.australia.gov.au/147> last accessed 3 June 2007.
[15]   *Commonwealth of Australia Constitution Act*, s 71.

On using analogy and metaphor in legal reasoning about the Internet

D Rowland, 'Conceptual views of a virtual world', Ch 19 in R Polcak, M Skop and
  D Smahel (eds), *Cyberspace 2005* (Conference proceedings), Masaryk University, 2006,
  p 179

Review questions for this chapter can be found on the book's Online Resource Centre
at www.oup.com.au/orc/fordersvantesson.

INTERNATIONAL LEGAL ASPECTS

OBJECTIVES // BY THE END OF THIS CHAPTER, YOU WILL:

O Be able to recognise the legal consequences of the Internet's international nature

O Be familiar with, and understand the connection between, the separate but interrelated issues of jurisdiction, choice of law, declining jurisdiction and recognition and enforcement of judgments

WHAT THIS CHAPTER IS ABOUT

As noted in Chapter 2, the Internet is international. One key consequence is that many, if not all, areas of Internet and e-commerce law involve international aspects. This chapter examines these international aspects to create a foundation for the rest of the book. When studying other chapters you should bear in mind the issues discussed here.

Here we explain the meaning of international law and clarify some of the slightly different meanings of the term 'jurisdiction'. We discuss the four different issues typically raised by jurisdiction problems: personal jurisdiction, choice of law, declining jurisdiction, and recognising and enforcing judgments. We consider examples of the way these rules are applied to the Internet, and describe technological developments that might ease the difficulties.

Private international law
Also known as 'conflict of laws', the area of law concerned with jurisdiction, choice of law, declining jurisdiction and recognition and enforcement of foreign judgments.

Convention
See *Treaty*.

Model code
A 'best practice' model typically suggested by an international organisation, aimed at harmonising and reforming an area of law.

Cybercrime
Crimes facilitated or aided by computing devices or the Internet, or committed where a computer or network is a target.

Conflict of laws
See 'private international law'.

WHAT IS INTERNATIONAL LAW?

So what do we mean when we speak of the international aspects of Internet and e-commerce law? The international aspects of virtually any area of law can be divided into four different areas of interest:

○   international instruments;
○   comparative law;
○   public international law; and
○   **private international law**.

International instruments are documents that reflect agreements between nations. They include **conventions**, treaties and **model codes** or laws. Several international instruments are relevant to Internet and e-commerce law, but we will not discuss them here—they are discussed throughout the text in their respective chapters. For example the Council of Europe's *Convention on Cybercrime* is discussed in the chapter addressing Internet and e-commerce crime (Chapter 16).

Comparative law focuses on the way different legal systems deal with different legal issues. While the area of Internet and e-commerce law is a fascinating lens to look through in a comparative context, this book does not aim to provide a comparative examination of Internet and e-commerce law. While some comparisons are made when dealing with particular topics, we focus on the principles applicable in Australia.

The third area of interest is public international law. This is mainly concerned with regulation of relationships between different nation-states. Thus, a typical situation in which public international law would be relevant is where two nation-states are in dispute about fishing rights in a particular body of water.

In recent years, a wider role for public international law has been recognised. In particular, establishment of various war crimes tribunals, and the increased impact of human rights law, have highlighted how public inter-national law also operates in the context of the relationship between states and individuals. Public international law is relevant to some of the chapters of this book, such as Chapter 16 on crime, and is discussed in those chapters.

This chapter focuses on the fourth area of interest. Private international law (or **conflict of laws** as it is also known in common law countries) relates to disputes between private parties. It is of crucial importance in most areas of law discussed in this book. The following brief example is illustrative.

EXAMPLE

Lou, who lives in Queensland, visits a website operated by a Swedish company but hosted on a server located in Belgium. From that website Lou orders a pair of clog shoes. Having received the order, the Swedish company contacts its manufacturing and distributions plant in Taiwan and the clogs are delivered to Lou via the post. Imagine that instead of getting a proper pair Lou receives two left shoes and the Swedish company refuses to rectify the mistake.

If Lou was considering taking the matter to court, perhaps the first question he would ask is in which country's court he should bring the action. Can he sue the Swedish company in a Queensland court, or does he have to travel to Sweden to bring action in a Swedish court? Or, can he perhaps take action in Belgium, as the server was located there—or even in Taiwan, as that is the place from which the shoes were posted? In legal terms, this is referred to as the question of *jurisdiction*. If for example Lou can bring his action in a Queensland court, it is said that the Queensland court has jurisdiction to hear the matter.

It is common for more than one court to be able to claim jurisdiction over a particular dispute. In the example above, it is possible that both a Swedish and a Queensland court could claim jurisdiction, and Lou could thus choose the country in which he wished to sue. We will discuss this and other slightly different meanings of jurisdiction in more detail below.

Once it has been established in which court the dispute is to be heard, that court would apply its *choice of law* rules to identify which country's law should be applied. For example an Australian court might apply the law of a foreign country. This could occur where the parties have agreed that a foreign law should be used to determine disputes arising as a consequence of a contract between them. The details of the Australian choice of law rules are examined below.

Having reached this stage, we know that a particular court can claim jurisdiction over the dispute, and which country's law the court will apply. However, even where a court *can* claim jurisdiction, the particular circumstances of the case may persuade a court to *decline to exercise jurisdiction*. This discretion might surprise many non-lawyers and is discussed in more detail below.

Assuming that the court chosen by Lou does not decline to exercise jurisdiction, it will apply the law identified by the choice of law rules and finally hand down a judgment. This takes us to the fourth and final element of private international law—recognition and enforcement. Let us say that Lou sued in a Queensland court and the court, having decided the dispute under Queensland law, handed down a judgment in Lou's favour. What would Lou do then? Unless the judgment can be recognised and enforced at a place where the Swedish company has assets, the judgment is virtually worthless. Swedish courts rarely, if ever, enforce foreign judgments, so Lou could not take his Queensland judgment there. If, however, the Swedish company had assets elsewhere—say in Hong Kong—and the courts there recognised the judgment, then Lou could enforce it in Hong Kong. The importance of recognition and enforcement is discussed in more detail below.

Before studying the issues of jurisdiction, choice of law, declining jurisdiction and recognition and enforcement in more detail, two more observations need to be made. First, the rules of private international law are part of each state's domestic law. Each state has its own rules of private international law—Australia has rules that might be different from those of other countries. Unlike the rules of public international law, the rules of private international law are not international in this narrow sense. However, a state may choose to adopt, as its rules of private international law, rules established by other states or some external organisation. For example a variety of rules of private international law in member states of the European Union stem from European Union law. Further, Australia has signed several international instruments that affect Australia's rules of private international law. One such example is the Hague Convention of 2 October 1973 on the Recognition and Enforcement of Decisions relating to Maintenance Obligations.

The second thing to note at this initial stage is that the rules of private international law are procedural rather than substantive. Substantive rules tell you what your rights are; procedural rules tell you how to enforce them. When copyright prevents others from copying your software without permission, this is a substantive right. To enforce that right you will need to know how to adduce (bring forward) evidence to the right court to get an **injunction**. These are procedural rules. Courts always apply their own procedural rules. On the other hand, as seen above, it is possible that the choice of law rules point to the application of a foreign country's **substantive law**.

Injunction
A court order whereby a party is required to do, or to refrain from doing, an act.

Substantive law
Law that tells you what your rights and duties are, as opposed to procedural law, which tells you how to enforce these rights.

Immovable property
Legal term referring to land and/or any permanent feature or structure above or below the surface.

Jurisdiction

One meaning of the term 'jurisdiction' was introduced above: that is, a court's power to hear a particular dispute. However, when looked at in more detail it becomes clear that this term has at least two different meanings. Its second meaning can be illustrated by the following sentence: 'An Australian court cannot exercise *jurisdiction* over **immovable property** located in another *jurisdiction*.' When first mentioned in this sentence, the term has the meaning previously discussed. However, when used the second time, it refers to what we might call a 'law area' such as a country or a state. Thus, expressed differently, the sentence could be: 'An Australian court does not have the power to hear a dispute over immovable property located in another law area (such as another country).'

Once these two different meanings are understood, we can consider how a court determines whether it has power to hear a dispute. A court's power may be limited by reference to the subject-matter of the dispute (known as subject-matter jurisdiction) or by reference to the parties involved in the dispute (personal jurisdiction).

Subject-matter jurisdiction refers to a court's jurisdiction to adjudicate a particular type of dispute. For example the Family Court does not have power to hear a patent dispute—the subject matter is outside its jurisdiction. A court's subject-matter jurisdiction is usually defined at the time it is created, and is largely uncontroversial. We do not need to discuss it further.

The more interesting form of jurisdiction for our purposes is personal jurisdiction, or *in personam* jurisdiction as it is also known. Under Australian law, and that of many other common law countries, the grounds upon which a court can claim personal jurisdiction can be grouped into three categories:

○   presence within the law area;
○   submission to the court's power; or
○   as allowed under relevant court rules.

The first two categories are relatively uncomplicated. Claiming jurisdiction (power to hear a dispute) over a defendant physically present in the relevant jurisdiction (law area) is common in all Australian states and territories[1] as well as other countries. Interestingly, an Australian court can claim jurisdiction on this basis whether or not the defendant is permanently located in the law area. Even a temporary visitor on holiday could be subject to the relevant jurisdiction—and this would surprise people from a civil law background. However, as discussed below, the negative impact of this is limited somewhat because a court could well decline to exercise its jurisdiction in these circumstances.

As for the second category, an Australian court can claim jurisdiction over a defendant that has submitted to its jurisdiction.[2] This would be the case where a party defends a legal action against it without raising any objections as to the issue of jurisdiction.

Jurisdiction based on the third category gives rise to the most disputes, and is of particular interest to us. While the finer details vary among the Australian states and territories, the main features are shared. A detailed examination of all the different grounds upon which jurisdiction may be founded within this category is beyond the scope of this book,[3] but the most relevant are listed. An Australian court can claim personal jurisdiction over a person located outside Australia where:

Domicile
The place of a person's permanent residence for legal purposes.

○   the defendant is **domiciled** or ordinarily resident in the relevant jurisdiction;[4]

---

[1]   P Nygh and M Davies, *Conflict of Laws in Australia*, 7th edn, Butterworths, Sydney, 2002, pp 46–47, making reference to *Evers v Firth* (1987) 10 NSWLR 22 and *Perrett v Robinson* [1985] 1 Qd R 83.

[2]   Nygh and Davies, pp 76–77. This jurisdictional ground is also available in all Australian states and territories.

[3]   Readers might refer to the relevant legislation: For NSW, see *Uniform Civil Procedure Rules 2005* (NSW); for Queensland see *Uniform Civil Procedure Rules 1999* (Qld); for NT see *Rules of the Supreme Court 1996* (NT); for WA see *Rules of the Supreme Court 1971* (WA); for SA see *Supreme Court Rules 1987* (SA); for Victoria see *General Rules of Procedure in Civil Proceedings 1996* (Vic); and for ACT see *Supreme Court Rules 1937* (ACT).

[4]   P Nygh and M Davies, *Conflict of Laws in Australia*, 7th edn, Butterworths, Sydney, 2002, p 68. This jurisdictional ground is available in all Australian jurisdictions.

○   the disputed property is within the relevant jurisdiction;[5]

○   the process is brought to enforce a foreign judgment or an arbitral award;[6] or

○   the process is brought seeking an injunction to compel or restrain the performance of any act within the relevant jurisdiction.[7]

In relation to contractual disputes, an Australian court may also claim jurisdiction, under the relevant court rules, where the proceeding relates to a contract:

○   made in the relevant jurisdiction;[8]

○   governed by the law of the relevant jurisdiction;[9]

○   designating the forum as appropriate;[10]

○   **breached** within the relevant jurisdiction;[11] or

○   made through an agent trading or residing within the relevant jurisdiction.[12]

Breach
A contravention of a legal duty, often one contained in a statute, contract or other legal document.

Torts
A collective name used to describe civil actions that provide remedies where wrongful conduct causes harm. Common tortious causes of action include negligence, nuisance, and defamation.

As far as **torts** are concerned, the jurisdictional rules vary slightly. In Western Australia, the Australian Capital Territory and Tasmania, jurisdiction in torts cases can be founded on the tort having been committed within the jurisdiction.[13] The rules of the other states and territories (Victoria, New South Wales, the Northern Territory, Queensland and South Australia) are even wider; they allow for jurisdictional claims both where the tort was committed within the jurisdiction and where the damage was sustained within the jurisdiction.[14]

In some circumstances these rules open the door to jurisdiction even though the defendant is another country. As we will see, there are still several practical difficulties to be overcome before it would be worth suing in an Australian court to obtain a remedy against someone who lives overseas.

---

5   Nygh and Davies, pp 68–69. This jurisdictional ground is available in all Australian jurisdictions.

6   Nygh and Davies, pp 74–75. Available in New South Wales.

7   Nygh and Davies, pp 72. This jurisdictional ground is available in all Australian jurisdictions.

8   Nygh and Davies, pp 58–60. Valid in all states and territories except the Australian Capital Territory.

9   Nygh and Davies, pp 60–61. Valid in all states and territories except the Australian Capital Territory.

10   Nygh and Davies, pp 68. Valid in New South Wales, Queensland, Victoria, South Australia and the Northern Territory.

11   Nygh and Davies, pp 61–63. Valid in all states and territories.

12   Nygh and Davies, pp 60. Valid in all states and territories except the Australian Capital Territory.

13   Nygh and Davies, pp 63–64.

14   Nygh and Davies, pp 63–66.

Choice of law

Just as in the case of jurisdiction, the choice of law issue gives rise to several problems in the Internet context. The first thing to note is that from a practical point of view the question of the applicable law may sometimes decide the outcome of the dispute. If for example the law of State A favours the plaintiff while the law of State B favours the defendant, the choice of law is crucial.

When it comes to contracts the court first examines whether the parties made a choice as to which substantive law should be applied. Typically, where two reasonably equal parties have made a choice, the court will respect their choice.[15] If two online traders have contractually agreed that the law of Singapore should be applied in any dispute, an Australian court would be likely to apply the law of Singapore. Special rules may apply where there is an inherent power imbalance between the parties. For example in contracts between a business and a consumer, special rules favouring the consumer may apply (see Chapter 6).

If the parties to a contractual dispute have not made any choice as to the applicable law, the court will seek to establish which law is most reasonably to be applied. In doing so the courts will take account of factors such as the place of contract formation, the place of performance of the contract, the currency stated in the contract and the language the contract is written in.[16]

In the context of torts, Australian courts apply the so-called law of the place of wrong (*lex loci delicti*). While this may sound like a rather logical and uncontroversial approach, that is not always so, as is illustrated in the study of the *Gutnick* case at the end of this chapter. Indeed, the acceptance of this approach is only recent in Australian courts. Until 2000[17] for domestic disputes and 2002[18] for international disputes, Australian courts applied a different choice of law rule—the *double actionability test*, which is still applied in some other common law jurisdictions such as Hong Kong.

Lex loci delicti
Literally, 'the law of the place where the delict [tort] was committed'; a rule used in Australian courts to determine the applicable law in tort cases.

Double actionability test
A two-stage test used in determining the choice of law question in tort actions in some common law jurisdictions. First, the wrong alleged must be actionable if it were to be committed within Australia. Second, the act must not have been justifiable by the law of the place where it was done.

---

15   *Gienar v Meyer* (1796) 2 H B1 603; 126 ER 728. See further: L Marasinghe, *Principles of International Trade Law*, Butterworth Asia, Singapore, 1998, p 16.

16   *The 'Assunzione'* [1954] 1 A11 ER 278. For a discussion of this approach see: 'Choice of Law' (1992) 58 *Australian Law Reform Commission Report* 94.

17   *John Pfeiffer Pty Ltd v Rogerson* (2000) 172 ALR 625.

18   *Regie National des Usines Renault SA v Zhang* (2002) 210 CLR 491.

Forum non conveniens
Literally, an 'inconvenient forum'. Refers to the discretionary power courts have to decline the exercise of jurisdiction in a particular matter.

Declining jurisdiction

Courts have a discretion to decline to exercise jurisdiction. As far as Australian courts (and the courts of other common law countries) are concerned, the most important ground is the doctrine of **forum non conveniens**.

A party may argue that, while the court has jurisdiction under the applicable rules, it should refrain from exercising it, as it is not a suitable forum for deciding the dispute. In most common law countries, a court will accept this argument if there is a more appropriate forum.[19] However, under Australian law, the test is whether the court finds itself to be a clearly inappropriate forum.[20]

A court might be persuaded that it is a clearly inappropriate forum on a number of grounds. It might for example be that the applicable law is that of another country, or that all the relevant witnesses and evidence are located in another country (here the decision would be based on procedural effectiveness). The court is likely to weigh up a number of factors such as the connection between the selected forum and the subject matter of the dispute as well as the parties. Thus, as hinted at above, where a person is brought under Australian jurisdiction due to a temporary presence in Australia, the court may take the extent of that person's contact with Australia into account in deciding whether or not to exercise jurisdiction.

The importance of the doctrine of *forum non conveniens* in the Internet context has been made clear by Kirby J:

> It seems to me [...] that that [the issue of *forum non conveniens*] is the place in which the Internet problem is going to be solved in the world. Countries are going to say, 'Of course we've got jurisdiction. The damage happened here or some other—we can serve here but it is much more convenient that this matter be litigated in another place'.[21]

While *forum non conveniens* is the most important ground on which Australian courts may decline jurisdiction, one other ground deserves mention as it has the potential to be of particular relevance in the Internet context. A court in a traditional common law jurisdiction may decline jurisdiction if its orders will be ineffective. This is relevant where the plaintiff is seeking an order such as an injunction aimed at affecting a foreigner's conduct. Simpson J commented on this difficulty in *Macquarie Bank Limited and Anor v Berg*:[22]

> It seems to me unsatisfactory to make orders the effectiveness of which is solely dependent upon the voluntary presence, at a time of his selection, of the person

---

[19]   *Spiliada Maritime Corporation v Cansulex Ltd* [1987] AC 460.
[20]   *Voth v Manildra Flour Mills Pty Ltd* (1990) 171 CLR 538.
[21]   Transcript of High Court hearing of *Dow Jones & Company Inc v Gutnick*, 28 May 2002, points 1484–1487.
[22]   [1999] NSWSC 526.

against whom the orders are made. The uncertainty of unenforceability is a factor adverse to the exercise of discretion in the plaintiff's favour.[23]

In other words a court may be reluctant to decide a dispute where its decision is likely to be ineffective. However, this issue was not explored further and was by no means determinative in the *Macquarie Bank* case.

Recognition and enforcement

The issues of recognition and enforcement of judgments are of central importance in any international dispute. Looked at from the defendant's perspective, the significance is highlighted by the following question: If there is no risk that the judgment can be enforced against you, why bother defending the court action? The significance for the plaintiff can be illuminated by asking the following question: If there is no chance of having the judgment enforced against the other party, why bother going to court?

In other words, before people decide to sue a foreigner they must evaluate the chances of having a favourable judgment recognised and enforced against the other party. Similarly, before rushing off to defend a lawsuit brought in a foreign state, one ought to evaluate the risk of an unfavourable judgment being recognised and enforced in any jurisdiction in which one has assets.

The rules regulating recognition and enforcement vary considerably among the various legal systems in the world. For example Sweden rarely enforces foreign judgments.[24] Under Australian law, foreign judgments may be recognised and enforced under two different schemes: under **statute** and at common law.

Recognition by statute is, procedurally, by far the easier of the two options. However, only judgments from a few selected states may be recognised under statute. Recognition at common law is open to judgments from any country, but is more complicated and requires the satisfaction of all four criteria of the following test:[25]

Statute
A law passed by Parliament, also known as an Act of Parliament or legislation.

O   the foreign court must have had jurisdiction recognised by the Australian court;

O   the foreign judgment must be final and conclusive;

O   the foreign judgment must have been granted between the same parties and in the same action; and

O   the foreign judgment must be for a fixed debt.

---

[23]   *Macquarie Bank Limited and Anor v Berg* [1999] NSWSC 526, paragraph 11.

[24]   M Bogdan, *Svensk Internationell Privat- och Processrätt*, 6th edn, Norstedts Juridik AB, Stockholm, 2004, p 311.

[25]   P Nygh and M Davies, *Conflict of Laws in Australia*, 7th edn, Butterworths, Sydney, 2002, pp 169–188.

APPLYING THE RULES OF PRIVATE INTERNATIONAL LAW TO THE INTERNET AND E-COMMERCE

The application of these rules to Internet disputes has been neither problem-free nor uncontroversial. Some commentators have gone so far as to suggest it simply is not possible to apply these types of rules to a 'borderless' communications medium such as the Internet.[26] There are several obvious problems:

○   There is an imbalance between the ease and cost-effectiveness of entering into cross-border contacts on the one hand and the difficulty and expense of solving cross-border disputes (which can be the result of those contacts) on the other.

○   If wide jurisdictional claims are allowed, those who operate websites may risk being sued just about anywhere in the world, while if wide jurisdictional claims are not allowed, a plaintiff may not have any reasonable access to justice.

○   As it may be virtually impossible for website operators to know in advance which law is going to be applicable in case of a dispute, they would have to abide by the strictest rules in the world to be 'on the safe side'.

○   There is a diminishing connection, and sometimes proportionality, between action and effects. The effects of an action can occur virtually anywhere, and be totally out of proportion to the action giving rise to it. This results in a widening of some of the jurisdictional rules such as those focused on the place of wrong.

○   There is a gap between reasonable grounds for jurisdictional claims and application of law claims on the one hand, and reasonable grounds for recognition and enforcement of foreign judgments on the other.

These problems are all highlighted in the *Gutnick* case, decided in the High Court of Australia in late 2002.

When the news of the High Court's decision reached the world, the reactions were strong. In particular, the media presented the judgment as a disaster with far-reaching consequences for the freedom of speech. For example the judgment was said to be:

a landmark court ruling that puts cyberspace publishers around the world on notice that they can be sued under Australia's strict defamation laws—and effectively in any of the 190 nations where defamation proceedings can be brought.[27]

Case law
The body of law made by judges whose decisions are, according to the doctrine of precedent, binding on other courts.

Defamation
A cause of action in torts law, which involves publication of material that unfairly impugns the reputation of another.

---

[26]   For example, D Johnson and D Post, 'Law And Borders—The Rise of Law in Cyberspace' (1996) 48 *Stan L Rev* 1367.

[27]   B Crawford and A Keenan, 'Court ruling threatens free Internet', *Australian IT*, 29 August 2001.

CASE EXAMPLE *DOW JONES & COMPANY INC V GUTNICK (2002) 210 CLR 575*[28]

AUSTRALIA, HIGH COURT OF AUSTRALIA, 2002

The plaintiff, Victorian businessman Joseph Gutnick, sought to sue Dow Jones in Victoria, and have Victorian law apply, due to an allegedly defamatory article published by Dow Jones. The relevant article was available both in physical copies of *Barron's Magazine* and on Dow Jones's subscription-based website. The paper version of the article had some fourteen subscribers in Australia (five of which were located in Victoria) of approximately 300 000 copies sold worldwide. Further, of approximately 550 000 people subscribing to the Internet version of the magazine, 1700 paid for the service using Australian-issued credit cards. Nevertheless, it was accepted that important business people in Victoria had indeed read the relevant article.

Before examining how the Court approached the private international law issues that arose in the case, it is interesting to note how differently the judges viewed the novelty of the Internet. Kirby J stated: 'Intuition suggests that the remarkable features of the Internet (which is still changing and expanding) makes it more than simply another medium of human communication. It is indeed a revolutionary leap in the distribution of information, including about the reputation of individuals.' In contrast, Callinan J stated: 'The Internet, which is no more than a means of communication by a set of interconnected computers, was described, not very convincingly, as a communications system entirely different from pre-existing technology.'

Despite this enormous difference in opinion, all judges ruled in Mr Gutnick's favour, holding that he could sue Dow Jones in Victoria and that Victorian law was applicable. Arguably, this conclusion was inevitable unless the Court had been willing to depart from existing legal principles. As far as jurisdiction was concerned, it was virtually impossible to argue that no damages had been suffered in Victoria, and since Mr Gutnick had limited his claim to damages suffered within Victoria and undertaken not to sue elsewhere, Victoria could not reasonably be a clearly inappropriate forum (indeed, no other forum could ever be as convenient as Victoria). Further, the question of the applicable law was determined applying settled, but controversial, principles developed more than 100 years earlier. As noted above, Australian law looks for the law of the place of wrong. Under **defamation** law, the place of wrong is the place of publication, and **case law** (for example *Duke of Brunswick and Luneberg v Harmer* (1849) 14 QB 184) has identified the place of publication as the place where the defamatory material enters the mind of a third person, rather than the place where the publisher acted. Thus, even though Dow Jones published the article in the USA, in the sense of having taken all the relevant steps to distribute the article there, Australian law does not place significance on that location.

In light of this it seems that as long as the plaintiff limits the claim to damages suffered in an Australian jurisdiction (here Victoria) due to publication in that jurisdiction, there is nothing in the Australian system to prevent the court from deciding the dispute and in doing so applying Australian law, even where only a small number of copies have been published in Australia.

---

[28]   Available at <www.austlii.edu.au/au/cases/cth/HCA/2002/56.html>.

While other states are clearly not bound to follow this Australian approach, and the statement above may thus seem overly dramatic, other jurisdictions have indeed looked to the *Gutnick* case in determining their approach to these issues. For example in referring to the High Court's judgment in the *Gutnick* case (among others), an English court stated:

> [I]t has long been recognised that publication is regarded as taking place where the defamatory words are published in the sense of being heard or read [...]. What is more, by analogy, the common law currently regards the publication of an Internet posting as taking place when it is down-loaded.[29]

Several Australian cases have referred to the *Gutnick* case. *National Auto Glass Supplies (Australia) Pty Limited v Nielsen & Moller Autoglass (NSW) Pty Limited*[30] involved an allegedly defamatory e-mail. The Court referred to the High Court's judgment in the *Gutnick* case and concluded: 'In the case of an international e-mail, ordinarily the place in the world at which the e-mail is read will be the place where the tort of defamation, if there be such a tort, is committed.'[31]

This statement raises at least two questions. First, if this is the rule that 'ordinarily' applies, under what circumstances does it not apply? Second, would a court adopt this approach also where a person does not read the e-mail on their computer screen, but instead prints it and moves to another jurisdiction before reading it? Presumably, we will not find answers to these questions until they are determined by the courts.

Situs

The place where an event happened or where property is located, which can be reasons for a court to exercise jurisdiction.

In *Australian Competition and Consumer Commission v 1Cellnet LLC*[32] Nicholson J, when considering a contravention of the *Trade Practices Act 1974* (Cth), used the High Court's decision in the *Gutnick* case to conclude that 'there is an authority that the destination of downloading can be the **situs** at which an offence is committed'.[33] This is worrying, as the *Gutnick* decision was based on long-established principles of defamation law—principles that cannot, and should not, readily be transferred to other areas of law.

Relevant technological advances

Australia's second most important case within the field of private international law and the Internet is also a defamation case (which pre-dates the *Gutnick* case). It involved an action in the NSW Supreme Court for an injunction against the publication of certain information on a website hosted in a foreign country.

---

29   *Don King v Lennox Lewis, Lion Promotions, LLC and Judd Burstein* [2004] EWHC 168 (QB) paragraph 15.

30   [2006] FCA 1386.

31   *National Auto Glass Supplies (Australia) Pty Limited v Nielsen & Moller Autoglass (NSW) Pty Limited* [2006] FCA 1386, paragraph 24.

32   [2004] FCA 1210.

33   *Australian Competition and Consumer Commission v 1Cellnet LLC* [2004] FCA 1210 paragraph 10. Available at <www.austlii.edu.au/au/cases/cth/federal_ct/2004/1210.html>.

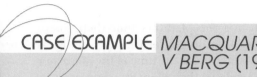

CASE EXAMPLE *MACQUARIE BANK LIMITED AND ANOR V BERG* (1999) NSWSC 526[34]

AUSTRALIA, SUPREME COURT OF NEW SOUTH WALES, 1999

The defendant (Mr Berg) had worked for the plaintiffs (the Macquarie Bank and some employees of the bank), but had subsequently taken action in the Industrial Relations Commission of NSW against his former employer. A website hosted in the US contained material alleged to defame the plaintiffs, who alleged that Mr Berg was responsible for the website. The plaintiffs sought an injunction preventing the publication of the website and the question was whether a New South Wales court could grant such an injunction. Simpson J did not grant the injunction, saying:

> An injunction to restrain defamation in NSW is designed to ensure compliance with the laws of NSW, and to protect the rights of plaintiffs, as those rights are defined by the law of NSW. Such an injunction is not designed to superimpose the law of NSW relating to defamation on every other state, territory and country of the world. Yet that would be the effect of an order restraining publication on the Internet. It is not to be assumed that the law of defamation in other countries is coextensive with that of NSW, and indeed, one knows that it is not. It may very well be that, according to the law of the Bahamas, Tazhakistan [sic], or Mongolia, the defendant has an unfettered right to publish the material. To make an order interfering with such a right would exceed the proper limits of the use of the injunctive power of this court.

Interestingly, it seems that the perceived lack of possibility of limiting the geographical spread of materials posted on the World Wide Web was determinative in the case, because Simpson J also noted:

> It is reasonably plain, I think, that once published on the Internet, material is transmitted anywhere in the world that has an Internet connection. It may be received by anybody, anywhere, having the appropriate facilities. Senior counsel conceded that, to make the order as initially sought, would have the effect of restraining publication of all the material presently contained on the website to any place in the world. Recognising the difficulties associated with orders of such breadth, he sought to narrow the claim by limiting the order sought to publication or dissemination 'within NSW'. The limitation, however, is ineffective. *Senior counsel acknowledged that he was aware of no means by which material, once published on the Internet, could be excluded from transmission to or receipt in any geographical area. Once published on the Internet material can be received anywhere, and it does not lie within the competence of the publisher to restrict the reach of the publication.* (emphasis added)

---

[34]   Available at <www.austlii.edu.au/au/cases/nsw/supreme_ct/1999/526.html>.

Geo-identification
The ascertaining of the geographical location of Internet users.

It was unfortunate for the plaintiffs that their senior counsel did not pay greater attention to relevant technological developments. There are—and were at the time of the *Macquarie Bank* case—technologies available that allow website operators to estimate the geographical location of those who visit their websites, thereby making possible geographically based access discrimination. Such **geo-identification** is becoming more widely used and is likely to have a significant impact on how courts approach issues of private international law in the Internet setting.

While geo-identification can be achieved in several ways, the most common approach is to focus on the website visitor's IP address. It works like this: when a person enters the appropriate Uniform Resource Locator ('URL') into their browser, or clicks on the appropriate hyperlink, an 'access-request' is sent to the server operating the requested website. As the server receives the access-request, it, in turn, sends a 'location request' (it forwards the access-seeker's IP address) to the provider of the geo-location service. The provider of the geo-location service has gathered information about the distribution of IP addresses, and built up a database of geo-location information. Based on the information in this database, the provider of the geo-location service gives the website server an educated guess as to the access-seeker's location.

There are currently several products on the market utilising this type of system.[35] However, their accuracy is difficult to gauge. Providers indicate the potential accuracy to be as high as 99 per cent at country level and approximately 92 per cent at city level. However, it should be remembered that providers are trying to sell their products, and the methods used to reach these impressive figures have been criticised. Further, a range of factors affect the accuracy of geo-location technologies. These factors can be divided into two categories: 'source problems' (associated with building up or collecting accurate geo-location data) and 'circumvention problems' (people seeking to circumvent the technologies).

These technologies will help address some problems associated with applying private international law rules to Internet conduct, but they may also have a negative effect. With an increased use of such technologies the Internet will inevitably be transformed from a relatively borderless dimension into a medium that takes account of geographical and legal borders, much like the 'real' world. In other words, with increased use of geo-identification, we stand to lose one of the Internet's main beneficial features—its 'borderlessness'.

---

[35]   A list of geo-location products, which can be tested for free, can be found on
      <www.svantesson.org>.

CONCLUDING REMARKS AND FURTHER READING

Our discussion of international law and the four elements of the jurisdiction issue in private international law will provide you with a basic understanding of the difficulties that pervade virtually all the topics studied in this book. Our treatment does not aim to be more than a good starting point. For those who would like to enhance their understanding, we provide some suggestions for further reading.

JL Goldsmith, 'Against Cyberanarchy' (1998) 65 U Chi L Rev 4

M Geist, 'Is There a There There? Towards Greater Certainty for Internet Jurisdiction' (2001) 16 Berkeley Tech L J 1

D Johnson and D Post, 'Law and Borders: The Rise of Law in Cyberspace' (1996) 48 Stan L R

Yee Fen Lim, *Cyberspace Law: Commentaries and Materials,* 2nd edn, Oxford University Press, Melbourne, 2007

D Svantesson, *Private International law and the Internet*, Klüwer Law International, 2007

Review questions for this chapter can be found on the book's Online Resource Centre at www.oup.com.au/orc/fordersvantesson.

04

CONTRACTUAL ISSUES

OBJECTIVES // BY THE END OF THIS CHAPTER, YOU WILL:

O Know how Australian legislation removes any doubt about whether electronic transactions are enforceable

O Appreciate why the time and place of formation of a contract may be important, and understand the difficulties in deciding when and where a contract is formed in the Internet environment

O Be aware of some of the arguments about the postal acceptance rule and when it might apply to modern electronic communications

O Understand the nature of shrinkwrap, clickwrap and browsewrap agreements and how they might be used to incorporate terms in an online contract

O Be aware of situations in which e-commerce traders might find their contracts unenforceable due to lack of contractual capacity

UNCITRAL
The United Nations Commission on International Trade Law.

Offer
The stated contractual terms on which the offeror promises to be bound if the other party (the offeree) accepts them. See also *Acceptance*.

WHAT THIS CHAPTER IS ABOUT

As new methods of electronic communication developed, an early issue was whether a contract entered into using these methods would be legally enforceable. In most countries, this is no longer contentious (if it ever was) because it has been addressed by legislation. We begin this chapter by explaining Australian provisions that recognise the validity of electronic contracts. Our discussion includes the **UNCITRAL** Model Law on Electronic Commerce on which the Australian legislation is based.

In deciding where and when a contract is formed, it is usually important to decide who made the **offer** and who accepted it. We describe the nature of an offer and who is likely to be regarded as the offeror in various e-commerce scenarios. We then broaden the enquiry to consider where and when **acceptance** takes place. We include a review of the postal acceptance rule and its possible place in the e-commerce environment, as well as the effect of electronic transactions legislation. The following section focuses on ways of incorporating contractual terms into online contracts. These are often described by the colourful phrases '**shrinkwrap**', '**browsewrap**' and '**clickwrap**'.

The final section in this chapter considers the risk faced by e-traders that the faceless party contracting with them may not have legal capacity. It gives an overview of situations in which this risk might arise.

ENFORCEABILITY OF ELECTRONIC CONTRACTS

When restrictions on commercial activity on the Internet were lifted in 1991 an early issue was whether contracts using the new technology would be enforceable. Common law legal systems have had little trouble adapting their laws to cater for new methods of communication in the past.[1] There is little doubt they would have been equally adaptable when considering contracts entered into using Internet technology.

A second (and more difficult) issue was whether the new communication methods would satisfy the various legislative requirements that certain contracts be in writing. Contracts typically required to be in writing include dispositions of land or interests in land, guarantees, credit contracts, bills of exchange, wills and contracts of insurance. Similar requirements exist in most countries. In some situations documents are also required to be signed. We focus on the writing requirement in this chapter, and leave discussion of the signature requirement for the next chapter.

Acceptance
The final, unqualified agreement with the terms of an offer that completes the formation of a contract.

Shrinkwrap
Where contractual terms are sealed inside the packaging of a product, so they are unavailable before the product is purchased.

Browsewrap
A method of attempting to incorporate terms into an online contract which relies on the customer voluntarily following a link and reading the terms.

Clickwrap
A method of incorporating terms into an online contract which requires the customer to indicate their assent by clicking on a button or other object before the agreement can be concluded.

---

[1]   Courts have, over hundreds of years, dealt with contracts formed by telephone, telex, telegram and facsimile. See for example *Brinkibon Ltd v Stahag Stahl und Stahlwarenhandelsgesellschaft mbH* [1983] 2 AC 34 (dealing with telexes); and *Reese Bros Plastics Ltd v Hamon-Sobelco Aust Pty Ltd* (1988) 5 BPR 11,106 (dealing with faxes).

In 1996 the United Nations Commission on International Trade Law (UNCITRAL) drafted a Model Law on Electronic Commerce that addressed both the enforceability issue and the writing issue.[2] The Model Law forms a flexible framework that allows individual countries to implement it in ways that suit their own requirements while at the same time achieving some international consistency. It has been widely adopted—more than 80 countries have implemented it in one way or another.[3]

Two general features of the UNCITRAL approach deserve mention. Soon after starting work on the Model Law, UNCITRAL recognised that it would need to be 'technologically neutral'—broad enough to cover future developments as far as possible. The second general feature was what it called 'functional equivalence'. Where electronic technology could achieve the same functions as paper-based technology, UNCITRAL tried to ensure it would be treated in the same way.

As a result of this approach, UNCITRAL was able to recommend laws that could be stated in a relatively straightforward way. Instead of examining every existing legislative provision and rewriting it, all that was necessary was to ensure that the use of electronic methods was not a barrier to enforceability—in other words, electronic methods that satisfactorily performed equivalent functions should be brought within the existing concept of 'writing'. It therefore recommended a provision that information generally[4]—and, more specifically, messages used in the formation of a contract[5]—should not be denied legal effect solely on the grounds that they were in an electronic form.

In 1999 the Australian Commonwealth Government passed the *Electronic Transactions Act 1999* implementing this recommendation. Section 8(1) provides:

> For the purposes of a law of the Commonwealth, a transaction is not invalid because it took place wholly or partly by means of one or more electronic communications.

According to the definition, an electronic communication is one that uses 'guided or unguided electromagnetic energy', whether in the form of data, text, images or speech.[6] The Act applies to commercial and non-commercial transactions.[7] Because of concerns about the limits of its constitutional power, the Commonwealth Government chose to restrict the scope of the Act to 'laws of the Commonwealth'. Since contract law is generally regulated by the states, this Act on its own would

---

2   United Nations Commission on International Trade Law (UNCITRAL), *Model Law on Electronic Commerce*, GA Resolution 51/162, GAOR 51st sess, 85th plen mtg, UN Doc A/Res/51/162 (1996) (with additional article 5bis as adopted in 1998 and Guide to Enactment) available at <www.uncitral.org> last accessed 27 April 2007.

3   For the latest adoption status, see <www.uncitral.org/uncitral/en/uncitral_texts/electronic_commerce/1996Model_status.html>.

4   *Model Law on Electronic Commerce*, article 5.

5   *Model Law on Electronic Commerce*, article 11.

6   *Electronic Transactions Act 1999* (Cth) s 5, definition of 'electronic communication'.

7   *Electronic Transactions Act 1999* (Cth) s 5, definition of 'transaction'.

not have had a wide impact. However, all the state and territory governments agreed to cooperate. They have all passed similar legislation, giving Australia a national legislative scheme.[8]

TIME AND PLACE OF CONTRACT FORMATION

Given that electronic transactions are enforceable, the next difficulty is deciding when and where the contract is formed. The *time* of formation can be important where deadlines are imposed, such as when determining liability for tax in a financial year, or when exercising an option before a certain date; the *place* of formation is one of the important factors taken into account in determining what law applies and which courts are likely to hear a dispute.[9]

We begin with a brief review of the relevant contract principles. The key requirements for a valid contract are:

O   two or more parties who are legally capable of entering a contract;

O   an agreement between them, usually identified by an offer and an acceptance of the offer;

O   valuable **consideration**[10] or alternatively a signed and witnessed formal document known as a deed;

O   a serious intention that the agreement be legally binding;

O   sufficient certainty about the terms of the agreement for it to be enforceable.[11]

We are concerned with the second of these requirements. The general principle is that a contract is formed when the parties have agreed on all its terms.[12] To identify the moment of agreement, communications between the parties are usually

Consideration
The giving of (or the promise to give) something of legal value in return for a promise, which is a requirement for a valid contract in most common law systems.

---

[8]   The equivalent Acts are: *Electronic Transactions Act 2000* (NSW); *Electronic Transactions (Victoria) Act 2000* (Vic); *Electronic Transactions (Queensland) Act 2001* (Qld); *Electronic Transactions Act 2003* (WA); *Electronic Transactions Act 2000* (SA); *Electronic Transactions Act 2000* (Tas); *Electronic Transactions Act 2001* (ACT); *Electronic Transactions (Northern Territory) Act 2000* (NT). In this book the various Acts are referred to collectively as the 'Electronic Transactions Acts'.

[9]   See Chapter 3 for a discussion of this and the other factors taken into account in deciding jurisdiction and choice of law.

[10]   Consideration distinguishes contracts from gifts or donations, which, unless recorded in a deed, are generally unenforceable for lack of consideration. International contracts under the Vienna Convention (discussed later) and contracts in civil law systems do not have this requirement. Further treatment of this topic is left to students of contract law.

[11]   See general texts on contract law for further details, such as L Willmott, S Christensen and D Butler, *Contract Law*, 2nd edn, Oxford University Press, Melbourne, 2005.

[12]   *Scammell v Ouston* [1941] AC 251; *Thorby v Goldberg* (1964) 112 CLR 597.

analysed to identify an offer being made, and an unconditional acceptance of that offer.[13] The normal rule is that the contract is formed when acceptance is communicated to the person making the offer—there is then a 'meeting of the minds'.[14] However, parties are at liberty to make different arrangements as to how and when their contract is to be concluded,[15] provided their arrangement is not illegal. This is consistent with the principle of freedom of contract.

We consider the application of these principles to online contracts under two headings: identifying the offer; and identifying the time and place of acceptance.

Identifying the offer

What, then, is an offer? It is a clear statement of the terms on which a person (the offeror) promises to be bound if the other party (the offeree) agrees. This is a narrower meaning than in everyday use. Advertising goods for sale in a newspaper, brochure or magazine might be described as an offer for sale in the everyday sense, but it is unlikely to be an offer in the legal sense.[16] The same goes for signs in shop windows,[17] even where words like 'special offer' or 'offer for sale' are used.[18] This is because, to be an offer in the legal sense, the seller must (a) disclose sufficient detail so that *all* the relevant terms of the contract would be known to the reader, and (b) intend that the reader could create a contract by merely replying 'yes'. We will explore the circumstances in which these conditions might be fulfilled shortly. The point to note for now is that by analogy, advertisements or catalogues on websites are generally unlikely to be legal offers.

After an offer is made, any method can be used to communicate acceptance or rejection, unless the offer itself or a statute requires a particular method. A rejection effectively terminates the offer.[19] An acceptance, in the legal sense, is a simple assent to the terms of the offer. If the offeree adds a new condition or proposes something different, this is not an acceptance, no matter how strongly it expresses agreement. It is a counter-offer, inviting the original offeror to accept or reject the new proposal.

---

[13]   Occasionally courts are unable to identify a clear offer and acceptance, but still conclude that a contract must have been formed at some stage during the negotiating process—see Denning MR in *Butler Machine Tool Co v Ex-Cell-O Corp* [1979] 1 WLR 401, 404 and Ormiston J in *Vroon BV v Foster's Brewing Group Ltd* [1994] 2 VR 32, 79–83. These situations do not raise issues peculiar to e-commerce and the Internet, so they need not concern us here.

[14]   *Entores Ltd v Miles Far East Corp* [1955] 2 QB 327; *Brinkibon Ltd v Stahag Stahl und Stahlwarenhandelsgesellschaft mbH* [1983] 2 AC 34, 41.

[15]   See for example *Carlill v Carbolic Smoke Ball Company* [1893] 1 QB 256, where the offeror was held to have waived the need for communication of the acceptance.

[16]   *Spencer v Harding* (1870) LR 5 CP 561; *Partridge v Crittenden* [1968] 2 All ER 421.

[17]   *Pharmaceutical Society of GB v Boots Cash Chemists (Southern) Ltd* [1953] 1 QB 401; *Fisher v Bell* [1961] 1 QB 394.

[18]   *Spencer v Harding* (1870) LR 5 CP 561; *B Seppelt & Sons Ltd v Commissioner for Main Roads* (1975) 1 BPR 9147.

[19]   *Hyde v Wrench* (1840) 49 ER 132.

There is no assumption that a particular party will always be the offeror. A shopkeeper could just as easily be the offeror or the offeree, depending on who made the last statement suggesting the terms (the offer) before the other party agreed (acceptance).

EXAMPLE

Imagine this exchange of e-mails:

Message 1—Andrew to Betty: 'I'm intending to sell my iPod. Before I advertise it, I thought I'd offer it to you. Are you interested?'

Message 2—Betty to Andrew: 'Yes, I'd like to buy it. I'd be prepared to pay $200 cash, but only if I can collect it before Sunday.'

Message 3—Andrew to Betty: 'You can have it before Sunday, but I can't accept less than $250. If you are happy to pay that, we have a deal.'

Message 4—Betty to Andrew: 'OK. I'll phone later to arrange a time to collect it.'

Despite using the term 'offer', message 1 cannot be an offer in the legal sense—it does not disclose essential terms such as the price or delivery details. It is just an enquiry or an invitation to discuss further (sometimes referred to as an 'invitation to treat'). Message 2 is beginning to look far more like an offer in the legal sense, provided the whole transaction is not interpreted as an unenforceable arrangement between friends. Betty would be the offeror and Andrew the offeree. A simple assent by Andrew would have resulted in a 'meeting of the minds' on the essential terms. However, Andrew rejects the offer in message 3, and makes a counter-offer. Andrew is now the offeror and Betty the offeree. In message 4, Betty accepts Andrew's counter-offer.

Might catalogues or advertisements on web displays ever amount to an offer? Some cases have interpreted advertisements or similar announcements as offers to 'the whole world' where this intention was sufficiently clear to a reasonable person.[20] In keeping with the principles discussed earlier, all the essential terms such as price, delivery and payment details would have to be disclosed as part of the advertisement or announcement. Static web displays that require users to enquire about prices or delivery details would not satisfy this requirement. The customer is likely to be regarded as making an enquiry; the trader's response, provided it contains sufficient details and anticipates a simple yes or no answer, is likely to be the offer.

More sophisticated interactive websites, with checkout systems that inform users of different options and allow them to enter payment and delivery details before sending the order, are more likely to be interpreted as legal offers, but there is still a difficulty. If they are offers, each customer who places an order is accepting the offer, and a contract is formed as soon as the order is received. In situations where web traders have limited stock, they would be in breach of contract if they received an unexpectedly large batch of orders and their stock ran out. Courts have recognised the danger of limitless liability in these situations—hence the traditional view that

---

[20]   *Carlill v Carbolic Smoke Ball Company* [1893] 1 QB 256.

it is normally the customer who makes the offer, giving the trader an opportunity to decide whether to accept it.[21]

Where the danger of limitless liability does not arise, it would be easier for a court to conclude that a web display was intended to be an offer. This might happen in two situations:

o   Where a web display makes it clear there are a limited number of products for sale, and they will be sold without limitation to the first to respond. Because the intention is clearly that the offer will lapse once all stocks are sold, the problem of limitless liability does not arise.[22]

o   Where there is no limit to the availability of the product being sold, a web display is more likely to be interpreted as an offer. This would be the case, for example, where software is made available for download.

Identifying the time and place of acceptance

Once we have identified the offer, we are one step closer to working out when the contract was formed. The normal approach has been well settled for years. It was restated in 1983 by Lord Wilberforce in the House of Lords:

> The general rule, it is hardly necessary to state, is that a contract is formed when acceptance of an offer is communicated by the offeree to the offeror. And if it is necessary to determine *where* a contract is formed ... it appears logical that this should be at the place where acceptance is communicated to the offeror.[23]

If a verbally expressed acceptance is drowned by the noise of an aircraft overhead so that it is not heard by the offeror, there is no contract. The acceptance will need to be repeated before there is a 'meeting of the minds'. The same thing applies if the line goes dead when the offeree utters an acceptance during a telephone conversation.[24] The parties would have to re-establish the connection, and the offeree confirm acceptance, before a contract would come into existence.

An unusual exception to the general rule, known as the 'postal acceptance' rule, developed in English common law. According to this rule, acceptance is complete as soon as it is posted if the parties must have contemplated that the post might be used as a method of acceptance.[25]

When applied strictly, this rule can have strange consequences. If a letter of acceptance disappears after posting and never arrives at its destination, there will still

---

[21]   *Grainger & Son v Gough* [1896] AC 325; *Pharmaceutical Society (GB) v Boots Cash Chemists (Southern) Ltd* [1952] 2 QB 795.

[22]   See Smithers J in *Reardon v Morley Ford Pty Ltd* (1980) 49 FLR 401, 407–408; and, in the USA see *Lefkowitz v Great Minneapolis Surplus Store Inc*, 86 NW 2d 689 (Minn 1957).

[23]   *Brinkibon Ltd v Stahag Stahl und Stahlwarenhandelsgesellschaft mbH* [1983] 2 AC 34, 41 ('*Brinkibon*').

[24]   Both these examples were discussed by Lord Denning in *Entores Ltd v Miles Far East Corp* [1955] 2 QB 327, 332.

[25]   *Henthorn v Fraser* [1892] 2 Ch 27 (HL), 33 (Lord Herschell).

be a contract, despite the offeror knowing nothing about it.[26] The offeror, not hearing from the offeree, may even have sold the goods to someone else in the meantime, but, without any fault, will still be in breach of the original contract with the offeree. What is more, the parties will frequently not be aware of the existence of the rule or its consequences. The parties can expressly or impliedly agree on a different time and place of formation,[27] but, in the absence of such an agreement, the rule is activated simply because the parties must have contemplated the use of the post for acceptance. Most common law countries have inherited this rule.

Applicability of the postal acceptance rule

There are several similarities between postal communications and some of the modern electronic methods. This has led to speculation that an equivalent of the postal acceptance rule might also apply—there might be an e-mail acceptance rule or SMS acceptance rule. For this reason, it is necessary to delve a little more deeply into the rule to assess the likelihood of a court in a common law country deciding that it should apply.

In 1983 the House of Lords was faced with the issue of whether the postal acceptance rule applied to telexes.[28] In deciding that generally it did not, the court reasoned that the normal rule applied to all communications that were instantaneous or virtually instantaneous. In using this phrase, the court was not concerned so much with the speed of the data travelling between the parties, but with whether the parties would have the opportunity to clear up any misunderstandings or problems promptly. By analogy with oral communications, if the technology allows the parties to respond to each other without undue delay, the court felt that the postal acceptance rule should not apply. On the other hand, the court recognised that, where messages are sent by post or via some similar independent third party for later delivery or collection, the postal acceptance rule would normally apply. This reasoning was consistent with previous court decisions applying the postal acceptance rule to telegrams,[29] but not to telephones or telexes.[30]

Synchronous or real-time communication methods are thus not problematic. Internet Relay Chat (IRC), or the popular MSN messaging service in which parties communicate with each other by exchanging typed text messages while both are online, would be treated as instantaneous, and the normal rule would apply. The same would hold for mobile phones, Voice over IP (VoIP) and videoconferencing. The analogy with the postal services is strongest when the communication method involves some delay between sending the message and receipt, so that there is no prospect of clearing up any misunderstandings or problems promptly. Where the

---

[26]   *Household Fire and Carriage Accident Insurance Co (Ltd) v Grant* (1879) 4 Ex D 216 (CA).

[27]   *Holwell Securities v Hughes* [1974] 1 All ER 161; *Tallerman & Co Pty Ltd v Nathan's Merchandise (Vic) Pty Ltd* (1957) 98 CLR 93; *Bressan v Squires* [1974] 2 NSWLR 460.

[28]   *Brinkibon* [1983] 2 AC 34.

[29]   *Cowan v O'Connor* (1888) 20 QBD 640.

[30]   *Entores Ltd v Miles Far East Corp* [1955] 2 QB 327.

parties contemplate that acceptance will be sent by e-mail, and the offeror only accesses the Internet by dial-up modem three times per week, there is an obvious analogy with the post. The offeror's Internet Service Provider acts like a post office, keeping the message in a mailbox until the offeror chooses to collect it. Other situations that may raise the issue include the use of SMS text messages where the recipient does not have their receiving device on all the time, or is habitually out of range; and use of a hosted e-commerce website, where the acceptance message is stored by the host server for later access by the offeror.

Some of these scenarios can be adequately dealt with on the basis of the general rule combined with the concept of 'deemed receipt'. In *Brinkibon* Lord Wilberforce suggested that, even with instantaneous methods of communication, actual communication of acceptance might not always be required. He referred to the example of a business contract where an acceptance sent by telex arrives outside normal office hours, suggesting that acceptance might be deemed to occur when the offeror would have had a reasonable opportunity to read the telex in the normal course of business the next day.[31] This 'deemed receipt' principle might well apply to situations where an offeror is not diligent about reading electronic messages (e-mail or SMS), and this could not reasonably be anticipated by the offeree. This might for example be appropriate where an offeror chooses to keep their receiving device turned off, or is habitually out of range.

Civil law
In the context of a legal system, refers to a system based primarily on the interpretation of statutory codes (like the legal systems of much of Europe) as opposed to systems based on the doctrine of precedent (like the English common law system).

The weight of academic opinion seems to be against extending the postal acceptance rule to modern communication methods.[32] Part of the reason is that the **civil law systems** do not have a similar rule and, given the global nature of e-commerce, it would be a concern if the rule were to take traders by surprise.[33] If it is to apply at all, the rule might be restricted to communication methods involving inevitable delays as a result of messages being handled and stored by third party intermediaries. The two most obvious examples of this are where e-mail messages are accessed periodically via dial-up modem and where a third party hosts an e-commerce website that is deemed to be making offers, and the offeror periodically accesses the host's server to gather the orders.

---

[31]   *Brinkibon* [1983] 2 AC 34.

[32]   See for example S Squires, 'Some Contract Issues Arising from Online Business–Consumer Agreements' (2000) 5 (1) Deakin LR 95; S Hill, 'Flogging a Dead Horse—the Postal Acceptance Rule and E-mail' (2001) 17 *J Con L* 151; S Christensen, 'Formation of Contracts by E-mail—Is it Just the Same as the Post?' (2001) 1 *QUTLJ* 22; and for a US view, see J C Dodd and J A Hernandez, 'Contracting in Cyberspace' (Summer 1998) *Computer Law Review and Technology Journal* <www.smu.edu/csr/Sum98–1-Dodd.pdf> last accessed 20 July 2007.

[33]   See the discussion on international contracts below.

In Australia there is one other complication. The only important High Court discussion of the postal acceptance rule occurred in 1957. The case was eventually decided on different grounds, but two of the judges said:

> [A] finding that a contract is completed by the posting of a letter of acceptance cannot be justified unless it is to be inferred that the offeror contemplated *and intended* that his offer might be accepted by [posting the letter]. (emphasis added)[34]

The words 'and intended' appear to introduce a significantly narrower approach. The traditional rule is triggered when the parties contemplate the use of the post for acceptance—they need not contemplate that the act of posting will *actually be* the acceptance. The judges' statement in this case indicates there would need to be evidence that the offeror *intended* the act of posting to be the acceptance. The effect of this rule would be less likely to take the parties by surprise—they will have agreed when the contract was to be regarded as formed, and voluntarily allocated the risk should the letter be lost. But because it was not part of the reasoning of the High Court's decision this statement is not regarded as binding, and has not been followed to date.[35] However, given the difficulties with the postal acceptance rule, it is possible that the High Court could again adopt this approach as a proper and more principled statement of the law.

The exact time and place of sending or receiving

In an electronic environment, the exact moment of sending or receiving a message is complicated because both sender and receiver are likely to have service providers that handle the sending, receiving and storing of their messages. The service provider's equipment may be in a different place—even a different country—from the sender or receiver of the message. There are numerous possibilities. Messages could be regarded as *sent* when the sender clicks the send button; or a split second later, when it leaves the device they are using; or if the sender has a network of devices under their control, when it leaves their network; or when it enters or leaves their service provider's system. Messages could be regarded as *received* when they enter the system belonging to the addressee's service provider; or a split second later, when stored and made available to the addressee; or when the addressee notices the existence of the message and clicks the read button; or when the message enters or is displayed on the addressee's local device.

---

[34]   Dixon CJ and Fullagar J in *Tallerman & Co Pty Ltd v Nathan's Merchandise (Vic) Pty Ltd* (1957) 98 CLR 93, 111.

[35]   In *Bressan v Squires* [1974] 2 NSWLR 460, Bowen CJ suggested that the statement was an unconsidered overstatement, and not intended to change the law at all.

Rather than considering the activity of each of the parties (such as clicking the send button, or clicking the retrieve or read button) the UNCITRAL approach is to focus on the time a message crosses a boundary between information systems. It distinguishes between information systems belonging to (or under the control of) three different parties: the message originator, an intermediary, and the addressee. The Australian implementation of this approach is well-represented by the provisions of the Federal Act:

14. Time and place of dispatch and receipt of electronic communications
Time of dispatch

(1) For the purposes of a law of the Commonwealth, if an electronic communication enters a single information system outside the control of the originator, then, unless otherwise agreed between the originator and the addressee of the electronic communication, the dispatch of the electronic communication occurs when it enters that information system.

(2) For the purposes of a law of the Commonwealth, if an electronic communication enters successively 2 or more information systems outside the control of the originator, then, unless otherwise agreed between the originator and the addressee of the electronic communication, the dispatch of the electronic communication occurs when it enters the first of those information systems.

If the contract is formed at the moment of sending the message (if for example an e-mail acceptance rule is held to apply) this will be interpreted as the moment the message enters the first information system outside the control of the originator of the message—in much the same way as the moment of posting would be regarded as when the sender of a letter places it in a post office box. Section 14 continues:

Time of receipt

(3) For the purposes of a law of the Commonwealth, if the addressee of an electronic communication has designated an information system for the purpose of receiving electronic communications, then, unless otherwise agreed between the originator and the addressee of the electronic communication, the time of receipt of the electronic communication is the time when the electronic communication enters that information system.

Designation of an information system is not defined. Presumably it includes the situation where an offeror (who will be the addressee) gives an e-mail address or a mobile phone number to the offeree (the originator) with the intent that it be used for communication. Where the offeror does not designate an information system, the Act comes close to implementing the common law position:

(4) For the purposes of a law of the Commonwealth, if the addressee of an electronic communication has not designated an information system for the purpose of receiving electronic communications, then, unless otherwise agreed between the originator and the addressee of the electronic communication, the time of receipt of the electronic communication is the time when the electronic communication comes to the attention of the addressee.

It is unclear whether it is merely the existence of the electronic communication or its contents that have to 'come to the attention of the addressee'. It is also unclear whether, if the general rule applies and the moment of contract formation is when the acceptance is communicated to the offeror, the time of receipt is taken to be the moment of communication.

None of these provisions addresses the fundamental issue of whether the postal acceptance rule applies. They merely clarify the exact time a message is 'sent' or 'received' without expressing a preference as to which is the moment of contract formation. The common law, as developed in cases, will continue to apply.

When it comes to the place of contract formation, the Act takes a slightly different view. Instead of joining the moment of contract formation with the place at which the event occurs, the Act takes a more pragmatic approach.

Place of dispatch and receipt

(5) For the purposes of a law of the Commonwealth, unless otherwise agreed between the originator and the addressee of an electronic communication:

  (a) the electronic communication is taken to have been dispatched at the place where the originator has its place of business; and

  (b) the electronic communication is taken to have been received at the place where the addressee has its place of business.

The section goes on to clarify: if there is more than one place of business, the one with the closer relationship to the transaction—or, failing that, the principal place of business—is the operative place. If there is no place of business, the ordinary place of residence is the operative place.

International contracts

Our discussion of the time and place of formation of a contract examined Australian law. It is relevant to Internet transactions between people in Australia. Where contracts are formed with people in other countries, Australian law might not apply—recall the issues raised in Chapter 3 on jurisdiction.

Which law applies is obviously an important issue—there are significant differences between Australian law and the law of other countries. For example civil law countries do not have an equivalent of the postal acceptance rule, so the discussion of this issue would be irrelevant if the law to be applied was that of France. Another important difference, beyond the scope of this book, is the requirement of consideration in the formation of a valid contract—a requirement in common law systems that is unknown in civil law systems.

The difficulties in deciding which law applies and which courts will hear disputes have existed since international trade first developed. Experienced international traders overcome the difficulties by agreeing in advance, perhaps as one of the terms of the contract, how disputes are to be resolved, including the relevant law. This is consistent with the principle of freedom of contract.

Most trading nations including Australia have acceded to the Vienna Sales Convention,[36] an international instrument sponsored by the United Nations. The states and territories also passed legislation adopting this convention in the late 1980s.[37] It applies to more substantial business contracts, rather than typical consumer purchases—it excludes sales by auction and goods bought for personal, family or household use. It applies automatically where the countries of all the contracting parties have adopted the **treaty**, or where the rules of private international law (see Chapter 3) determine that an acceding country's law applies to the contract.

Treaty
An agreement formed under international law by states and/or international organisations.

The Convention does not support the postal acceptance rule. It provides that 'acceptance of an offer becomes effective at the moment the indication of assent reaches the offeror'.[38] Article 24 clarifies this by providing:

> an offer, declaration of acceptance or any other indication of intention 'reaches' the addressee when it is made orally to him or delivered by any other means to him personally, to his place of business or mailing address or, if he does not have a place of business or mailing address, to his habitual residence.

Despite the clarification provided by article 24, there is still scope for argument over exactly where and when the contract is formed. In the online environment, where communications are handled by web or e-mail servers, it is difficult to know how a court would interpret one's 'business or mailing address'.

To address these and other issues, the United Nations adopted a new Convention in 2005 on the Use of Electronic Communications in International Contracts.[39] There are substantial similarities, but also subtle differences, between this Convention and the Australian Electronic Transactions Acts which, as we have seen, were based on the earlier (1996) UNCITRAL Model Law on Electronic Commerce.[40] We will not explore these similarities and differences here, since Australia has not acceded to the Convention. The accession rate has been particularly slow,[41] partly because the

---

[36] *United Nations Convention on Contracts for the International Sale of Goods* ('Vienna Sales Convention'), 1489 UNTS 3, 19 ILM 668 (Vienna, 11 April 1980) <www.uncitral.org/pdf/english/texts/sales/cisg/CISG.pdf> last accessed 21 July 2007. The acceding countries are listed at the Status page, available at <www.uncitral.org>.

[37] *Sale of Goods (Vienna Convention) Act 1986* (NSW); 1986 (Qld); 1987 (Vic); 1986 (SA); 1986 (WA); 1987 (Tas); 1987 (ACT); 1987 (NT).

[38] Vienna Sales Convention, article 18(2).

[39] *United Nations Convention on the Use of Electronic Communications in International Contracts,* GA Res 60/21 UN Doc A/RES/60/21 (23 November 2005), available at <www.uncitral.org> last accessed 27 April 2007.

[40] See previous discussion on UNCITRAL Model Law.

[41] As of May 2007, only ten states had taken the preliminary step of signing the Convention (Central African Republic, China, Lebanon, Madagascar, Senegal, Sierra Leone, Singapore, Sri Lanka, Paraguay, and the Russian Federation) and none had actually ratified it. The latest status can be seen at <www.uncitral.org>.

Convention takes an extremely flexible approach, allowing states to implement a complex regime of exceptions and exemptions.[42]

THE TERMS OF THE CONTRACT

The offer–acceptance analysis assists in determining the time and place of formation of a contract. One of the other requirements for an enforceable agreement is that there is agreement on all the terms. Terms are usually expressed by the parties, either orally or in writing, as part of the negotiations prior to formation of the contract. They can also be incorporated into the contract by reference to other documents.[43] Even without a clear expression of the terms, they might be implied from the parties' conduct or the surrounding circumstances.[44] In some contracts, terms might also be imposed by legislation.[45] If the important terms are unclear, the contract may be void from the outset.[46]

Once a contract is formed, neither party can vary its terms or impose new terms without the consent of the other. For example the issue of a ticket or receipt containing terms may be ineffective if it occurs after the contract is formed. This principle developed at a time when most contracts were formed by parties negotiating in each others' presence or by exchanging letters through the post. It presents some practical difficulties in the modern context, where many contracts are based on a standard set of terms and are entered into quickly without opportunities for individual negotiation.[47] In the e-commerce environment sellers need to include detailed terms in many online contracts, but buyers are unlikely to want to take the time to read them all before deciding to buy. We will approach these difficulties by considering three expressions coined to describe some of the solutions: shrinkwrap, browsewrap and clickwrap. Before dealing with these expressions, we mention the special case of signed documents, although a detailed consideration of **electronic signatures** will wait until Chapter 5.

Electronic signature
A method of electronically authenticating the identity of a person who sends a message.

---

[42] For further reading on this topic, see C Connolly and P Ravindra, 'First UN Convention on eCommerce Finalised' (2006) 22 *Computer Law and Security Report* 31.

[43] *Parker v SE Railway* (1877) 2 CPD 416.

[44] *'The Moorcock'* (1889) 14 PD 64; and see the discussion in *Codelfa Construction v State Rail Auth (NSW)* (1983) 1149 CLR 337.

[45] For example, warranties are imposed in consumer contracts for supply of goods and services under the *Trade Practices Act 1974* (Cth) and state Sale of Goods Acts.

[46] *Scammell Ltd v Ousten* [1941] AC 251.

[47] The use of standard contractual terms in a mass market setting reduces transaction costs, which would otherwise be borne by the consumer. There is thus a sound policy reason for allowing the practice.

Signed documents

In the offline world, one way of reducing the risk of the other party being able to dispute the terms of the contract is to ensure they are contained in a signed document. In this context, signatures have achieved a special legal significance—the act of signing is taken as confirmation that the signer is agreeing with the contents of the document. It is the signer's responsibility to read the terms, or take any risks involved in not reading them.[48] As always, there are exceptions to this rule, but they need not concern us now.[49]

As we will see in Chapter 5, electronic signatures are a little cumbersome. Fortunately, while they perform similar functions to traditional signatures, they appear to be unnecessary in ensuring that a buyer is agreeing to the terms. A well-designed clickwrap agreement (without a signature) appears to be adequate. Given that most online contracts are likely to be unsigned, we need to consider other ways in which terms might be incorporated into a contract in the digital environment.

Shrinkwrap

The shrinkwrap problem is best illustrated by an example.

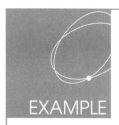

EXAMPLE

Anna buys a laptop from her local computer shop. It is manufactured by a Taiwanese company and supplied in a box sealed with cellophane or plastic film (shrinkwrap). She pays for it and takes it home. On opening it, she finds a five-page document inside the box entitled 'Terms and conditions of purchase'. One of the terms states that the law of Taiwan applies to any dispute between buyer and manufacturer. Is this term enforceable?[50]

In Chapter 6 we deal with consumer protection laws that might apply. Leaving them aside, we focus here on the general principle that, once a contract is formed, neither party can change the terms or impose new terms without the other's agreement.[51]

---

[48]   *L'Estrange v Graucob Ltd* [1934] 2 KB 394; *Toll (FGCT) Pty Ltd v Alphapharm Pty Ltd* (2004) 219 CLR 165.

[49]   Exceptions include situations where the person misrepresents the effect of the clause, where the document is not contractual in nature, where there is a fundamental mistake about the nature of the document (*non est factum*), and where it is signed after the contract is formed. Details of these arguments and the supporting cases can be found in texts on contract law.

[50]   This scenario is common with computer software, where the terms defining copyright and other rights are contained in an 'end-user licence' that is sealed in the package of software.

[51]   The principle is most often seen in what are commonly described as the 'ticket cases'. The best known are probably the UK case of *Thornton v Shoe Lane Parking Ltd* [1971] 2 QB 163 and the Australian High Court case of *Oceanic Line Special Shipping Co Inc v Fay* [1988] 62 ALJR 389.

Based on this principle, Anna would have a strong argument that clauses in the 'Terms and conditions' document do not apply, since she only learnt of them after she bought the computer. They are post-contractual. 'Shrinkwrap' describes situations like this where one party seeks to impose terms that were inaccessible by the other until after the contract was formed. Early US cases suggested the terms would be unenforceable.[52] Although these cases were based largely on an interpretation of the Uniform Commercial Code, they are consistent with the general principle in common law.

The Taiwanese manufacturer might suggest a more sophisticated analysis. It would argue that the contract is not really formed at the time Anna 'buys' the product in the shop, but at some later stage when she has had the opportunity to read the terms. Analogies can be drawn with similar situations in the offline world. In 1975 the Australian High Court regarded the issuing of an airline ticket by an airline or travel agent as the making of an offer, but felt that, even though the fare was paid, the contract should not be regarded as being formed at that time.[53] The contract was seen as being formed some time later, either when the passenger had a reasonable opportunity to consider the terms on the ticket and failed to object,[54] or at the latest when the passenger actually took their seat on the plane.[55]

Later US cases have more readily accepted this approach.[56]

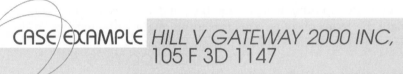

CASE EXAMPLE HILL V GATEWAY 2000 INC, 105 F 3D 1147

USA, SEVENTH CIRCUIT COURT OF APPEALS, 1997

Mr and Mrs Hill bought a computer from Gateway via a call centre and paid by credit card. They were not satisfied with the machine. When they sued for damages, Gateway objected that the agreement accompanying the computer required any dispute to be heard by an arbitrator. The Hills argued this documentation was post-contractual and therefore inapplicable (the shrinkwrap argument). The court rejected this argument. The crucial reason was that the documentation advised customers that if they did not return that the machine within 30 days, they were taken to be agreeing to the terms. The court held that the contract had only been formed at the end of the 30-day period, and that Mr and Mrs   >>

---

52   *Vault Corp v Quaid Software Ltd*, 655 F Supp 750 (ED La, 1987); *Step-Saver Data Systems v Wyse Technology*, 939 F 2d 91 (1991); and *Arizona Retail Sys v Software Link*, 831 F Supp 759 (D Ariz 1993).

53   *MacRobertson Miller Airlines v CoT* (1975) 133 CLR 125.

54   Ibid 137 (Stephen J).

55   Ibid 133 (Barwick CJ), 146 (Jacobs J).

56   *ProCD Inc v Zeidenberg* 86 F3d 1447 (7 Cir 1996); *Hill v Gateway 2000 Inc* 105 F3d 1147 (7 Cir 1997); *MA Mortenson Company Inc v Timberline Software Corporation* 970 P2d 803 (Wash App 1999).

>> Hill had had an opportunity to read the terms and reject them before the contract was formed. Easterbrook J said:

> Payment preceding the revelation of full terms is common for air transportation, insurance, and many other endeavors. Practical considerations support allowing vendors to enclose the full legal terms with their products. Cashiers cannot be expected to read legal documents to customers before ringing up sales ... Writing provides benefits for both sides of commercial transactions. Customers as a group are better off when vendors skip costly and ineffectual steps such as telephonic recitation, and use instead a simple approve-or-return device. Competent adults are bound by such documents, read or unread.

In *Gateway*, the specific reference to a 30-day period assisted in the conclusion that the contract was only formed after delivery of the product. In accordance with the freedom of contract principle, the seller of Anna's computer in our earlier example could legitimately tell Anna that, before the contract is to be regarded as final, she is to take the machine home and read all the documentation. But as in the airline ticket example, even without specific words being used the surrounding circumstances might show that the contract only comes into force some time after the order is placed and payment made—in other words when the purchaser has had a reasonable chance to assimilate the terms on offer. This reasoning might gain credence in the online world.

Browsewrap

Early traders taking advantage of the speed and reach of the Web soon encountered the problem of how best to incorporate terms into their online contracts. When advertising their products, the easiest solution was merely to create a page containing contractual terms, with links to that page from other relevant pages. The link was often in small print at the bottom of the page. This method, which relies on users browsing the page of terms by following the link of their own accord, is what is meant by browsewrap. There is generally no requirement that users follow the link, nor any proof they have done so—users are presumed to have agreed because the terms are available on the website, and the user has chosen to proceed with the transaction.

If it can be proved that the user actually read the terms, and still chose to proceed with the transaction, there would be an objective indication of assent, and the user would be bound. Computer logs may be able to prove that the page of terms was downloaded to a machine used by the user, and this might be sufficient to satisfy a court that the user read the terms. But, in the absence of this proof, would users still be bound, even where the user have not read the terms?

By analogy with established case law, the answer depends on two overlapping but slightly different enquiries: were the provisions so obvious that a reasonable user would have noticed them (before the contract was formed)?[57] And, even if not so obvious, did the seller take reasonable steps to bring them to the user's attention? If the answer to either of these questions is yes, users would be bound, since *they* would be at fault for not noticing and reading the provisions. Objectively, they will be taken to have agreed by going through with the transaction.[58]

In deciding whether notice was reasonable, a court would weigh up, among other things, how obvious the terms were and what alternatives existed for bringing them to the users' attention.

CASE EXAMPLE *SPECHT V NETSCAPE COMMUNICATIONS CORP* 150 F SUPP 2D 585

US DISTRICT COURT FOR THE SOUTHERN DISTRICT OF NEW YORK, 2001

Netscape operated a 'SmartDownload' website for freely available programs. Specht and others claimed that the SmartDownload system contained code that allowed Netscape to track the activities of users, and this amounted to illegal surveillance. Netscape attempted to avoid the litigation by enforcing their 'terms of agreement', which provided that 'all disputes relating to this agreement ... shall be subject to final and binding **arbitration** in Santa Clara County, California'. The terms were available by clicking a link below the download button; attention was drawn to this link by text in a box (also below the download button) saying 'Please review and agree to the terms of the Netscape SmartDownload software license agreement before downloading and using the software'.

Judge Hellerstein described this 'please review' clause as an invitation, not a clear condition of download. The act of downloading was not enough to indicate assent. The court distinguished this case from the shrinkwrap and clickwrap scenarios in which users were required to perform an unambiguous act *before* they could download or use the software.

Arbitration
An out-of-court process by which the parties to a dispute submit their differences to the judgment of an impartial person or group appointed by mutual consent or statutory provision.

---

[57] This is sometimes expressed by asking whether the document in question (brochure, ticket, receipt, etc) was an obviously contractual document. See *Parker v SE Railway* (1877) 2 CPD 416, 422; *Mendelssohn v Normand* [1970] 1 QB 177 (CA) 182.

[58] *Balmain New Ferry v Robertson* (1906) 4 CLR 379.

It is likely that an Australian court would reach a similar conclusion.[59] Apart from the impracticality of making the link to the page of terms so obvious that it cannot fail to attract the users' attention, what makes the browsewrap argument weak is that technology provides a viable and more acceptable alternative—the clickwrap agreement.

Clickwrap

A clickwrap agreement, as its name suggests, is one in which users are required to click on a button or link to indicate their acceptance of the terms and their willingness to proceed. This can be implemented by program code in the design of websites and software. The safest model from the trader's point of view is one that presents the terms on screen, with the 'I agree' button below the page of terms. It is also possible to have a button on screen that refers to the terms available on a different page but asks the user to confirm they have read the terms and agree with them. In either case, the essence of a clickwrap agreement is that, unlike browsewrap, some positive act of assent is required before users can proceed with the transaction.

Again, the leading cases are American. In 1998 the Northern District court in California held such an agreement to be binding,[60] and there is no reason why an Australian court would not follow suit.

THE LEGAL CAPACITY OF THE OTHER PARTY

A contract is an agreement between two or more people. When contracting over the Internet, the parties will often not have seen or dealt with each other before, and it will be difficult to gauge the other's age or mental state. It is also difficult to enforce one's rights across international boundaries. This combination of factors gives rise to increased opportunities for fraud. The well-known expression 'on the Internet, no one knows you are a dog' encapsulates this difficulty. In this section we give a brief overview of situations in which someone with whom you have contracted might have limited capacity.[61]

All legal systems have rules relating to legal capacity. The usual approach is to regard all parties to a contract as having legal capacity unless and until proven otherwise. The most common limitations involve minors and people with mental disabilities, although we will also mention issues with corporations and aliens.

---

59   See also *Evagora v eBay Australia & New Zealand* [2001] VCAT 49. A US court reached an opposite conclusion about the enforceability of terms in *Register.com Inc v Verio* (unreported, US Court of Appeals, Second Circuit, 23 January 2004), but the facts involved a blatant misuse of the WHOIS database by automated and continuous access for mass marketing purposes.

60   *Hotmail Corporation v Van$ Money Pie Inc*, not reported in F Supp, 47 USPQ 2d 1020, 1998 WL 388389 (ND Cal, 16 April 1998). See also *In re RealNetworks Inc Privacy Litigation*, not reported in F Supp 2d, 2000 WL 631341 (ND Ill, 8 May 2000).

61   Other issues related to anonymity are discussed in other chapters, notably authenticating someone's identity (Chapter 5) and Internet fraud (Chapter 16).

Minors   The common law regarded all persons under 21 as minors, having limited capacity to contract. However, the 'age of majority' has been reduced to 18 in all Australian jurisdictions.[62] The law is not uniform across Australia, but the broad approach in all states and territories except New South Wales still follows the common law. This approach is that a contract with a minor is regarded as voidable at the minor's option.[63] The minor can choose to perform the contract, thus treating it as valid; or the minor can choose to avoid the contract.[64] This is a dilemma for e-traders, particularly those involved in the entertainment industry, since statistics show that users in the 14–24-year old age group are very active in this area.[65]

New South Wales introduced a different scheme altogether in 1970.[66] The broad approach taken under its legislation is that a minor is presumed to be bound by any beneficial contract they make, unless it can be shown they did not have the necessary understanding of what they were doing.

Mental disability (including the influence of alcohol or drugs)   Mental health legislation provides for the appointment of guardians for people who are generally incapable of managing their own affairs. Once a person is certified under the legislation, contracts made by them without the assistance of their guardian are void.[67] A contract made by an uncertified person, on the other hand, is regarded as valid until it is proved that they were incapable of understanding the nature of the transaction at the time it was made and that the other contracting party knew (or ought to have known) this.[68] They are thus perfectly capable of making valid contracts during lucid intervals, and can even ratify contracts made while suffering from the disability.[69] In the case of intoxication or the influence of other drugs, it would have to be 'an extreme state ... that deprives a [person] of [their] reason'[70] before common law would invalidate the contract. But where the other party has taken unfair advantage of a lesser state of intoxication, a court might still grant relief under the principle of unconscionability.[71]

---

[62]   *Minors (Property and Contracts) Act 1970* (NSW); *Age of Majority Act 1977* (Vic); *Age of Majority Act 1974* (Qld); *Age of Majority (Reduction) Act 1971* (SA); *Age of Majority Act 1972* (WA); *Age of Majority Act 1973* (Tas); *Age of Majority Act 1974* (ACT); *Age of Majority Act 1971* (NT).

[63]   Although this general statement provides a useful overview, it should be treated with caution, since the term 'voidable' is used in a rather loose and ambiguous way. For further details, see a general text on contract law, such as N Seddon and M Ellinghaus, *Cheshire and Fifoot's Law of Contract*, 8th Australian edn, LexisNexis Butterworths, 2002, p 797.

[64]   There are two broad exceptions: if a contract is for the 'necessities of life' (such as food and essential clothing) or a beneficial employment contract, it is binding on a minor.

[65]   The Department of Communications, Information Technology and the Arts (DCITA), *Online Statistics*, Doc ID 57471, 12 February 2007 (citing Nielsen/Net Ratings), available at <www.dcita.gov.au> last accessed 27 April 2007.

[66]   *Minors (Property and Contracts) Act 1970* (NSW).

[67]   *Gibbons v Wright* (1953) 91 CLR 423, 439. Note that legislation in some states does allow the innocent party certain rights.

[68]   *Hart v O'Connor* [1985] 1 AC 1000, 1018–1019.

[69]   *Gibbons v Wright* (1953) 91 CLR 423, 441–443, 449.

[70]   *Blomley v Ryan* (1956) 99 CLR 362, 404–405 (Fullagar J).

[71]   *Blomley v Ryan* (1956) 99 CLR 362.

Corporations   The traditional view was that any non-natural legal entity such as a corporation could only make valid contracts to the extent authorised by its constitution—any contract exceeding its objects or powers was void (*ultra vires*). This doctrine, which could take blameless consumers by surprise, has been amended by statute in Australia. Corporations generally have the full contractual capacity of a natural person. Even if a corporation's contractual powers are restricted by its constitution, the other party can enforce the contract unless they knew—or should have known—that the corporation did not have the power.[72] Companies or other legal entities not registered under the Corporations legislation may still be affected by the *ultra vires* doctrine.[73]

Aliens   There is no restriction on the capacity of foreign nationals during peacetime. However, according to common law, when there is a state of war between Australia and another country nationals of that country can no longer enter into valid contracts. Nor may they use Australian courts to enforce contracts made before the outbreak of war. There may be some interesting cases ahead based on this principle in the current climate of the war on international terrorism.

It can be seen from this brief discussion of capacity that the faceless and arm's-length nature of Internet transactions presents several traps for unwary traders.

CONCLUDING REMARKS AND FURTHER READING

We have seen that electronic contracts are enforceable, but that there are still a number of difficulties deciding where and when they are formed. The Electronic Transactions Acts do provide some answers when trying to decide on the exact moment of dispatch or receipt of a message, but the applicability of the postal acceptance rule is still uncertain. Well-designed clickwrap and shrinkwrap agreements appear to be enforceable, and facilitate the incorporation of relevant terms in online contracts.

Here are some suggestions for further reading on these topics.

On contract issues

S Squires, 'Some Contract Issues Arising from Online Business–Consumer Agreements' (2000) 5 (1) Deakin LR 95

On the applicability of the postal acceptance rule

S Christensen, 'Formation of Contracts by E-mail: Is it Just the Same as the Post?' (2001) 1 QUTLJ 22

S Hill, 'Flogging a Dead Horse: The Postal Acceptance Rule and E-mail' (2001) 17 J Con L 151

---

[72]   *Corporations Act 2001* (Cth), ss 124–125.
[73]   *Humphries v The Proprietors 'Surfers Palms North' Group Titles Plan 1955* (1993–1994) 179 CLR 597.

On incorporating terms

F M Buono and J A Friedman, 'Maximizing the Enforceability of Click-Wrap Agreements' (2000) 4 J Tech L and Policy 3

P Johnson, 'All Wrapped Up? A Review of the Enforceability of 'Shrink-wrap' and 'Click-wrap' Licences in the United Kingdom and the United States [2003] EIPR 98

E Wong and A Lawrence, 'From Shrink to Click and Browse: Ensuring the Enforceability of Web Terms' (2004) 7 *Internet Law Bulletin* 61

Review questions for this chapter can be found on the book's Online Resource Centre at www.oup.com.au/orc/fordersvantesson.

05

AUTHENTICATION AND SIGNATURES

OBJECTIVES // BY THE END OF THIS CHAPTER, YOU WILL:

○ Appreciate the security and authenticity concerns when communicating over open networks

○ Know how cryptography is used to address these problems

○ Understand how public key systems are used to 'sign' and 'seal' electronic documents

○ Appreciate the role played by digital certificates and certification authorities

○ Know how legislation recognises the use of electronic signatures

○ Be aware of some non-legislative initiatives that encourage the use of electronic signatures

WHAT THIS CHAPTER IS ABOUT

Cryptography
The study of methods of keeping information secret by transforming the information into something unintelligible except to a person who knows the secret method of decoding it.

In Chapter 2 we described the open nature of the Internet—the transmission of data is not private or secure. The global reach of the Internet also means that communications, particularly those involving e-commerce, often involve people who do not know each other. This environment lends itself to fraud. In this chapter we focus on technological attempts to limit the opportunities for fraud, and the extent to which the law has recognised these technologies.

We begin by describing the open network problems. Solutions to these problems generally involve **cryptography**, so this leads us to a basic explanation of what cryptography is and how it works.

We describe the two main systems, and how they resolve some or all of the open network problems. Our description includes an explanation of digital signatures and certificates.

Our discussion then moves on to the law, and how it has responded to these technological solutions. We deal mainly with the Electronic Transactions Acts[1] and the recognition of electronic signatures.

Note that there is some overlap between this chapter and Chapter 16. In this chapter we focus on cryptography as it is used to protect the transmission of data over the Internet. Cryptography is equally useful in protecting stored data from hackers and **computer viruses**, but we leave discussion of the extent to which criminal law protects against these threats until the chapter on computer crime.

Computer virus
Used in a broad sense to mean all malicious or unwanted software that spreads onto hardware without the knowledge or permission of the user.

OPEN NETWORK CONCERNS

There are three basic concerns when using open communication systems:

1   Messages are not private or secret—we will call this the *confidentiality* problem.
2   Messages are not secure from being tampered with—we refer to this as the *message integrity* problem.
3   You cannot be certain who you are dealing with—we call this the *identity* problem.

The answer to these problems has been to use various forms of cryptography. Until the 1970s, most cryptographic systems depended on the exchange of a **key** known only to the sender and the receiver of the message. With the Internet, this raises a fourth problem—it is impossible to exchange the key over an open network without compromising its secrecy. We call this the *key exchange* problem.

We will spend some time describing cryptographic systems, and how they address these four problems, since an appreciation of the technology is important in understanding the prospects for legal regulation.

Message integrity
The status of a message that can be proved not to have been altered during transmission.

Key
A secret method used to protect data in a cryptographic system.

---

[1]   The various Acts passed by the federal, state and territory governments are referred to collectively as the 'Electronic Transactions Acts'—details of the individual Acts are listed in Chapter 4.

TECHNOLOGICAL SOLUTIONS

A cryptography primer

While the traditional aim of cryptography is to keep communications private, modern cryptography extends far beyond this—it is used to sign documents and pay money, for example. The basic idea is the same, though. A secret method (known as a key) is used to transform a message[2] into something that is unintelligible. Once encrypted, no one should be able to understand the message without knowing the key. Decryption is the process of applying the key to transform the encrypted message back to its original state.

In the digital environment data are represented as a string of bits (binary digits, represented by 0s and 1s). What is needed is a method of mixing up the bits so they no longer make sense. Cryptographic methods usually consist of an **algorithm** and a key. The algorithm is the sequence of steps to be followed in transforming the message; the key is the secret data used to make the result unintelligible. Here is a simple illustration. The algorithm might be: (1) divide the original message into blocks of 16 bits; (2) generate a random sequence of 16 bits to use as a key; (3) with the first block of 16 bits from the original message, go through each bit, and, if the bit in the same position in the key is 0, the bit in the original message stays the same; but if the bit in the same position in the key is 1, the bit in the original message changes to its opposite value; (4) do this with each of the remaining blocks of 16 bits from the original message. The message will be substantially mixed up in a random way through use of the key.

Algorithm
A list of steps or instructions for accomplishing a task.

Imagine the first two characters (16 bits) of the message are 'Hi'. The following table illustrates the application of the algorithm. The second row shows the 16 bits that represent these two characters (step 1 of the algorithm). The next row contains a random 16-bit key (step 2 of the algorithm). In step 3, each binary number from step 1 will either change or stay the same, depending on the value in the key. The final row shows the two characters '$z'—these are the encrypted characters that would be displayed as a result of the new sequence of 16 bits.

TABLE 1   **A SIMPLE ENCRYPTION ALGORITHM AND KEY**

First two characters of message	H								i							
Step 1 (first 16 bits of message in binary code)*	0	1	0	0	1	0	0	0	0	1	1	0	1	0	0	1
Step 2 (random 16-bit key)	0	1	1	0	1	1	0	0	0	0	0	1	0	0	1	1
Step 3: in each column, if key = 0, bit from step 1 stays the same (s); if key = 1, bit changes (c), resulting in transformed bits	s	c	c	s	c	c	s	s	s	s	s	c	s	s	c	c
	0	0	1	0	0	1	0	0	0	1	1	1	1	0	1	0
Encrypted characters represented by transformed bits	$								z							

* Using the American Standard Code for Information Interchange (ASCII code)

To decrypt the message, the process is reversed. While sender and receiver both need to know the key in advance, they can generate a fresh key each time they use the system. Even if someone intercepting the message knows the algorithm, if they do not know the random key, the message will be difficult to work out. Note that we say it is *difficult*—not impossible.[3] Given enough time, all cryptographic systems are capable of being cracked, if not by luck or guesswork, then by trying every possible combination until the solution is found—the brute force method. In the above example there are 2^{16} (65 536) possible combinations for the key. Modern computers can test this number of combinations in fractions of a second. If the key was 32 bits, there would be 2^{32} (in round numbers, 4294 million) possibilities. Obviously the longer the key and the more complex the algorithm, the more difficult it would be to crack. For practical purposes, all that is necessary is to choose a system likely to take so long to crack that by the time it *is* cracked it will no longer matter. With small or quick transactions, a system that is safe for a week or two may be sufficient; for national security agencies, several decades may be necessary.

Predictions as to how secure a product might be are, to a large extent, rough estimates that depend on the processing power of the computers used to crack them. DES, the Data **Encryption** Standard selected by the US Government in 1976, uses a 56-bit key, which gives approximately 72 quadrillion possible combinations. It was thought DES would take decades to crack, but, as machines became more powerful, estimates had to be revised. In 1997 it took 96 days; and in 1999 it took 56 hours.[4] By 1998, the US Government had approved a stronger version, known as Triple DES,[5] and in 2002 replaced it with a different system—the Advanced Encryption Standard (AES)— which can use key sizes of 128, 192 or 256 bits.[6]

Encryption
The process of transforming information into something unintelligible except to a person who knows the secret method of decoding (decrypting) it.

Secret key (single key or symmetric system)
A cryptographic system in which the same key, known to both sender and receiver, is used to encrypt and decrypt a message. See also *Public key (asymmetric) system.*

Single key (secret key or symmetric) systems

DES, AES and the other illustrations above are all **symmetric systems**. The same key, known to both sender and receiver, is used to encrypt and decrypt the message. Do these systems solve the open network problems we identified?

---

2   We focus on examples involving the transmission of messages over the Internet. It should be noted that cryptography is equally useful in protecting stored data.

3   Cryptographic literature describes these 'almost impossible to solve' problems as computationally infeasible.

4   See the Electronic Frontier Foundation's account of the DES Challenges and its efforts to crack them, available at <www.eff.org/Privacy/Crypto/Crypto_misc/DESCracker> last accessed 27 April 2007.

5   Triple DES applies DES encryption three times using three different keys.

6   See section 3.3 in RSA Laboratories, *Frequently Asked Questions About Today's Cryptography* (2000, Version 4.1) <www.rsa.com/products/bsafe/documentation/certj212html/rsalabs_faq41. pdf> last accessed 22 July 2007; and see Enrique Zabalas's animated Flash illustration of AES for Conxx at <www.conxx.net/rijndael_anim_conxx.html> last accessed 22 July 2007.

Provided the key is kept secret, they clearly solve the confidentiality problem, since no one can understand the message without knowing the key. They also provide satisfactory solutions to the integrity and identity problems. While outsiders *can* change the message, any alteration will be random guesswork, because the encrypted message is unintelligible. If altered, when the message reaches its destination and is decrypted, it is unlikely to make sense, so the receiver will know it has been corrupted. On the other hand, if the message does make sense when decrypted with the agreed key, this shows it is unlikely to have been tampered with. It must also have been sent by someone who knew the key, and, unless the key has been compromised, this authenticates the identity of the sender.

The major disadvantage of symmetric systems is that the key has to be known to both parties before the message is sent. This does not suit most e-commerce situations. If the key were exchanged over the Internet at the same time or shortly before the secured transaction, it would defeat the purpose, since anyone could see the key. Having to use other communication methods to agree on the key, or agreeing on the key at some other time and place, would destroy the spontaneity needed. Internet communications require a secure way of exchanging the secret key at the time the message is initiated.

Public key (asymmetric) systems

Public key or (asymmetric) system

A cryptographic system in which two different but related keys are used to encrypt and decrypt a message. One key is made public, the other is kept private, and the private key cannot easily be derived from the public key.

A system that does not require advance knowledge of a secret key was developed in 1976. Researchers came up with an algorithm that generates two keys, not just one.[7] The pair of keys are related to each other in such a way that either of them can be used to encrypt a message; but once encrypted, the message can *only* be decrypted by using the other related key. Unlike a symmetric system, the same key *cannot* be used to unlock the message. The second important feature of the algorithm is that even if you know one of the keys, it is effectively impossible to work out the related key.

These features mean that one key can be kept private and the other—the **public key**—made accessible to anyone who might want to use it. Later, we'll discuss distributing public

---

[7]   The initial breakthrough, known as the RSA algorithm (after the first letters of the names of the three researchers who refined it), is used widely in the Internet environment. We leave those interested in understanding the technology to pursue this interest on their own, but here are some useful starting points: for a description of the RSA algorithm's use of prime factoring and modular arithmetic, see section 3.1 in RSA Laboratories, *Frequently Asked Questions About Today's Cryptography* (2000, Version 4.1) <www.rsa.com/products/bsafe/documentation/certj212html/rsalabs_faq41.pdf> last accessed 22 July 2007; for a simple illustration of how this is implemented, see the description by DI Management Services at <www.di-mgt.com.au/rsa_alg.html> last accessed 22 July 2007; for alternative algorithms used in public key systems, including discrete logarithms, elliptic curves, and lattices, see section 2.3, 'Hard Problems' in RSA Laboratories' FAQ.

keys through trusted third parties, but, for the moment, imagine that an e-trader makes their public key available by putting it on their website. This makes several scenarios possible.

'Sealing' a message

If you wanted to communicate securely with the e-trader, you could access their public key to encrypt your message. Once encrypted, only the related private key can decrypt the message—and only the e-trader has it. This achieves confidentiality. As with symmetric systems, any changes to the message will be random, and are unlikely to be intelligible. So this achieves message integrity as well. It does not, however, prove your identity to the e-trader, since anyone could access the e-trader's public key and pretend to be you. Using the public key system in this way solves the confidentiality, message integrity, and key exchange problems, but not the identity problem. It is often described as the equivalent of sealing a message in an envelope.

'Signing' a message

Now imagine the second possibility—the e-trader's private key is used to lock a message before sending it to you. On receipt, you would access the e-trader's public key and use it to decrypt the message. If you are able to decrypt it successfully, then you know only the private key could have locked the message. So whoever owns the related private key must have sent the message. This establishes the e-trader's identity—provided you can trust the source of the public key. But the message is not confidential because anyone could access the e-trader's public key and decrypt the message. Can you rely on the integrity of the message? If others can decrypt it, could they also make intelligible changes to it? As it turns out, the integrity of the message is not compromised. This is because, if an interceptor wants to fool you after changing something, they will need the e-trader's private key to encrypt the message again. If they encrypt it with any other key, your attempt to decrypt it with the sender's public key would fail, and you would know the message had been corrupted. So, using a public key system in this way solves the identity, message integrity and key exchange problems—but not the confidentiality problem. Because encrypting a message with a private key authenticates the identity of the sender, it was seen as the equivalent of a real-world signature and came to be known as a digital signature.

In summary, using one pair of related keys only solves three of the four open network problems at a time. To solve all four at once—to sign and seal a message—it is necessary to use two pairs of asymmetric keys. Before describing how this is done, we give brief descriptions of two other, more efficient ways of using public key systems.

Using a public key to establish a session key

Public key systems are rarely used to encrypt the whole message. They require longer key lengths and are generally much slower (in the order of 1000 times slower) than symmetric systems. It is far more efficient to use a hybrid system in which a public key is used initially, but only to exchange a fresh symmetric key. The symmetric key, known as a session key, is used for the duration of the interaction, after which it expires.

This process happens behind the scenes, with software handling the exchange. A user accessing an e-trader's secure website using, say, Microsoft Internet Explorer just gets feedback that they have accessed a secure site.[8] The software on the user's machine will have looked up the public key belonging to the e-trader (more about the use of certificates to obtain this information shortly); confirmed what symmetric key system the e-trader is using; generated a suitable symmetric key; encrypted this key with the e-trader's public key and sent it to the e-trader. The e-trader's server will decrypt the message using their private key—and, as we have seen, only they can do so—and the software will then start using the symmetric key to exchange encrypted messages.

Using a hash function for more efficient digital signatures

Encrypting the whole of a long message is extremely slow. If all that is required is to confirm the identity of the sender, there are more efficient ways of using a public key system to sign the message. Consider the e-trader encrypting only one sentence of a message with their private key. If the receiver can successfully decrypt that sentence with the e-trader's public key, it would equally authenticate the identity of the e-trader. However, while we gain in efficiency, the integrity of the rest of the message would not be assured—it would remain unencrypted.

A one-way hash function provides a solution that achieves efficiency as well as message integrity. Also known as a message digest or fingerprint, a one-way hash function is a mathematical formula that operates on a message of variable length, converting it into a much smaller fixed-length number. It is like the check sum used with credit card numbers. A good hash function must be hard to reverse (hence described as one-way); unlikely to produce the same hash value from two different messages; and sensitive enough that even a small change in the message will cause a drastic change in the hash value produced.[9]

Armed with this useful function, the sender's computer can calculate a hash value for a message. The sender's private key is then used to encrypt only the hash value. This encrypted hash value is attached to the plain text of the message (the digital signature), and sent to the recipient, as in Diagram 1.

---

8   Feedback depends on the settings. It usually involves a padlock symbol in the status bar; the protocol in the URL showing https instead of http; and the display of warning messages when accessing or leaving the secure site.

9   Microsoft's Base Cryptographic tools support a number of different hash algorithms. For those seeking more information about them, they are Message Authentication Code (MAC), Message Digest 2 (MD2), Message Digest 5 (MD5), and Secure Hash Algorithm (SHA). See the Microsoft website at <http://msdn2.microsoft.com/en-au/library/ms904264. aspx> last accessed 3 June 2007.

DIAGRAM 1   SENDING A SIGNED MESSAGE USING A HASH ALGORITHM

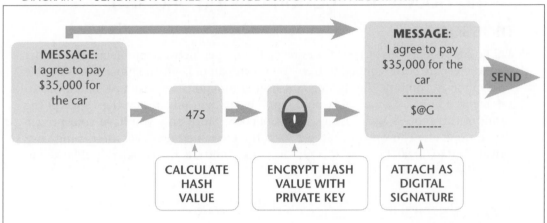

Message integrity is now easy to prove. The receiver (Diagram 2) takes the plain text, and independently calculates its hash value. The sender's public key is also used to decrypt the digital signature part of the message, giving the original hash value. If the two hash values are the same, the receiver knows that nothing has changed in the message, and that only the sender could have used the related private key to send the correct hash value. This is the most common form of digital signature. As before, it does not achieve confidentiality.

DIAGRAM 2   RECEIVING AND AUTHENTICATING THE SIGNED MESSAGE

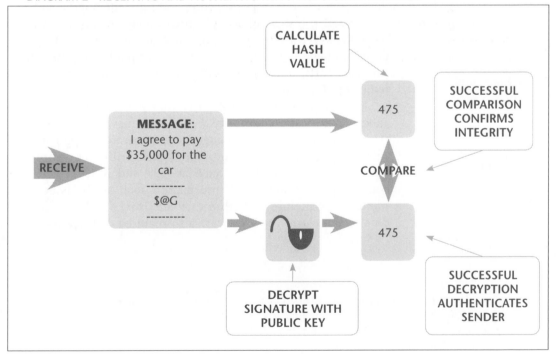

Using double encryption to sign and seal messages

Public key systems can be used to address all four open network problems. The sender and receiver are both required to have their own pair of keys. The process uses double encryption to combine the signing and sealing functions we have just described. An e-trader sending you a message would sign it using their private key, then encrypt the result of this process again using your public key. Since only you have your private key, no one else can open or tamper with the encrypted message. After using your private key to 'break the seal' (decrypt it), you would use the e-trader's public key to check the signature.

Key distribution and certificates

The use of a public key system is only effective if you can be certain the public key belongs to the e-trader. In our discussion, we asked you to imagine that the e-trader makes the key available on their website. This method of distributing the key creates problems. It enables a third party to create a website and distribute a bogus public key, pretending to be the e-trader. It also enables a 'man in the middle attack' where someone intercepts the user's initial download of the e-trader's public key, and impersonates the e-trader by substituting their own public key.

An independent third party is needed to verify that the public key is genuine—in other words, that the e-trader and user *are* talking to each other. The trusted third party must initially use other data to verify the identity of the e-trader. The third party then bundles the e-trader's name and public key together and signs the bundle with their own private key. The e-trader, instead of sending their public key on its own, sends this package (called a digital certificate) to the user. Anyone can verify the third party's signature by using the third party's public key, and, if the third party is trusted, can thus be confident the e-trader's public key is genuine.

Certification authority

In cryptography, a trusted third party who issues a digital certificate that attests to the authenticity of a public key, thus validating the person, organisation, or server noted in the certificate.

An independent third party that issues certificates is called a **certification authority** (CA). Sometimes the CA is also the distributor of software systems that generate key pairs for their customers. The most common digital certificates comply with recognised standards, such as X9[10] and X.509.[11] They usually contain additional information such as the issuer's name, the signature algorithm they are using and the expiry date of the certificate.[12] CAs are also required to keep up-to-

---

[10]   This is actually a suite of standards issued by the American National Standards Institute (ANSI) for the financial and banking industries in the USA.

[11]   A common standard issued by the International Telecommunications Union (ITU-T), recognised by both Microsoft Internet Explorer and Netscape.

date lists of certificates that have been revoked, for example because they are known to have been compromised.

Other methods of authenticating identity

There are four broad ways of authenticating identity:

○ by reference to something the user has (for example an identity card, smartcard or a private key related to a public key);

○ by reference to something the user knows (for example a password or phrase, a **personal identification number** or a secret key);

○ by reference to some unique feature of the user (for example fingerprint, retina pattern, DNA sequence, or other biometric identifiers); and

○ by reference to some unique thing the user does (for example signature or gait).

Personal Identification Number (PIN)
An alphanumeric string of digits used to identify an individual.

Biometrics
The use of unique personal characteristics (such as fingerprints) to identify a person or authenticate their identity.

Stronger authentication results if a combination of methods is used—known as layered or multi-factor authentication. **Biometrics**—identifying humans based on their unique features or behaviour—offers useful possibilities. Fingerprint technology is well established in forensics, and is beginning to be used on many computer systems to authenticate the identity of a user. These systems have the advantage that they do not depend on remembering secret information (unlike passwords or PINs), nor can they be stolen or easily transferred to others.[13] However, on the Internet, the data generated by a fingerprint reader for example still must be sent to a server to be compared with a database, and a message sent back confirming or denying an acceptable match. The integrity of these messages needs to be assured, so we will still have to rely on cryptographic solutions in combination with biometrics.

One of the consequences of the development of other methods of authentication has been a change in the terminology. As described earlier, the term 'digital signature' first came to mean a signature applied with a public key system. These days, when referring to all possible methods of authenticating identity, the term 'electronic signature' is generally used. A digital signature is a type of electronic signature.

---

[12]   For further details, see section 5.3, 'Cryptography Standards' in RSA Laboratories, *Frequently Asked Questions About Today's Cryptography* (2000, Version 4.1) <www.rsa.com/products/bsafe/documentation/certj212html/rsalabs_faq41.pdf> last accessed 22 July 2007.

[13]   As to the reliability of current fingerprint technology, however, see Dan Svantesson, 'Whose Fingerprints, and with What Flavour, Would You Like Today?' (August 2005) 11(7) *Privacy Law and Policy Reporter* 201.

LEGAL RECOGNITION OF ELECTRONIC SIGNATURES

When signatures are used

Signatures are not a general requirement for the formation of a contract. Parties *choose* to sign documents to make it more difficult for the contents to be denied later. They are more difficult to deny because, in a formal setting, the names of the signatories and witnesses are usually recorded and the signatures can be verified by handwriting experts. Verifying the signature makes it easy to prove that the signatory knew, or ought to have known, of the contents of the document.

While there is no general signature requirement, a number of statutes call for a signature to make certain documents legally effective. Examples include contracts for the sale of land or interests in land, guarantees (in some states), wills, credit contracts, bills of exchange and certain certificates by company directors.

In common law, a signature includes any mark put on a document with the intention that it will be binding. It does not have to use the person's name or be written by hand.[14] On the other hand, some statutes require signatures to be made with the name or autograph of the party signing. Some also require a signature to be 'under the person's hand', which excludes signing by an agent. Where a statute merely requires a document to be signed and provides nothing further, the wide common law rules would normally apply. How should the law treat these signature requirements in the digital environment?[15]

Alternative approaches to electronic signatures

In 1998, an Australian report on e-commerce found it useful to categorise electronic signature legislation into three broad groups:[16]

○   Signature-enabling legislation merely recognises the legality of electronic signatures without defining them. It usually provides that they have the same effect as paper-based signatures. This is also known as a 'minimalist' approach, and, as we will see, the Australian legislation is an example. The legislation does not have to be long or detailed, so it is fairly easy to implement, but it is relatively unhelpful because it does not specify what qualifies as a valid electronic signature.

○   Prescriptive legislation specifies exactly what qualifies as a valid electronic signature, often giving details of the algorithm and acceptable key lengths for certain purposes. The disadvantage of this approach is that it entrenches a

---

[14]   *R v Moore; Ex Parte Myers* (1884) 10 VLR 322.

[15]   See S Christensen, 'Moving the Statute of Frauds to the Digital Age' (2003) 77(7) *ALJ* 416.

[16]   *Electronic Commerce: Building the Legal Framework*, Report of the Electronic Commerce Expert Group to the Attorney-General 'ECEG Report', 31 March 1998, paragraph 3.2.2, available at <www.ag.gov.au> last accessed 27 April 2007.

particular technology and discourages the development of other technologies. It also requires the legislation to be changed if the chosen technology becomes outdated or new systems become commercially acceptable.

o   Criterion-based legislation is somewhere between these approaches. It sets out general criteria for an electronic signature. The criteria can be expressed in neutral language that does not favour one technology over others. For example it may require that the signature method must be unique to the person using it and capable of independent verification. On the other hand, this might not give sufficient guidance because it precludes the laying down of acceptable algorithms and key lengths.

While the report speculated that it may be possible to gain maximum advantage by combining these approaches,[17] it concluded that Australia should implement the approach recommended in UNCITRAL's Model Law on Electronic Commerce[18]—a minimalist or signature-enabling approach. As we saw in the previous chapter, the Commonwealth Government not only passed an Act[19] largely following the Model Law, but also persuaded all the states and territories to pass similar legislation, so Australia has a national scheme.[20]

The signature provision in the Electronic Transactions Acts

The signature provision in the New South Wales Act is s 9.[21] It reads:

Signatures

(1) If, under a law of this jurisdiction, the signature of a person is required, that requirement is taken to have been met in relation to an electronic communication if:

(a) a method is used to identify the person and to indicate the person's approval of the information communicated, and

(b) having regard to all the relevant circumstances at the time the method was used, the method was as reliable as was appropriate for the purposes for which the information was communicated, and

(c) the person to whom the signature is required to be given consents to that requirement being met by way of the use of the method mentioned in paragraph (a).

---

[17] ECEG Report, paragraph 4.5.11.

[18] UNCITRAL, *Model Law on Electronic Commerce*, GA Resolution 51/162, GAOR 51st sess, 85th plen mtg, UN Doc A/Res/51/162 (1996) (with additional article 5bis as adopted in 1998 and Guide to Enactment) available at <www.uncitral.org> last accessed 27 April 2007.

[19] The *Electronic Transactions Act 1999* (Cth).

[20] Details of the Acts in all the states and territories appear in Chapter 4. In this book the various Acts are referred to collectively as the 'Electronic Transactions Acts'.

[21] *Electronic Transactions Act 2000* (NSW). There are equivalent provisions in the Acts of the Commonwealth and all the states and territories.

While it could be argued this is a criterion-based approach, the requirements are so broad that it would be more accurate to categorise it as minimalist.

As we have seen, secret and public key systems do identify the person. Usually the message itself will expressly (or impliedly, from its context) indicate the person's approval of the information. As for the reliability requirement, this will presumably depend on the purpose of the communication and the suitability of the algorithm and key length for that purpose. The section does not require verification of the integrity of the message, so the digital signatures we described perform an extra function that is not required under the Act.

Biometric systems would identify the person equally well. When used with suitable cryptographic systems protecting the security of the data, they are likely to satisfy the reliability requirement. But what if the data generated by a fingerprint reader were sent without encryption? Or could an unencrypted e-mail message sent from an account that can be proved to belong to the sender satisfy the section? Courts have been prepared to accept the latter argument for some purposes,[22] but until senior appellate courts interpret the meaning of the reliability requirement in several different situations it is difficult to know what amounts to an acceptable signature.

While the uncertainty of this broad approach may be frustrating, it has several advantages. The flexibility enables courts to recognise that different transactions require different levels of security, and that signature methods may become less secure over time. It also does not favour one technology over others.

The last point to be made in dealing with the Electronic Transactions Acts is that each state lists certain exemptions in regulations made under its own Act. There is some consistency—the Acts do not generally apply to contracts for the sale of land or to legal proceedings. But there are differences between the states. For example New South Wales exempts polls and elections;[23] Tasmania exempts wills and powers of attorney.[24] Despite the attempt to have a national scheme, there are thus crucial differences in the detail.

The attribution provision in the Electronic Transactions Acts

Might you be liable if someone pretending to be you sends electronic messages or signs documents in your name? The Electronic Transactions Acts have a provision that deals with this situation:[25]

---

[22]   See *McGuren v Simpson* [2004] NSWSC 35 (18 February 2004) (e-mail acknowledgment of a debt held to satisfy the writing and signature requirements for interrupting the limitation period on a claim); and *Faulks v Cameron* [2004] NTSC 61 (11 November 2004) (e-mail correspondence held to constitute a written and signed separation agreement under the *De Facto Relationships Act 1991* (NT)).

[23]   *Electronic Transactions Regulations 2007* (NSW), regs 4 and 7.

[24]   *Electronic Transactions Regulations 2001* (Tas), regs 4 and 5.

[25]   *Electronic Transactions Act 1999* (Cth) s 15, and equivalent sections in the other Acts. Later subsections make it clear this does not affect the law of agency.

Attribution of electronic communications

(1) … unless otherwise agreed between the purported originator and the addressee of an electronic communication, the purported originator of the electronic communication is bound by that communication only if the communication was sent by the purported originator or with the authority of the purported originator.

Thus if someone orders goods using your e-mail address, you will not have to pay. If someone hacks into your computer, accesses an e-trader's website and enters an electronic contract in your name, you would not be bound by the contract. Even if the person signed the message with your private key, you would not be bound.

The initial impression given by this broad provision requires some qualification. In the first place, the section says 'unless otherwise agreed …'. If you already have a relationship with the e-trader, you may have agreed to their terms and conditions, which might specify that orders made from your machine are deemed to be yours, whether you approved them or not. Second, it is important to note the use of the word 'bound'. Not being *bound* is not the same as not being *liable* if you did not send or authorise the message. You might not be bound by the contents of the message, but if you were **negligent** in allowing the hacker access to your machine in the first place, you might still be liable in tort law for any loss suffered by the other party.

Negligence
A cause of action in torts law where one party who owes a 'duty of care' to another breaches that duty by failing to meet the standard of care expected of a reasonable person, resulting in material damage.

Model Law on Electronic Signatures

After the Commonwealth Act was passed, UNICTRAL released a Model Law on Electronic Signatures.[26] While it has no immediate legal effect until implemented by legislation in each country, it is interesting to note the way our law might develop in future. It recognises the vagueness of the earlier approach, and tries to fill out what is meant by the phrase 'as reliable as appropriate'. Article 6(3) provides:

An electronic signature is considered to be reliable for the purpose of satisfying the requirement … if:

(a) The signature creation data are, within the context in which they are used, linked to the signatory and to no other person;
(b) The signature creation data were, at the time of signing, under the control of the signatory and of no other person;
(c) Any alteration to the electronic signature, made after the time of signing, is detectable; and
(d) Where a purpose of the legal requirement for a signature is to provide assurance as to the integrity of the information to which it relates, any alteration made to that information after the time of signing is detectable.

---

[26] UNCITRAL, *Model Law on Electronic Signatures*, GA Res A/RES/56/80, 12 December 2001, available at <www.uncitral.org> last accessed 27 April 2007 (includes Guide to Enactment).

While this is a criterion-based approach, the Model Law also recognises the advantages of a prescriptive approach. In article 7 it contemplates delegating a power to a public or private body to decide in advance whether a signature system satisfies article 6. In other articles, the Model Law outlines the responsibilities of signatories, certification authorities and relying parties.[27] For example signatories must exercise reasonable care to avoid unauthorised use of their signatures, and must use reasonable efforts to notify relying parties if their signature is compromised. The final article addresses international harmonisation. It provides that foreign electronic signatures and certificates have the same legal effect if they offer a 'substantially equivalent level of reliability'.

Whether and when Australian law is likely to be updated along these lines remains to be seen.

OTHER INITIATIVES

Many other initiatives are designed to encourage security, trust and confidence in e-commerce. To round off this chapter, we mention a small selection.

Gatekeeper and other Federal Government initiatives

The Federal Government has taken the view that apart from providing certification services for government agencies, its role is mainly to develop infrastructure and policies. The implementation of certification services for the private sector has been left to market forces.

The certification service developed for government agencies is known as Gatekeeper. This is a public key infrastructure (PKI) that uses digital certificates to certify public keys. Suitable organisations (pubic and private) can apply for accreditation and issue certificates. All Commonwealth government agencies are required to use this system when online authentication is required for themselves, their customers or trading partners. Gatekeeper has not been successful as anticipated—some service providers (notably Telstra and PriceWaterhouseCoopers) have let their accreditation lapse.[28] In September 2006 the Australian Government Information Management Office (AGIMO) released a new framework for the Gatekeeper system in an attempt to make it less complex and more affordable.[29]

---

[27]   Articles 8–11.

[28]   The list of current and former accredited or recognised service providers is available at <www.agimo.gov.au/infrastructure/gatekeeper/accredited> last accessed 27 April 2007.

[29]   See AGIMO, *Gatekeeper Public Key Infrastructure (PKI) Framework*, September 2006, and the notes introducing the framework at <www.agimo.gov.au/infrastructure/gatekeeper> last accessed 27 April 2007.

The work on revitalising Gatekeeper was part of a Federal Government focus on security and confidence during 2004–2006.[30] A number of similar frameworks have been developed, or are now being developed:[31]

o   The Australian Government e-Authentication Framework (AGAF) for Business was released in 2005. It goes further than the Gatekeeper approach, aiming to match the risk level of the transaction to an appropriate authentication mechanism. An equivalent AGAF for Individuals is still under development.

o   The Australian Government Smartcard Framework has been released in part. The Overview and Principles and the Smartcard Handbook were released in June 2006; the remainder is still under development. Its aim is to provide greater convenience in accessing government services through smartcards, and to protect the cards and enhance the privacy and security of cardholder information.

Project Angus

Project Angus is very similar to Gatekeeper. It is a certification system for the private sector developed by four major Australian banks. Other financial institutions are also able to participate. It is designed as an authentication system for the banks' business customers who are involved in e-commerce. Angus certificates are globally interoperable—they comply with and can be recognised by Gatekeeper and Identrus.

Project Identrus

This project started with the cooperation of several large European financial institutions in 1999. Its original aim was for financial institutions to act as certification authorities for their corporate e-commerce customers, to promote trusted relationships with the institutions and with each other. It led to the registration of a separate company offering international certification services.[32]

CONCLUDING REMARKS AND FURTHER READING

A good understanding of the law relating to online authentication can only be achieved with an equally good understanding of the technology. With this in mind, we have spent some time in this chapter explaining encryption technology and how it is used to sign

---

[30]   Department of Communications, Information Technology and the Arts, *Strategic Framework for the Information Economy 2004–2006: Opportunities and Challenges for the Information Age*, July 2004, available at <www.dcita.gov.au/communications_and_technology/policy_and_legislation/australias_strategic_framework> last accessed 27 April 2007.

[31]   Details can be seen on the AGIMO website at <www.agimo.gov.au/infrastructure/authentication> last accessed 27 April 2007.

[32]   See the IdenTrust company profile, available at <www.identrust.com/company/index.html> last accessed 27 April 2007.

and seal digital documents. This should help you to understand the difficulty faced when considering how to achieve legal recognition of the technology, and in analysing the merits of those choices.

Our suggestions for further reading on this subject follow.

On the technology

RSA Laboratories, *Frequently Asked Questions About Today's Cryptography* (2000, Version 4.1) available at <www.rsa.com/products/bsafe/documentation/certj212html/rsalabs_faq41.pdf>

On appropriate forms of legislation (among many other issues)

Chapter 3 in *Electronic Commerce: Building the Legal Framework*, Report of the Electronic Commerce Expert Group to the Attorney-General 'ECEG Report', 31 March 1998, available at <www.ag.gov.au>

Model laws

UNCITRAL, *Model Law on Electronic Signatures*, GA Res A/RES/56/80, 12 December 2001, available at <www.uncitral.org> (includes Guide to Enactment)

On satisfying signature requirements in law

S Christensen, 'Moving the Statute of Frauds to the Digital Age' (2003) 77(7) ALJ 416

Review questions for this chapter can be found on the book's Online Resource Centre at www.oup.com.au/orc/fordersvantesson.

06

CONSUMER PROTECTION

OBJECTIVES // BY THE END OF THIS CHAPTER, YOU WILL:

○ Have developed an understanding of the different considerations relevant to consumers as opposed to businesses

○ Be able to identify those e-commerce situations where consumer protection law applies

○ Be familiar with the most central consumer protection provisions in Australian law

WHAT THIS CHAPTER IS ABOUT

Transactions in which the buyer is a private individual are common online. This chapter discusses such transactions and how they are different from those where the buyer is not a private individual.

While this chapter focuses on consumer concerns, it does not address *all* relevant issues. Many are addressed in other chapters. The example of Jack is illustrative.

EXAMPLE

Jack, who lives in Queensland, buys a CD from a website operated by a New Zealand company called Kiwikiwi. When placing the order for the CD Jack has to enter his postal address, e-mail address and credit card details. When the CD arrives it turns out that Kiwikiwi has posted the wrong CD. In addition, Jack starts receiving spam e-mails from a range of New Zealand-based companies, and a few days later he finds that Kiwikiwi has made his credit card details freely accessible on their website, which has resulted in his credit card being used by other people making purchases online.

This example involves areas of law dealt with in other parts of this book, which are clearly relevant to consumers. The collection and distribution of Jack's personal information may be regulated by privacy law (discussed in Chapter 9), and the spam e-mail may be subject to spam regulation (discussed in Chapter 10). This situation also raises private international law and contractual issues (discussed in Chapters 3 and 4 respectively). It should be obvious that the reader must also read other chapters of this book to get a complete picture of the issues facing consumers in e-commerce.

WHO IS DEFINED AS A CONSUMER?

The necessary starting point when discussing consumer protection is the definition of *consumer*—we need to know who is classed as a consumer. While this might seem like a trivial task it is not as easily done as might first be thought. The definition varies throughout the world. In the majority of legal systems, as well as in several important international instruments, a consumer is defined as a natural person acting outside her or his professional capacity.[1]

Australia has, however, opted for a much wider definition. In s 4B of the most important consumer protection instrument in Australia, the *Trade Practices Act 1974* (Cth), a distinction is drawn between a business engaging in a transaction for consumption (a business consumer), and a business engaging in its primary area of trade. Businesses are treated like consumers and given the same protection as consumers where they contract for goods or services, and:

o   the purchase was not for re-supply or otherwise for being used up or transformed in trade or commerce; and

---

[1]   See for example Hague Convention of 30 June 2005 on Choice of Court Agreements, article 2(1), and Council Directive 2000/31/EC of 8 June 2000 on certain legal aspects of information society services, in particular electronic commerce, in the Internal Market, article 2(e).

○   the purchase was either for goods or services of a kind ordinarily acquired for personal, domestic or household use, or for an amount lower than the prescribed amount (currently $40 000).

While the wide Australian approach is unusual, it is not without merit. Imagine a situation where a small business purchases software from a large retailer. The large retailer will certainly be the stronger party and the small business may be in as weak a bargaining position as a private consumer would be when purchasing the same software from the same retailer.

DISTINCTION BETWEEN B2B, B2C AND C2C

Having discussed what is meant by the term 'consumer', we can draw some distinctions between different types of transactions commonly occurring online. Where two businesses transact, the transaction is commonly referred to as a business-to-business (B2B) transaction. So for example where IKEA purchases a sophisticated computer system from IBM, we can talk of a B2B transaction taking place. In contrast, where a natural person acting outside her or his professional capacity purchases a book from Amazon.com, a business-to-consumer (B2C) transaction takes place.

While the two types of transaction mentioned above have commonly occurred online for a relatively long period of time, the third category, consumer-to-consumer (C2C) transactions are more recent. In a C2C transaction neither of the parties is acting in their professional capacity, and a typical example of such a transaction is where one natural person purchases some object from another natural person via eBay.com.[2]

These different types of transaction warrant different treatment. A transaction between two major corporations such as IKEA and IBM will be scrutinised by both parties' lawyers, and both parties are likely to be fully informed about its legal implications. However, when consumers buy books from a website they may not be aware of the legal implications. In virtually all B2C contracts the terms of the contract are determined in advance by the business and set out in its standard terms and conditions. In C2C contracts neither party is likely to be fully aware of the legal implications, or to worry about entering a formal contract.

This brings us to the core of the consumer protection problem. On one hand, consumers are vulnerable and need to be protected, otherwise they will not feel confident enough to engage in e-commerce. On the other hand, if the law is overly protective of consumers' rights and ignores the needs of businesses, businesses will not engage in e-commerce. A suitable balance needs to be struck between these interests.

---

[2]   Auctions, including Internet-based auctions, give rise to a range of particular issues. They are not discussed here, and the reader is referred to (for example) A Sorensen and M Webster, 'Internet Auctions, Consumer Protection and the Trade Practices Act' (2003) 6 (8) *Internet Law Bulletin*; and A Reynolds, 'E-auctions: Who Will Protect the Consumer?' (2002) 18 J Con L 75.

Bait advertising
An appealing but insincere advertisement for a product or service where the main purpose is not to sell at the advertised price, but to lure consumers so there is an opportunity to sell a different or more expensive product.

Unconscionable conduct
Unfair or unreasonable conduct in business transactions that goes against good conscience.

Misleading or deceptive conduct
Any conduct in trade or commerce which misleads or deceives or is likely to do so.

Misrepresentation
A false statement of fact; to be actionable in tort law, it must be made intentionally or negligently and must induce a person to act on it to their detriment.

Imposed terms
Certain conditions and warranties imposed on contracts by the law.

Many countries address the special needs of B2C and C2C transactions, as opposed to B2B transactions. While they take different approaches to the problem, they all have special rules that mitigate the effect of the strong power imbalance in B2C transactions. We now move on to examine the consumer protection landscape in Australia.

THE IMPACT OF THE *TRADE PRACTICES ACT 1974* (CTH)

As already mentioned, the most important consumer protection instrument in Australia is the *Trade Practices Act 1974* (Cth) ('TPA'). It aims to 'enhance the welfare of Australians through the promotion of competition and fair trading and provision for consumer protection'.[3]

The TPA covers several topics of relevance to e-commerce. For example s 54 regulates the offering of gifts and prizes and s 57 deals with **bait advertising**. However, the most important areas are the regulation of **unconscionable conduct** (ss 51AA, 51AB and 51AC), **misleading or deceptive conduct** (s 52), **misrepresentations** (s 53) and **imposed terms** (ss 69–74).

Another relevant provision is s 67 of the TPA, which affects the choice of law. It provides:

Where:

(a)   the proper law of a contract for the supply by a corporation of goods or services to a consumer would, but for a term that it should be the law of some other country or a term to the like effect, be the law of any part of Australia; or

(b)   a contract for the supply by a corporation of goods or services to a consumer contains a term that purports to substitute, or has the effect of substituting, provisions of the law of some other country or of a State or Territory for all or any of the provisions of this Division;

this Division applies to the contract notwithstanding that term.

In other words, this provision ensures that corporations do not avoid the application of the TPA simply by nominating a foreign law as the applicable law.

---

[3]   *Trade Practices Act 1974* (Cth) s 2.

The Commonwealth has power to legislate in relation to international and inter-state trade and commerce[4] as well as postal, telegraphic and telephonic services.[5] Under the TPA it uses this power to expand the applicability of certain provisions— including ss 51AA–AC, s 52, s 53 and ss 69–74—to the acts of natural persons, even though the provisions themselves seem limited to corporations. For certain provisions of the TPA a reference to a corporation includes a person where that person engaged in conduct involving the use of postal, telegraphic or telephonic services, or took place in a radio or television broadcast.[6] So for example when s 52 states: 'A corporation shall not, in trade or commerce, engage in conduct that is misleading or deceptive or is likely to mislead or deceive', it is in reality saying:

> A corporation [or a person, not being a corporation, who is engaged in conduct involving the use of postal, telegraphic or telephonic services, or taking place in a radio or television broadcast] shall not, in trade or commerce, engage in conduct that is misleading or deceptive or is likely to mislead or deceive.

Similarly, s 6 extends the application of certain provisions to persons (not just corporations) where they engage in trade or commerce among the Australian states and territories.

Unconscionable conduct

The concept of *unconscionable conduct* developed in case law long before the TPA. The first provision dealing with unconscionable conduct in the TPA—s 51AA—simply ensures that where the more specific sections (ss 51AB and 51AC) do not apply, an action can still be brought in reliance on 'unwritten law' (case law).

So what is unconscionable conduct in case law? The concept of unconscionability is very broad and general. Typically, someone is acting unconscionably where they knowingly (whether due to actual or constructive knowledge) exploit an innocent party's special disadvantage.[7] Special disadvantage can stem from a variety of aspects of the weaker party's personality, such as age, gender, health, drug dependence, or level of education.[8]

One difficulty is that e-traders may not be in a position to properly evaluate whether the other party acts under some special disadvantage. While the requirement of knowledge of the special disadvantage ought to minimise the problems stemming from this, it would still be prudent for web businesses to avoid situations in which they could be seen to be exploiting a special disadvantage.

---

4   *Commonwealth of Australia Constitution Act* s 51(i).
5   *Commonwealth of Australia Constitution Act* s 51(v).
6   *Trade Practices Act 1974* (Cth) s 6, and see further: *Australian Competition and Consumer Commission v Chen* [2003] FCA 897, *Dataflow Computer Services Pty v Goodman* (1999) 168 ALR 169 and *Australian Competition and Consumer Commission v Kaye* [2004] FCA 1363.
7   See for example *Commercial Bank of Australia Ltd v Amadio* (1983) 151 CLR 447.
8   See for example *Blomley v Ryan* (1956) 99 CLR 405.

Sections 51AB and 51AC are more specific. Section 51AB puts in place special rules for the way corporations may conduct themselves in relation to consumers.[9] Having made clear in subsection 1 that a court will take account of all the circumstances in evaluating whether or not conduct is unconscionable, s 51AB(2) gives some examples of particular indicators of unconscionability that courts may consider. For example the courts will look at:

○   'the relative strengths of the bargaining positions of the corporation and the consumer';[10]

○   'whether, as a result of conduct engaged in by the corporation, the consumer was required to comply with conditions that were not reasonably necessary for the protection of the legitimate interests of the corporation';[11]

○   'whether the consumer was able to understand any documents relating to the supply or possible supply of the goods or services';[12]

○   'whether any undue influence or pressure was exerted on, or any unfair tactics were used against, the consumer or a person acting on behalf of the consumer by the corporation or a person acting on behalf of the corporation in relation to the supply or possible supply of the goods or services';[13] and

○   'the amount for which, and the circumstances under which, the consumer could have acquired identical or equivalent goods or services from a person other than the corporation'.[14]

As s 51AC largely repeats the provisions of s 51AB, but in the context of B2B transactions, it will not be discussed here.

Misleading conduct and deceptive conduct

Section 52 is by far the most important consumer protection provision in Australian law. Indeed, seeing the diversity of legal proceedings in which s 52 is raised, it could be suggested that it is the most important section in all Australian legislation. It has been raised in actions ranging from pure consumer protection to cases involving one trader trying to prevent another trader from using similar packaging for its products (passing off: see Chapter 14), and even defamation cases. Here it is examined primarily as a tool for consumer protection in the strict sense.

The enormous versatility of s 52 stems from its simplicity—subsection (1) states: 'A corporation shall not, in trade or commerce, engage in conduct that is misleading or deceptive or is likely to mislead or deceive.' Subsection (2) makes clear that the more specific provisions of the TPA do not limit the scope of s 52. As a consequence, s 52 is often pleaded as a 'catch all' alongside more specific provisions of the TPA.

---

9   Note that a similar provision is found in *Fair Trading Act 1989* (Qld) s 39.
10   *Trade Practices Act 1974* (Cth) s 51AB(2)(a).
11   *Trade Practices Act 1974* (Cth) s 51AB(2)(b).
12   *Trade Practices Act 1974* (Cth) s 51AB(2)(c).
13   *Trade Practices Act 1974* (Cth) s 51AB(2)(d).
14   *Trade Practices Act 1974* (Cth) s 51AB(2)(e).

So how is this broadly worded provision applied in practice? The question of whether conduct is misleading or deceptive is addressed by asking whether a hypothetical member of a relevant section of the public would be misled or deceived. A court will typically start by seeking to identify the relevant section of the public at which the conduct was aimed.[15] For example the relevant section may be identified by reference to factors such as age, gender, interests and geographical location.

Once the relevant section of the public has been identified the court will focus its attention on how weaker-than-average individuals within that section—but 'not persons whose reactions are extreme or fanciful'[16]—would respond to or interpret the relevant conduct.[17] It is not necessary to prove that anybody actually has been misled and/or deceived to be successful. However, proof of this is **admissible** and may be persuasive.[18]

Having said this, the courts have acknowledged that when applying s 52 'everything must depend on an appropriately detailed examination of the specific circumstances of the case',[19] and a study of available cases reveals a considerable diversity of approach.

> **Admissible evidence**
> Evidence that is admissible in court—it is required to be relevant, not overly prejudicial, and reliable.

Misrepresentations

Like unconscionable conduct, *misrepresentations* are actionable at common law and under the TPA. Actions for misrepresentation at common law are not restricted to consumer contracts. Like s 52, the TPA provision on misrepresentations (s 53) is not restricted to consumer contracts. However, here we will focus only on the TPA protection of consumer contracts.

Section 53 of the TPA outlines a wide range of specific types of representations that a corporation is prevented from making 'in connexion with the supply or possible supply of goods or services or in connexion with the promotion by any means of the supply or use of goods or services'.[20] These include false representations:

o   'that goods are of a particular standard, quality, value, grade, composition, style or model or have had a particular history or particular previous use';

o   'that services are of a particular standard, quality, value or grade';

o   'that goods are new';

o   'that a particular person has agreed to acquire goods or services';

o   'that goods or services have sponsorship, approval, performance characteristics, accessories, uses or benefits they do not have';

o   'that the corporation has a sponsorship, approval or affiliation it does not have';

---

[15]   *Taco Company of Australia Inc and Anor v Taco Bell Pty Ltd and Ors* (1982) ATPR 40–303.

[16]   *Campomar Sociedad, Limitada v Nike International Limited* (2000) 202 CLR 45.

[17]   *Taco Company of Australia Inc and Anor v Taco Bell Pty Ltd and Ors* (1982) ATPR 40–303.

[18]   *Taco Company of Australia Inc and Anor v Taco Bell Pty Ltd and Ors* (1982) ATPR 40–303.

[19]   *Butcher v Lachlan Elder Realty Pty Limited* (2004) 218 CLR 592, 615.

[20]   *Trade Practices Act 1974* (Cth) s 53.

○   'with respect to the price of goods or services';
○   'concerning the availability of facilities for the repair of goods or of spare parts for goods';
○   'concerning the place of origin of goods';
○   'concerning the need for any goods or services'; and
○   'concerning the existence, exclusion or effect of any condition, warranty, guarantee, right or remedy'.

Similarly to breaches of s 52, a breach of s 53 can result in the court ordering the offending corporation to pay damages.[21] Courts can also grant injunctions restricting the offending corporation's conduct,[22] and have power to make a wide range of other orders.[23] Finally, unlike breaches of s 52, a breach of s 53 can amount to an offence leading to a criminal prosecution.[24]

The role of the Australian Competition and Consumer Commission

ACCC
Australian Competition and Consumer Commission, responsible for administering the *Trade Practices Act 1974* (Cth).

Contravention
See *Breach*.

The *Australian Competition and Consumer Commission* (**ACCC**) is an independent statutory authority. Its primary responsibility is making sure that individuals and businesses comply with relevant federal law in the areas of competition, fair trading and consumer protection. Most importantly for this context, the ACCC administers the *Trade Practices Act*. The ACCC informs individuals and businesses of their rights and obligations under the TPA, and investigates **contraventions**.

Only courts are entitled to make a determination as to whether a contravention has occurred, but the ACCC can bring suspected contraventions before the courts. If the offending party acknowledges its contravention, the ACCC can accept formal administrative settlements or undertakings from the offending party instead of bringing the matter before a court.

The ACCC has brought actions before the courts in several Internet-related matters.[25] However, of the Internet-related cases brought by the ACCC, the *Chen* case (see case example) has drawn the most attention.

---

21   *Trade Practices Act 1974* (Cth) s 82.
22   *Trade Practices Act 1974* (Cth) s 80.
23   *Trade Practices Act 1974* (Cth) s 87.
24   *Trade Practices Act 1974* (Cth), Pt VC.
25   See for example *Australian Competition and Consumer Commission v 1Cellnet LLC* [2004] FCA 1210.
26   Available at <www.austlii.edu.au/au/cases/cth/federal_ct/2003/897.html>.
27   *Australian Competition and Consumer Commission v Chen* [2003] FCA 897, paragraph 61.
28   *Australian Competition and Consumer Commission v Chen* [2003] FCA 897, paragraphs 47–48.

CASE EXAMPLE *AUSTRALIAN COMPETITION AND CONSUMER COMMISSION V CHEN (2003) FCA 897*[26]

AUSTRALIA, FEDERAL COURT OF AUSTRALIA, 2003

The *Chen* case involved a US-based person, Mr Chen, who operated a website from which he was selling tickets to, among other venues, the well-known Sydney Opera House. The first page of the website was virtually identical to that of the official website for the Sydney Opera House. The tickets were sold at highly inflated prices and a number of them were not valid. The ACCC argued that Mr Chen had acted in violation of certain provisions of the TPA (including ss 52 and 53), and sought an injunction restricting Mr Chen from continuing, or resuming, his conduct. The Court took particular notice of how an injunction granted by an Australian court might be viewed and used by overseas consumer protection agencies (in this case the Federal Trade Commission of the United States of America). The Court clearly took account of the close cooperation that exists between the ACCC and the FTC and noted:

> While domestic courts can, to a limited extent, adapt their procedures and remedies to meet the challenges posed by cross-border transactions in the Internet age, an effective response requires international co-operation of a high order.[27]

Having acknowledged the difficulties associated with enforcing such an injunction, the Court nevertheless ruled in favour of the ACCC.

The ACCC also sought a declaration that Mr Chen had acted in contravention of certain provisions of the TPA (including ss 52 and 53). The Court made the declaration:

> I have taken into account the fact that the Sites no longer contain information relating to the Sydney Opera House and no longer purport to provide a facility for booking tickets at the venue. I have also taken into account that the current registrant of the domain name 'sydneyopera.org' appears to have no connection with the respondent. However, I do not infer from these facts that there is no threat that the respondent will not resume his pattern of blatantly misleading and deceptive conduct in relation to the Sydney Opera House. The respondent has not appeared in the Court to explain what has happened in relation to the Sites and, of course, no undertakings have been given to refrain from misleading conduct in the future, either to this Court or to the United States authorities. The respondent appears still to be associated with at least two of the Sites and, given the pattern of misleading and deceptive conduct revealed in the evidence, there can be no assurance that the respondent will not use the Sites or create other web sites to convey misleading information to Australian consumers (and consumers elsewhere) about the availability and sale of tickets to Sydney Opera House events. [...]
>
> [T]he public interest in protecting Australian consumers from misleading conduct often warrants the making of a declaration. A declaration also marks the Court's disapproval of the respondent's conduct and, if appropriate, can be used to inform consumers of the dangers posed by the respondent's operation of the Sites. I think that these considerations justify making a declaration in the present case in the terms to which I have referred.[28]

The *Chen* case leads us to another of the ACCC's important functions—its involvement in international cooperation. The ACCC represents Australia in several different international organisations such as the International Competition Network (ICN). Most importantly, as far as online consumer protection is concerned, the ACCC is a member of the International Consumer Protection and Enforcement Network (ICPEN). This is 'a membership organisation consisting of the trade practices law enforcement authorities of more than two dozen countries'.[29] One of the more interesting activities conducted by ICPEN is its 'Sweep Day'. During a sweep day the member organisations search the WWW for a targeted online activity such as get-rich-quick schemes (targeted in 2004). ICPEN is also involved in the operation of a website aimed at addressing cross-border e-commerce complaints.[30] Bearing in mind the enforcement problems identified in Chapter 3 it could be suggested that initiatives such as ICPEN are the only viable way to address online consumer issues. It simply is not enough for one (or a few) countries to take these issues seriously because as long as unethical businesses can operate from 'safe havens', consumers can never get adequate redress.

THE TPA AND STATE-BASED LEGISLATION

The rules found in the *Trade Practices Act* are mirrored to a degree in state-based Acts.[31] In some cases, these Fair Trading Acts go even further than the *Trade Practices Act*. For example, drawing upon the European Union's experience, the Victorian *Fair Trading Act 1999* regulates certain unfair contractual terms.[32] This is a useful approach, which would be worth considering in the other states and territories.

The applicability of the state-based Fair Trading Acts is illustrated by a dispute involving online auction site eBay.

 **CASE EXAMPLE** *EVAGORA V EBAY AUSTRALIA AND NEW ZEALAND PTY LTD (2001) VCAT 49*[33]
AUSTRALIA, VICTORIAN CIVIL AND ADMINISTRATIVE TRIBUNAL, 2001

The plaintiff (Mr Evagora) had placed a bid for a computer using the respondent's online auction service. The bid was successful and payment was made. However, the seller never delivered the computer.

The Australian police told Mr Evagora that they were unable to assist, arguing that the seller was outside their jurisdiction. Mr Evagora then sought compensation from eBay.   >>

---

29   <www.icpen.org>.
30   <www.econsumer.gov>.
31   See for example *Fair Trading Act 1989* (Qld) and *Fair Trading Act 1999* (Vic).
32   See *Fair Trading Act 1999* (Vic), Part 2B.
33   Available at <www.austlii.edu.au/au/cases/vic/VCAT/2001/49.html>.

>>   The basis for the claim was that various statements made on eBay's website had induced Mr Evagora to use the respondent's services:

> In support of his position, Mr Evagora provided to the Tribunal copies of various pages from the internet including eBay's homepage, and the 'bidding page'. The homepage includes a prominent clickable graphic which states in large letters 'Buy with confidence. ebay insured. Automatically insured'. In smaller letters appear the words 'Conditions Apply'. There is also a smaller clickable graphic in the centre of the page which includes 'why eBay is safe'. The 'bidding page' includes the following statement in bold type: 'eBay purchases are insured'. He noted there are no warnings that buyers buy online at their own risk.[34]

Mr Evagora argued that, in light of eBay's having a condition limiting the insurance to $270, the statements referred to above violated the *Fair Trading Act 1999* (Vic). In particular, he suggested that ss 9 and 11, which relate to misleading and deceptive conduct (similar to TPA s 52), and s 12, which addresses misrepresentations (similar to TPA s 53), had been contravened.

Predictably, the respondent referred to the terms and conditions that Mr Evagora had agreed to when signing up to use the respondent's services. These contained several clauses limiting eBay's liability. Mr Evagora, who was not particularly computer literate, confessed to not having read the terms and conditions, which consisted of a twelve-page document with numerous links to additional text.

Interestingly, the Tribunal found in Mr Evagora's favour:

> I am satisfied on the evidence before me, that Mr Evagora was induced to participate in an online auction by the clear representations by the Respondent, as contained on its homepage, that it was safe to do so, and that all purchases were automatically insured. Furthermore, I am not satisfied the proviso 'Conditions Apply' provides sufficient notice to buyers that the available insurance cover is limited. Even if the Respondent had been able to successful [sic] rely on this proviso to absolve itself of any liability, the statement 'eBay purchases are insured' on the 'bidding page' is of itself a clear representation that I find the Applicant was entitled to rely upon.
>
> It would appear the [sic] eBay have assumed a level of sophistication of its users that is not reasonable in all the circumstances. It is true that many people have a good knowledge and understanding of the internet but increasingly, those with limited experience are beginning to use it. These people are often attracted to sites such as that operated by the Respondent as an alternative means of purchasing goods. The Respondent has an obligation to its consumers to ensure that any limitations associated with the use of its online auction facility are clearly notified to prospective users. It is not sufficient to have a 12-page User Agreement with numerous clickable links that in many respects contradicts the clear representations contained on the homepage and the 'bidding' page. Where limits apply they must be clearly spelt out. In this instance, I do not accept Mr McSweeney's submission that it would not have been possible to include a notation 'limit of $270 applies' under the prominent insurance graphic on the homepage, or under the notation on the bidding page.[35]

---

[34]   *Evagora v eBay Australia and New Zealand Pty Ltd* [2001] VCAT 49, paragraph 2.
[35]   *Evagora v eBay Australia and New Zealand Pty Ltd* [2001] VCAT 49, paragraphs 15–16.

While the Fair Trading Acts of other states are not identical to the *Fair Trading Act 1999* (Vic), it is likely that a similar result could have been reached in other states, or indeed, under the *Trade Practices Act 1974* (Cth).

Imposed terms

Statutes impose[36] terms on some contracts. In Australia this happens under the TPA and the various Sale of Goods Acts.[37] Under the TPA, terms are only imposed on B2C contracts; under the Sale of Goods Acts terms are also imposed on B2B and C2C contracts. From the e-commerce perspective, the most interesting requirement for imposed terms is that the contract must relate to the sale of 'goods'. As discussed below, there has been some dispute as to whether software should be classed as goods.

While parties can decide that the imposed terms under the Sale of Goods Acts will not apply to their contract,[38] the terms imposed under the TPA cannot be avoided.[39] The TPA takes the view that this freedom could easily be abused, resulting in terms being dictated by businesses, to the consumers' disadvantage. Other than this, the differences between the terms imposed by the TPA and by the state Sale of Goods Acts are minimal. We will focus on the TPA, as it is more likely to apply to consumers engaged in e-commerce.

One last observation needs to be made before we examine the imposed terms. The law distinguishes between conditions and warranties. Put simply, a *condition* is a term of the contract that is so central that where one party acts in breach of it, the other party has a right to terminate the contract immediately. A *warranty*, on the other hand, is a contractual term that is not of the same fundamental importance as a condition. A breach of a warranty would normally only give the other party the right to claim damages, not the right to terminate the contract.

Terms imposed by the TPA include:

○   conditions and warranties as to title;[40]
○   a condition that the goods correspond with their description;[41]
○   conditions that goods will be of merchantable quality and/or fit for their purpose;[42]

---

[36]   Literature typically talks about implied terms without distinguishing between those situations where the parties themselves act in a manner that warrants the terms being part of the contract (truly implied terms) and those situations where the parties' conduct is irrelevant because the law makes the terms mandatory (imposed terms).

[37]   *Sale of Goods Act 1896* (Qld), *Sale of Goods Act 1923* (NSW), *Goods Act 1958* (Vic), *Sale of Goods Act 1895* (SA), *Sale of Goods Act 1895* (WA), *Sale of Goods Act 1954* (ACT), *Sale of Goods Act 1972* (NT), *Sale of Goods Act 1896* (TAS).

[38]   See for example *Sale of Goods Act 1896* (Qld) s 56.

[39]   *Trade Practices Act 1974* (Cth) s 68.

[40]   *Trade Practices Act 1974* (Cth) s 69.

[41]   *Trade Practices Act 1974* (Cth) s 70.

[42]   *Trade Practices Act 1974* (Cth) s 71.

o   conditions relating to sales by sample;[43] and
o   certain warranties in relation to services.[44]

The conditions and warranties as to title have the effect of ensuring that the provider (the business) cannot supply goods it does not have a right to supply, and that the receiver (the consumer) has a right of quiet possession once the goods have been supplied.

Where goods are sold by description otherwise than by auction, the TPA imposes a condition that the goods correspond with their description. The concept of a 'sale by description' is wide: 'The term "sale of goods by description" must apply to all cases where the purchaser has not seen the goods, but is relying on the description alone.'[45] Virtually all products sold online would be sales by description, and where Australian law applies, must consequently correspond with their description.

The conditions as to quality and fitness for purpose are arguably the most complex of the imposed terms. The condition that goods must be of merchantable quality is of great relevance. Put simply, unless goods sold are of merchantable quality the consumer can terminate the transaction. Whether or not goods are of merchantable quality needs to be determined case by case, and in making the assessment a court would have regard to factors such as the description of the goods and the price charged.[46]

The condition that goods be fit for their purpose is only of relevance where the consumer has made clear to the seller the particular purpose for which the goods are required. However, where the purpose is the purpose for which the goods are ordinarily used, the consumer does not need to have made specific reference to that purpose. A typical e-commerce transaction would not involve the buyer outlining any particular purpose for the goods and the condition would not be of relevance. However, one can easily imagine exceptions. For example a person makes a posting on a discussion board stating that she needs goods for a particular purpose. If another person then contacts her seeking to sell particular goods there would be a condition that the goods are indeed fit for the purpose originally stated. Thus, while not as widely relevant as merchantable quality, fitness for purpose may be of relevance in some e-commerce transactions.

The conditions relating to sale by sample—that the bulk of the goods must correspond with the sample—would rarely be of relevance in e-commerce transactions and is not discussed further.

Section 74, which outlines certain warranties in relation to services, states that a corporation that is providing a service must render that service with 'due care and skill and that any materials supplied in connexion with those services will be reasonably fit for the purpose for which they are supplied.'[47] The same section also contains a requirement that the services rendered be fit for their purpose where the consumer has made clear the purpose for which the services were required.[48]

---

[43]   *Trade Practices Act 1974* (Cth) s 72

[44]   *Trade Practices Act 1974* (Cth) s 74.

[45]   *Varley v Whipp* [1900] 1 QB 513, 516.

[46]   *Trade Practices Act 1974* (Cth) s 66(2).

[47]   *Trade Practices Act 1974* (Cth) s 74(1).

[48]   *Trade Practices Act 1974* (Cth) s 74(2).

Can software be 'goods'?

Internet service provider (ISP)

An entity that uses a *carrier's* telecommunications facilities, usually in combination with their own servers and other equipment, to provide access to the Internet. See also *Carriage service provider* (CSP).

As mentioned above, the Sale of Goods Acts are not applicable if the product sold cannot be classed as *goods*. Thus a contract under which one party undertakes to act as an **Internet Service Provider** (ISP) for another party in exchange for a certain amount of money would not fall within the scope of the Sale of Goods Acts. The TPA imposes terms in relation to both goods and services, but the imposed terms are not the same and are provided under different sections. So the classification of a product as goods or a service may also be of relevance under the TPA.

It may be obvious that providing an ISP service does not constitute a sale of goods, and that the sale of a physical book is a sale of goods. However, difficulties arise in the e-commerce setting, particularly with digital products. Can an e-book be goods, and would it be accurate to classify a music file or a computer game as goods?

Both the TPA and the Sale of Goods Acts contain sections dealing with the definition of 'goods'.[49] However, neither of those definitions gives any indication whether software can be classed as goods. Although no guidance can be found in the legislation, case law has clarified the issue to some extent. The most important case regarding whether software can be classed as goods under Australian law is the *Amlink* case.

CASE EXAMPLE *AMLINK TECHNOLOGIES PTY LTD AND AUSTRALIAN TRADE COMMISSION (2005) AATA 359*[50]

AUSTRALIA, ADMINISTRATIVE APPEALS TRIBUNAL, 2005

The *Amlink* case related to whether a particular software product was to be considered as goods for the purpose of a grant application. Senior Member McCabe concluded:

> If the program had been commissioned by the purchaser and written (or even modified) to its specifications, the contract of supply is likely to be a supply of know-how or intellectual property rather than goods. The situation is different once the product is sold as a tangible commodity after being copied or mass-produced. At that point, the products cease to be know-how and become goods.[51]

>>

---

49   See *Trade Practices Act 1974* (Cth) s 4(1) and for example *Sale of Goods Act 1896* (Qld) s 3(1).
50   Available at <www.austlii.edu.au/au/cases/cth/aat/2005/359.html>.
51   *Amlink Technologies Pty Ltd and Australian Trade Commission* [2005] AATA 359, paragraph 42.

>> Further, in explaining this conclusion, Senior Member McCabe stated:

> The fact the licence agreement places restrictions on the use of the product after sale does not make it much different to music CDs and DVD movies—products that are clearly goods. The requirement for an access code is apparently an innovative attempt to combat **piracy** which might rob the producers of revenue. It is merely a more sophisticated protection than the regional coding system used in DVDs. That evidence does not change my conclusion. The existence of 24-hour service is also not determinative: help-desks and other forms of the [sic] round-the-clock assistance are available as part of the purchase price of many goods, such as computers and cars.[52]

Piracy
In the Internet context, the unlawful copying or distributing of copyright protected material.

In reaching these conclusions, Senior Member McCabe made clear that Australian law recognises software as goods in some circumstances. Unfortunately, he stopped short of discussing whether software that is not attached to a physical medium amounts to goods. Australian law is still unclear on this point.

There are arguments in favour of, and against, classing software as goods. Software clearly lacks several key characteristics of things we normally regard as goods. For example software is intangible and can be reproduced without any loss of quality. On the other hand, the better approach might be to focus on the consequences of the classification. If software itself is not classed as goods, a person downloading software from the Internet would not enjoy the same level of protection as a person purchasing the same software on a CD from a shop. One would certainly question why already vulnerable online consumers should be less protected than those visiting physical shops—this would have a negative impact on the development of online B2C commerce.

As noted in other chapters (for example Chapter 8, dealing with e-commerce taxation), the question of whether software is to be regarded as goods or services is of relevance in relation to a wide range of legal questions.

CONCLUDING REMARKS AND FURTHER READING

In this chapter we have discussed consumer protection in the e-commerce setting. We highlighted the way there are competing policy objectives that need to be considered in the regulatory approaches, and discussed some of the difficulties.

We conclude with the observation that, in the majority of e-commerce transactions, the values involved are so small that few people would consider taking legal action. In light of this, it is important that suitable, fair and workable Alternative Dispute Resolution

---

[52]   *Amlink Technologies Pty Ltd and Australian Trade Commission* [2005] AATA 359, paragraph 43.

(ADR) schemes be developed. This is not to say that legal protection of consumers is unnecessary—even though legal action will be a last resort, suitable laws are needed to strengthen the consumer's position in resolving disputes.

Further reading on the topic of consumer protection in the context of the Internet and e-commerce might include:

ACCC, *Tips for good business online* available at <www.accc.gov.au>

Yee Fen Lim, *Cyberspace Law: Commentaries and Materials,* 2nd edn, Oxford University Press, Melbourne, 2007

L Smith, 'Global Online Shopping: How Well Protected is the Australian Consumer?' (2004) 12 (2) *Competition and Consumer Law Journal* 163

D Svantesson, 'B2C Sales and Consumer Protection', in R. Polčák (ed), *Introduction to ICT Law: Selected Issues,* Masaryk University, Brno, Czech Republic, 2007

Australian Government Treasury, *Australian Guidelines for e-commerce* (2006) available at <www.treasury.gov.au>

OECD Guidelines for Consumer Protection in the Context of Electronic Commerce (1999) available at <www.oecd.org>

Review questions for this chapter can be found on the book's Online Resource Centre at www.oup.com.au/orc/fordersvantesson.

07

PAYMENT SYSTEMS

OBJECTIVES // BY THE END OF THIS CHAPTER, YOU WILL:

O Understand the nature of payment systems, and be familiar with the types of established payment products

O Be aware of the role of intermediaries and the need for clearance and settlements

O Recognise which laws, regulatory bodies and codes of conduct apply to payments systems

O Know how established products and new and emerging products are being used for online payments

WHAT THIS CHAPTER IS ABOUT

In Chapter 4 we discussed issues that arise when contracts are formed over the Internet. The transfer of money is an important part of most contracts, and this chapter explores how payments are made in the Internet environment. Familiarity with the concepts discussed in Chapter 5 (authentication and signatures) and Chapter 6 (consumer protection) will be useful in understanding some of the points discussed.

We start with an explanation of what is meant by a payment system. We also mention the established non-cash products and some of the terms used in describing them—terms like intermediaries, clearances and settlements. Our attention then turns to the way payment systems are regulated, including the two main codes of conduct that might apply.

The final part of this chapter looks at the way established payment products are used on the Internet and at the development of new products that might suit the requirements of Internet payments even better.

AN INTRODUCTION TO PAYMENT SYSTEMS

Cheque
An unconditional order in writing addressed by a person to a financial institution, signed by the person giving it, requiring the institution to pay a sum of money on demand.

Negotiable instrument
A written and signed document that entitles the holder to receive a payment, and which can be transferred in such a way as to give the new holder an unconditional right to payment, even if the transferor did not have such a right. Examples include cheques and promissory notes.

Digital cash
Digital data representing value that can be transferred as the equivalent of money.

A payment is a transfer of value from one person to another. It is usually made with money, although delivering goods or performing services might also amount to payment in some circumstances. Before the digital age it was easy to understand the transfer of money—it involved handing over tangible objects such as cash, **cheques** or other **negotiable instruments**. In modern financial systems the concept is far more complex. Money in the form of **digital cash** ('network money') is transferred through the exchange of data over electronic networks, facilitated by the use of cards, computers and other devices. When distilled to their essentials, however, all payment systems require two things: a *product* that facilitates the transfer—often by holding or representing value—and a *channel* through which the transfer takes place.[1]

Products and channels

With cash, the *product* consists of notes or coins that have value; the *channel* is physical delivery, for example over a shop counter. Most products, including cash, can be used in more than one channel. Thus cash can also be delivered through the post or by an agent. For a non-cash example, consider a credit card: the product consists of the plastic card and the arrangements for its use; channels include using the card over a shop counter, by telephone or on the Internet.

Products or channels that require the parties to be in each other's presence, or depend on physical delivery—like cash—are obviously unsuited to payments over the Internet. Our focus will therefore be on non-cash products that can be used over electronic channels such as websites or e-mail.

---

[1]   Centre for International Economics and Edgar, Dunn & Company, *Exploration of Future Electronic Payments Markets*, Report for DCITA, June 2006, p 13 available at <www.dcita.gov.au> last accessed 26 July 2007.

Established non-cash products

For those with little background in payment systems we give a brief description of the four well-established non-cash products in general use:

1   *Cheques* involve written and signed instructions that authorise a customer's financial institution to pay a sum of money to the merchant. Similar paper-based products such as bills of exchange, travellers' cheques and money orders could also be included in this category.

2   *Credit cards* involve an arrangement with a financial institution for the cardholder to be given credit up to a specified limit. When the cardholder uses the card in the agreed way, this gives authority to the financial institution to pay the amount involved to the merchant, and to debit the cardholder's account. Charge cards and store cards are similar, since they also give credit.

3   *Debit cards* enable access to funds already in a cardholder's account. They are used in conjunction with ATMs and EFTPOS terminals,[2] both of which enable funds to be transferred from the cardholder's account in real time. Prepaid phone cards and similar **stored value cards** might also be considered to fall into this category.

> **Stored value card (SVC)**
> A card that permits the electronic storage and use of prepaid value; also known as an electronic purse or wallet.

4   *Direct entry payments* were implemented so a customer could give a financial institution standing instructions to transfer funds on a regular basis. There are two varieties. Direct credit is where the *customer* issues the instruction to the bank to transfer funds to other accounts. A common example of this would be an employer instructing its bank to pay wages on a particular day of the week to all employees. Direct debit is where a customer authorises their bank to accept instructions *from the merchant* to transfer funds to the merchant. This enables trusted creditors who are entitled to regular payments such as insurance premiums or loan repayments to initiate the payments themselves directly from their customer's account.

Part of our discussion in this chapter will focus on the extent to which these products have been (or can be) adapted or used over electronic channels. We will also identify deficiencies in this range of products, and discuss new or emerging systems (sometimes described as virtual cash or e-money). Before we move on to these topics, however, there are a few more introductory concepts you will need to know.

Intermediaries, clearance and settlement

Unlike cash payments, which involve two parties, non-cash products involve three or more parties. Simpler schemes, such as Diners' Club and American Express charge cards, are three-party systems. The card issuer has a direct contractual relationship with both the merchant and the cardholder. The merchant, who has previously agreed to accept payments from customers using the card, collects the card details from the

---

2   Automated Teller Machines and Electronic Funds Transfer at Point of Sale terminals.

cardholder. The merchant then requests payment from the card issuer; the card issuer credits the merchant's account and debits the cardholder's account.

Most non-cash products typically involve at least four parties, because banks (known as payment intermediaries) do the actual paying and collecting. Here is a simple outline of the process: after a transaction, the merchant sends the cheque or transaction details to their own bank for collection; the merchant's bank (known as the acquiring bank) requests payment from the customer's bank; the customer's bank verifies their customer's instruction and honours the request to pay, debiting the customer's account; on receiving the funds, the merchant's bank credits the merchant's account.[3]

With the large quantities of transactions they handle, banks cannot afford to go through this process separately for every transaction. Central clearing and settling systems, in which all banks participate, have therefore developed. A **clearing organisation** (clearing house) collects payment requests from all the acquiring banks and transmits them to the relevant paying banks; the paying banks validate the requests and confirm their intention to pay. However, settlement of the debt between the banks does not occur immediately, unless it is a large or urgent transaction. The banks accumulate transactions, and after setting them off against each other, settle them in a batch—at the end of the day, for example.

In Australia the Australian Payments Clearing Association (APCA) manages clearing for cheques, **direct entry payments**, debit cards, ATMs and high-value payments. Other independent clearing systems include those for credit cards (MasterCard and VISA) and the Bpay system.

Settlement of the accumulated transactions is done through the Reserve Bank of Australia (RBA). Each financial institution has an exchange settlement account with the RBA, and the funds are effectively transferred between the banks by making entries in the RBA's settlement accounts at a regular time each business day.

Payment intermediaries charge each other interchange fees for clearing and settling payments, and these costs are passed on, one way or another, to users. Non-cash systems thus tend to be more expensive to the consumer than cash. As we will see later, relative cost of products is one of the factors that determine their popularity.

Clearing organisation
An organisation that gathers payment instructions from collecting banks, and transmits them to paying banks, seeking confirmation that the payment instruction will be honoured.

Direct entry payments
A payment system enabling the transfer of funds by entering the transaction directly in the accounts of the paying and receiving institutions so that it has immediate effect. A direct credit is where the paying party initiates the transaction; a direct debit is where the receiving party initiates the transaction.

---

[3]   In reality there are often five or six parties. For example, the customer's bank might issue a credit card, but might have a relationship with a larger credit card organisation like VISA or MasterCard—a fifth party. As we will see, clearances are usually handled by a separate intermediary known as a clearing house—a sixth party.

Thinking about the RBA's role in settlements might make you wonder who regulates payment systems.

THE REGULATION OF PAYMENT SYSTEMS

The borderless nature of the Internet, combined with the potential for new unregulated payment systems, has worried regulatory bodies for some time. Risks include damage caused by deficiencies in the reliability and integrity of the systems; damage to the reputation of the whole financial system; and legal risks such as fraud, privacy and money laundering. Despite these concerns, authorities are reluctant to over-regulate, since too much supervision would hamper innovation. The general approach taken by authorities is that regulation is only needed where market forces are proving inadequate in protecting the system.[4]

General supervision

After a comprehensive review,[5] extensive reforms were made to the financial services industry (including payment systems) in 1998. Two federal government bodies now have wide supervisory powers:

O   The RBA is responsible for controlling risk to the whole financial system (which includes the payment system). It also promotes efficiency and competition. The main source of its power is the *Reserve Bank Act 1959* (Cth). In 1998 the Payment Systems Board (PSB) was set up within the RBA to give advice on payment system policy.

O   The Australian Securities and Investment Commission (ASIC) is responsible for market integrity and consumer protection across the whole financial system. It is empowered by the *Corporations Act 2001* (Cth) and *Australian Securities and Investments Commission Act 2001* (Cth). It promotes the adoption of, and monitors compliance with, industry standards and codes of practice.

A number of other agencies have narrower supervisory roles, the most important of which are the Australian Prudential Regulation Authority (APRA), which supervises banks, insurance companies, building societies and superannuation funds; and the Australian Competition and Consumer Commission (ACCC), which looks after the competition and access provisions of the *Trade Practices Act 1974* (Cth). Each of these roles gives the agency some say in the operation of payment systems.

---

4   See for example the discussion by the Basel Committee on Banking Supervision, *Risk Management for Electronic Banking and Electronic Money Activities*, March 1998 <www.bis. org/publ/bcbs35.htm> last accessed 27 April 2007.

5   Treasury, *Financial System Inquiry: Final Report* (Wallis Commission Report), March 1997 <http://fsi.treasury.gov.au/content/publications.asp> last accessed 26 July 2007.

Banking business

Banking business
Defined under the *Banking Act 1959* (Cth) to involve both the taking of money on deposit and the making of advances.

Authorised deposit-taking institution (ADI)
A financial institution that is authorised to conduct banking business under the *Banking Act 1959* (Cth).

The *Banking Act 1959* (Cth) provides that the carrying on of **'banking business'** can only be undertaken by a corporation that is an **authorised deposit-taking institution** (ADI) or has received a determination that authorisation is not required.[6] Banking business means taking money on deposit *and* making advances—both activities are required.[7] Thus an institution that restricts itself to only one of the activities—a retailer making advances by offering credit on a store card, for example—is not engaging in banking business. As we will see, however, this does not mean they are free from regulation. On the other hand, some financial institutions, such as building societies and credit unions, do conduct banking business and must have ADI status even though they do not call themselves banks.

The authorisation requirement is intended to ensure that, in the interests of stability and confidence in the financial system, financial institutions have sufficient assets and suitable management structures. The *Banking Act* offers little direct protection for customers or consumers. However, all major Australian financial institutions have adopted a voluntary code of conduct—the Code of Banking Practice—developed by the Australian Bankers' Association.[8] We refer to some of its provisions when dealing with specific products later.

The *Payment Systems (Regulation) Act*

Besides the broad regulation of banking business, payment systems are directly regulated under the *Payment Systems (Regulation) Act 1998* (Cth). Where an institution is not already an ADI under the *Banking Act*, and wishes to operate a payment system that involves storing value that can be used to pay—such as stored value cards or travellers' cheques—it will need authorisation.[9]

The RBA can also 'designate' a payment system, which then gives it wide power to:

o   ensure a fair access regime for others wishing to participate in the system;
o   make standards to be complied with;

---

[6]   *Banking Act 1959* (Cth) s 8. The authorising body is the Australian Prudential Regulation Authority (APRA).

[7]   *Banking Act 1959* (Cth) s 5, definition of banking business. This is consistent with the common law view (*Commissioners of the State Savings Bank of Victoria v Permewan Wright & Co Ltd* (1915) 19 CLR 457, 470–471; and see A Beatty, M Aubrey and R Bollen, 'E-Payments and Australian Regulation' (1998) 21 *UNSWLJ* 489, 509).

[8]   Australian Bankers' Association, *Code of Banking Practice*, May 2004 <www.bankers.asn.au/Default.aspx?ArticleID=446> last accessed 27 April 2007.

[9]   This is a simplified description of the requirement relating to a 'purchased payment facility' in s 22 (as read with ss 9 and 23–25) of the *Payment Systems (Regulation) Act 1998* (Cth).

○   arbitrate disputes;

○   give directions to participants.[10]

Designations that have been made under the Act include credit cards (VISA and MasterCard)[11] and EFTPOS and VISA debit cards.[12] Possible designation of the **Automated teller machine (ATM)** system has been postponed while the industry tries to reach agreement on self-regulation.[13] Access regimes and standards, including fee benchmarks, have been imposed on the designated systems.[14] The regulatory provisions were not well received by industry players—first VISA and MasterCard and then EFTPOS applied for judicial review of the RBA decisions—but the RBA has been successful in defending its actions.[15]

The EFT Code of Conduct

While regulation under the *Payment Systems (Regulation) Act 1998* (Cth) is of benefit to consumers, it does not directly affect the relationship between consumers and their financial institutions. This is left to another code of conduct, originally developed in 1991 to cover the use of ATM and EFTPOS machines. Under ASIC's direction, it was expanded in 2002 to cover all electronic funds transfers. These include telephone and **Internet banking** (a form of **electronic banking**), using a credit card over the phone or Internet (but not using one over the counter with a signature) and using a stored value card.[16] Complaints under this code and the Code of Banking Practice are handled by the Banking and Financial Services Ombudsman. We will mention a number of the EFT Code's provisions when dealing with specific products below.

Automated teller machine (ATM)
A networked terminal that enables cash withdrawals from an account with a financial institution; it may also provide account-related information or permit funds to be transferred between accounts.

Internet banking
A form of electronic banking in which access to products and services is provided via the Internet.

Electronic banking
Electronic provision of banking products and services, including use of electronic terminals, the Internet, telephone and wireless networks.

---

10   *Payment Systems (Regulation) Act 1998* (Cth), Part 3 (ss 10–21).

11   See relevant media releases and gazette notices at 'Reform of Credit Card Schemes in Australia', available on RBA website at <www.rba.gov.au> last accessed 27 April 2007.

12   See relevant media releases and gazette notices at 'Reform of Debit Card Systems in Australia', available on RBA website at <www.rba.gov.au> last accessed 27 April 2007.

13   See 'Reform of the ATM System in Australia', available on RBA website at <www.rba.gov. au> last accessed 27 April 2007.

14   See the collection of relevant documents on the RBA website at 'Payment System Reforms', available at <www.rba.gov.au> last accessed 27 April 2007.

15   See *VISA International Service Association v Reserve Bank of Australia* [2003] FCA 977 and *Australian Retailers Association v Reserve Bank of Australia* [2005] FCA 1707. There have been continuing complaints, and the RBA's payment system reforms are due for review during 2007–2008.

16   EFT Code of Conduct, cl 1. The Code is available at <www.fido.asic.gov.au> last accessed 27 April 2007.

Other provisions

The *Corporations Act* gives ASIC power to regulate financial markets and service providers. Under these provisions licences are required, for example, to operate clearing and settlement facilities[17] and to acquire, issue or dispose of non-cash payment facilities.[18]

In controlling tax evasion, organised crime and money laundering, the federal government requires certain financial institutions to verify the identity of people opening an account and to report all cash transactions of $10000 or more, and any other 'suspect transactions', to AUSTRAC (the Australian Transaction Reports and Analysis Centre).[19] Existing financial institutions are covered; operators of electronic cash or stored value systems are also likely to fall under the system.[20]

Any system based on giving credit also has to comply with the Uniform Consumer Credit Code. The Code is implemented in legislation in all the states and territories, and governs all credit transactions in Australia.[21] Credit providers must explain the consumer's rights in a clear and easy to understand written document. They also have certain obligations—for example they must not enter contracts with consumers who would find it difficult to make the required repayments, and they must be prepared to modify contracts if consumers lose their jobs or become ill. A court can also order changes to a credit contract if it is considered unjust.

Desirable attributes of Internet payment systems

Micropayments
Payments involving fractions of the normal units of value, such as 1/2 cent—useful in e-commerce, for example to pay per page viewed in a document.

A 2006 report produced for the federal government identified 'six Cs' that shape the choice of a payment system.[22] They provide useful criteria by which we can judge the efficacy of the various payment products we discuss next. In summary they are:

1   Capability—is the technology reliable and capable of delivering the required service?

2   Cost—are the costs low compared with the underlying value of the transaction and alternative systems?

3   Convenience—is the system easy to use, available when needed, quick and efficient? Is it flexible and cost-effective enough to handle **micropayments** and large amounts?

---

[17]   *Corporations Act 2001* (Cth), Part 7.3.

[18]   *Corporations Act 2001* (Cth), Part 7.6 as read with s 766C, s 763A(1)(c) and 763D(1).

[19]   *Financial Transaction Reports Act 1988* (Cth), which is being phased out and replaced over 24 months by the *Anti-Money Laundering and Counter-Terrorism Financing Act 2006* (Cth), but the verification and reporting requirements will be substantially the same. See details provided by AUSTRAC at <www.austrac.gov.au/aml_ctf.html> last accessed 27 April 2007.

[20]   A Tyree and A Beatty, *The Law of Payment Systems*, Butterworths, 2000, p 103.

[21]   See explanations and links to relevant documents, including legislation in the states and territories, at <www.creditcode.gov.au> last accessed 27 April 2007.

[22]   Centre for International Economics and Edgar, Dunn & Company, *Exploration of Future Electronic Payments Markets*, Report for DCITA, June 2006, p 38, available at <www.dcita. gov.au> last accessed 26 July 2007. See also G J H Smith, *Internet Law and Regulation*, 3rd edn, Sweet & Maxwell, 2002, pp 491–492.

4   Coverage—is it widely accepted (nationally and internationally) and does it enable payments through a number of channels (not just the Internet) to a wide range of recipients (family, friends, merchants)?

5   Confidence—is it trusted and well understood, encouraging a belief in its integrity?

6   Confidentiality—is it secure and does it protect the privacy of personal information?

These factors ought to be kept in mind as we consider the way established products are used on the Internet, and what new or emerging systems might be successful.

USE OF CONVENTIONAL PRODUCTS

We start with credit cards, since they are by far the most popular payment system used in e-commerce.[23]

Credit cards

When using a credit card over the counter a signature authenticates the cardholder's identity and verifies the cardholder's authorisation to pay the amount due. When used over the telephone or Internet, the card details (name, card number and expiry date, which are all apparent on the face of the card) are disclosed, but there is no additional attempt to verify identity or the authorisation to pay. This makes unauthorised use of the card easy. Who bears this risk?

The primary source of obligations in these circumstances will be the contract between the cardholder and issuer, but the contractual provisions will have to comply with the EFT Code of Conduct, and, in the case of an ADI card issuer, the Code of Banking Practice.[24] The EFT Code specifies a number of situations in which the cardholder is not liable for unauthorised use of the card.[25] These include where the account institution's employees or agents have been fraudulent or negligent and where the access method has been forged, is faulty, or has expired or been cancelled. A cardholder is also not liable for any unauthorised transactions after he or she has notified the institution that the card is lost or stolen. Cardholders may be liable up to the time of notification if they contributed to the loss—for example by maintaining poor card security or delaying the notification.[26]

---

23   A recent survey reported credit cards had 81 per cent of the Internet payment market: Centre for International Economics and Edgar, Dunn & Company, *Exploration of Future Electronic Payments Markets*, Report for DCITA, June 2006, p 87, available at <www.dcita. gov.au> last accessed 26 July 2007.

24   All institutions that allow EFT transfers have adopted the EFT Code; and all major banks have adopted the Code of Banking Practice.

25   EFT Code of Conduct, cl 5.

26   On lost, stolen or misused cards, see also clause 23 of the Code of Banking Practice, although it is less specific than the EFT Code.

To avoid the dangers of transmitting credit card details over the Internet most e-traders provide secure servers and communication methods using the encryption techniques discussed in Chapter 5. If a user were persuaded to provide credit card details without any method to secure the information, this might amount to a contribution to any loss that occurred as a result.

The protection afforded to consumers by the EFT Code means financial institutions carry most of the risk of unauthorised card use. They could protect themselves better by having some authentication requirement, such as a PIN to be used when ordering over the phone or Internet, but so far they have chosen not to. Presumably if abuse of credit cards becomes too big a problem they will introduce such a system.

Cheques

Until the 1970s cheques were the only non-cash system used for consumer-type payments,[27] but since the introduction of card-based systems they have been decreasing in popularity.[28] Cheques are regulated by the *Cheques Act 1986* (Cth) and are a type of negotiable instrument. This basically means that—like cash—where a cheque is lost or stolen, a subsequent innocent receiver of it might have a good title to the money.

Cheques are required to be drawn on an ADI, and to be in writing and signed.[29] Although (as we saw in chapters 4 and 5) the *Electronic Transactions Act 1999* (Cth) recognises electronic communications and signatures, cheques and other negotiable instruments have been specifically excluded from the operation of the Act.[30] Until this exclusion is lifted, electronic cheques are not feasible in Australia—at least not in the sense of being negotiable instruments. Electronic communications that do not purport to be cheques, but still instruct your bank to do things with your account, should be treated on the same basis as any other instruction—but such an arrangement is probably more accurately described as a direct entry scheme.

Debit cards

Debit cards have a number of features that would make them suitable for e-commerce. They are well known and well used in Australia. The transaction is processed instantaneously, so there is no delay in getting payment. If there are insufficient funds in the account, the transaction is rejected. Authorisation is by means of a Personal Identification Number (PIN) that is relatively secure, compared with credit cards. The EFT Code protects consumers from unauthorised use in the same way as with credit cards.

---

[27]   Bank for International Settlements, *Payment Systems in Australia*, June 1999 (2nd revised edn), paragraph 2.2.1, (known as the 'Red Book') <www.bis.org/publ/cpss31.pdf> last accessed 27 April 2007.

[28]   Centre for International Economics and Edgar, Dunn & Company, *Exploration of Future Electronic Payments Markets*, Report for DCITA, June 2006, p 34, Chart 3.5 (citing RBA statistics), available at <www.dcita.gov.au>.

[29]   *Cheques Act 1986* (Cth) s 10.

[30]   *Electronic Transactions Regulations 2000* (Cth), Schedule 1, Items 19 and 22.

The difficulty with debit cards is that as presently used, they require the cardholder to be physically present at an ATM or EFTPOS terminal. Could a suitably cheap card reader be produced and attached to personal computers and other Internet devices? The dilemma is that a critical mass is needed before the card readers will be sufficiently inexpensive; but people are unlikely to use them until they are cheap and ubiquitous.

Direct entry

The use of direct entry systems has developed beyond their original purpose, which was to give standing instructions to perform multiple transfers. They now enable instructions to be given for a single transaction. This is done through the telephone or Internet banking service provided by all major Australian financial institutions. A customer can log on to the service, authenticating himself or herself with a password or PIN, and use electronic communications to transfer funds to someone else's account at another institution.

The disadvantage of transferring funds this way is that the customer has to know the merchant's account details—and most merchants would be reluctant to make their account details known to casual e-commerce customers. It is a system that is useful to parties with an established relationship of trust, and is used more often for business-to-business payments than in consumer transactions.

RECENT AND EMERGING PRODUCTS

Recent and emerging products can be divided into two broad categories: those that use intermediaries to facilitate use of conventional payment products and those that try to replicate the functions of money with new electronic products.

Intermediaries facilitating conventional products

Some products involve intermediary services using electronic channels to facilitate access to conventional payment products. We will describe two well-entrenched systems (Bpay and PayPal), and mention likely developments with other similar systems.

Bpay

Bpay is a direct entry system for paying bills, facilitated by a company set up in 1997 as a joint venture between some of Australia's major financial institutions.[31] It uses established telephone and Internet banking channels. This is the way it works: the merchant sends the customer an invoice through normal postal services. The invoice displays the merchant's unique Bpay Biller Code and the customer's Reference Number (CRN). Customers access their own financial institution's phone or Internet banking service, and select the Bpay option.[32] They enter the amount they wish to pay with

---

31   See 'About Bpay' on the Bpay website at <www.bpay.com.au> last accessed 26 July 2007.

the relevant Biller Code and CRN. The customer's bank then validates the payment and gives the customer a receipt number. The details are sent through Bᴘᴀʏ to the merchant's bank, which credits the merchant's account.

Bᴘᴀʏ is not an ADI, and does not engage in banking business. However, it has subscribed to the EFT Code of Conduct. Since customers use their own financial institution's phone or Internet banking channel, and this is also subject to the EFT Code, customers are relatively well protected from unauthorised transactions.

PayPal

PayPal developed in the USA as a payment system for online auctions, and was acquired by eBay in 2002. It is available in 103 countries, and enables anyone with an e-mail address and a credit card, debit card, or bank account to send or receive payments.

PayPal has a number of different payment models and account types. Here is a brief description of a typical website-based transaction: The seller registers with PayPal and offers it as a payment method. When paying, the buyer selects PayPal and fills in personal details, including their e-mail address and nominated account, giving PayPal authority to collect the money. This information is encrypted and transmitted to PayPal. PayPal sends an e-mail to the buyer seeking confirmation of the payment request. On receiving confirmation, PayPal collects the funds and credits the seller's account. A seller can receive funds from a buyer's credit card account without first having to have an agreement with the card issuer. This facilitates less formal e-commerce transactions between individuals or small businesses.

A slight variation on this model—using e-mail to communicate with both parties—enables one to pay other individuals or family members without having to register with PayPal first. The payer initiates the transaction, providing the same information to PayPal. PayPal e-mails the recipient, notifying them of the payment and asking what they want done with the funds. Funds can be left in a PayPal account for use in other PayPal transactions, deposited in a bank account, or sent by cheque through the post.

While PayPal has achieved a sizeable market, and claims this is based on trust, it has not been without its share of controversy. It is frequently criticised for freezing merchant accounts for long periods without sufficient reason,[33] and has been required to change its dispute resolution practices as a result of litigation on a number of occasions.[34] It is not licensed as a bank in Australia, nor is it a designated payment system. In the USA it is licensed as a money transmitter on a state-by-state basis.

---

[32] All Australian institutions that offer phone or Internet banking allow payments through Bᴘᴀʏ.

[33] See for example Radley Balko, 'Who Killed PayPal?', 27 August, 2005, Cato Institute, (which includes a good overview of the development of PayPal) at <https://cato.org/pub_display.php?pub_id=4405> last accessed 26 July 2007; and complaints sites such as <www.aboutpaypal.com> last accessed 27 April 2007 and <http://paypalsucks.com> last accessed 27 April 2007.

[34] *In re PayPal litigation* 218 FSupp 2d 1185 (ND Cal 2002); and *Craig Comb, et al v PayPal, Inc* Case No. CV-02-01227-JF (PVT) (ND Cal 2002).

Other developing intermediary-based systems

There are other services similar to those provided by PayPal, but they do not match PayPal's market presence. Products have also been proposed or tried that make use of existing billing systems. They enable payments to be made by adding the amount owed to the user's existing account with a mobile phone or digital television provider.

New hardware-based products

Single-purpose prepaid stored value cards have been in use in Australia for some time.[35] They are used for such things as telephone services, public transport, vending machines and photocopying. Some are rechargeable—further credit can be transferred onto them when needed. Prepaid card-based systems can also be multi-purpose, but this requires all the merchants wanting to use the system to agree on the specifications.

The more sophisticated card-based products use smartcards rather than magnetic-strip cards. Mondex is the best known of these.[36] Smartcards include a small processing chip and circuit board on the card. This makes them more useful because they can store more information and perform processing and authentication functions that are not possible on a magnetic-strip card. They can be used with wireless technology like radio frequency identification (RFID), allowing transfers without physical contact. This includes transfers from card to card—much like cash. For this reason they are often described as **electronic purses** or wallets. Having this type of system incorporated into a mobile phone— a wallet phone—is a likely development, as is the increasing use of biometric authentication systems.

Electronic purse
See *stored value card.*

The major disadvantage of hardware-based products is they require a card reader whenever a payment is to be made, and, like EFTPOS, it is impracticable to have card readers on all computers accessing the Internet. They can generally be used for purchases of any size, but the card-handling infrastructure is too expensive for them to be cost-effective with really small payments.

New software-based products

To avoid the expense of cards and card readers, several products have been developed using software and encryption techniques. A software token or 'coin' is created by an issuing institution and given value by transferring funds from the user's existing bank or credit card account. Like a physical coin, this token is transferred to the merchant when payment is required. The merchant can deposit the token to redeem its value from the issuing institution, or can spend the token by transferring it to someone else.

By using encryption and signatures, the token can be made anonymous, so there is no traceable record—at least in the token itself—of who made the payment. Tokens

---

[35]   One of the earliest was the prepaid Telstra Phonecard, introduced in 1997.
[36]   Mondex is part of the MasterCard WorldWide suite of smart card products—see
<www.mondex.com>.

can be generated to represent very small amounts, since the infrastructure costs are relatively low—the product depends only on software and network communication. This system is regarded as the closest electronic products are likely to get to real cash.

Software-based products have not been very successful—the original DigiCash suffered financial difficulties;[37] and Cybercash, despite being bought by PayPal,[38] remains relatively unknown. If they do achieve critical mass in the financial services market they are likely to be regulated, since they would otherwise be very convenient for money laundering.

CONCLUDING REMARKS AND FURTHER READING

The regulation of payment systems can be seen as a large-scale balancing act. It has to take account of the need for a stable financial system in which the public has confidence; the need to be able to develop and test innovative new payment products without over-regulation; the need for efficient financial institutions to be able to reap sufficient rewards; and the interests of consumers in being protected from insecure and costly systems. This chapter should provide you with a good understanding of how this balance is achieved in Australia.

Our treatment has, of necessity, been brief—financial systems and their regulation are topics worthy of much deeper study. Our recommendations for further reading include:

Centre for International Economics and Edgar, Dunn & Company, *Exploration of Future Electronic Payments Markets*, Report for DCITA, June 2006, available at <www.dcita. gov.au>

A Tyree and A Beatty, *The Law of Payment Systems*, Butterworths, Sydney, 2000

M van Rafelghem, 'Plastic and the Internet: Rights of Consumers in Australia', November 2005 19(3) *Commercial Law Quarterly* 3

Review questions for this chapter can be found on the book's Online Resource Centre at www.oup.com.au/orc/fordersvantesson.

---

[37] A team of enthusiasts appears to have taken over the name and is trying to resurrect it— see <www.digicash.com/about.htm> last accessed 27 April 2007.

[38] See <www.cybercash.com> last accessed 27 April 2007.

08

TAXATION

O Be able to appreciate the difficulties associated with taxing e-commerce

O Have a solid understanding of how Australia taxes e-commerce

O Have an understanding of the international dimensions of e-commerce taxation

WHAT THIS CHAPTER IS ABOUT

Various aspects of human activity are subject to tax. For example when we earn an income, that income is usually taxed, and when we purchase certain products, we pay tax. As it is a commercial activity, e-commerce is also affected by tax law.

This chapter examines the way Australian taxes affect e-commerce. It also provides an overview of other tax issues to which Australian e-commerce businesses may be exposed, and examines the broader question of why it is so difficult to tax e-commerce activities.

AUSTRALIAN TAXES AFFECTING E-COMMERCE

Income tax
A personal tax levied on annual income.

Goods and services tax (GST)
A value-added tax of 10% on most goods and services sold in Australia.

Withholding tax
A tax that is paid directly to the taxation authorities by a third party on behalf of a taxpayer. The best example is the PAYG system in which employers deduct tax from an employee's wages and pay it directly to the tax office.

E-commerce activities carried out in Australia may be subject to a range of different types of tax. The three most important taxes for e-commerce are:

○　**Income tax**;
○　**Goods and services tax (GST)**; and
○　**Withholding taxes**.

Income tax is, as the name indicates, a tax imposed on a person's income. It applies to residents as well as non-residents. Under Australian tax legislation residents of Australia pay income tax on their worldwide income, while non-residents pay income tax only on their Australian income. Income tax is regulated through the *Income Tax Assessment Acts 1936* and *1997* (Cth), and is discussed in more detail below as it is associated with a range of difficulties in the e-commerce context.

On 1 July 2000 a new tax came into place in Australia. An Act titled *A New Tax System (Goods and Services Tax) Act 1999* (Cth) introduced a consumption tax popularly referred to as GST. Under the GST scheme a tax is imposed on the supply of goods and services. While the burden of collecting the tax is placed on the business supplying the goods or service, it is the final consumer who carries the burden of paying the tax. Interestingly for our purposes, GST is typically not applicable where goods or services are exported from Australia. However, GST may be payable where goods or services are imported into Australia. As is discussed below, this type of consumption tax raises several interesting and complex issues in the e-commerce context.

The government has imposed various withholding taxes on Australians. A common feature of such taxes is that they are withheld at the source from dividends, interest payments and royalties. One of the most important withholding taxes is pay as you go tax (PAYG). PAYG is conceptually a part of income tax. Under the PAYG scheme, an employer or other person hiring labour deducts tax from the employee's salary—with the consequence that the employee has paid a large part of their income tax month by month or fortnightly, instead of having to pay a lump sum at the end of the financial year. While it is just as relevant for e-commerce businesses as for conventional businesses, PAYG tax does not give rise to any particular difficulties in the e-commerce context and will not be discussed further.

Having identified the different types of taxes that may be of relevance for e-commerce, we can examine how those taxes work in the e-commerce environment. However, first it is useful to discuss some internationally recognised general principles of taxation.

The OECD's influence on Australian tax law

The **Organisation for Economic Co-operation and Development (OECD)** is an international organisation. Its work is aimed at 'economic and social issues from macroeconomics, to trade, education, development and science and innovation'.[1] In 1998 the OECD stated five fundamental principles of taxation.[2] Those principles are as follows:

> **Organisation for Economic Co-operation and Development (OECD)**
> An organisation formed by 30 economically developed nations, which meet regularly to agree on policies for economic cooperation and development.

- O   Neutrality—tax rules need to produce a neutral and equitable treatment of different forms of e-commerce transactions, as well as between e-commerce transactions on the one hand, and conventional transactions on the other.
- O   Efficiency—compliance costs must be minimised.
- O   Certainty and simplicity—like other legal rules, taxation rules should be clear and simple.
- O   Effectiveness and fairness—tax evasion and avoidance must be minimised.
- O   Flexibility—taxation systems 'should be flexible and dynamic to ensure that they keep pace with technological and commercial developments'.[3]

While some of these principles may be overly ambitious, they are of great importance for Australia as they have been endorsed by the Australian Tax Office (ATO).

Australian taxes applied to e-commerce

The two Australian taxes that are examined in detail here are income tax and GST. We start with income tax, which arguably is less controversial than GST.

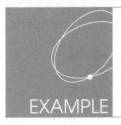

EXAMPLE

Jim is an Australian citizen residing in Australia. He operates a subscription-based online tax law information website from which he derives income each year. Being an Australian resident, the general rule is that Australia can claim income tax from Jim, regardless of the location of those who pay Jim—the website visitors.

---

[1]   See website at <www.oecd.org>.

[2]   OECD, 'Electronic Commerce: The Challenges to Tax Authorities and Taxpayers', an informal round table discussion between business and government, provided by Robert N Mattson.

[3]   Ibid.

Due to the Internet's global reach it is common for online businesses to come into contact with people from other jurisdictions. Had Jim in our example on page 105 been a resident of New Zealand, Australia could not rely on residency as a basis for taxation. However, Australia could have taxed Jim if the income had its *source* in Australia. When assessing the source of the income, the focus is placed on the location where the person trades or renders services, and account is taken of factors such as the place where the contract was made and the place where the contract was performed.

Should Jim have operated his website as a company, the question of how we determine the residence of a company would also have arisen. It has been stated:

A company is resident in Australia if:

○   it is incorporated in Australia, or
○   it carries on business in Australia and has either its central management and control in Australia or its voting power controlled by shareholders who are residents.[4]

Permanent establishment
A fixed place from which a business is wholly or partially conducted, making its profits taxable in that place.

A system of tax based on residency and also on source of income could lead to double taxation. However, such a result is commonly avoided by international tax agreements.

Under most tax agreements, Australia is limited to taxing non-residents in relation to profit derived from business carried on through a '**permanent establishment**' in Australia. The term has been defined to mean a 'fixed place of business through which the business of an enterprise is wholly or partly carried on'[5]. However, this definition does not make entirely clear when an e-commerce business is a permanent establishment. For example we must ask:

○   Can a website targeting Australia be a permanent establishment?
○   Can a website hosted on a server in Australia be a permanent establishment?

These questions were discussed in *Tax Determination TD 2005/2*. There the question was whether a resident of a country with which Australia has a tax treaty has a permanent establishment in Australia based solely on the sale of stock through a website hosted by an Australian Internet Service Provider (ISP).

It was concluded that non-residents are not seen to have a permanent establishment in Australia by virtue of the website alone. However, this conclusion is subject to limitations. It is applicable provided:

(a)   … the taxpayer, as a resident of the country with which Australia has a tax treaty, is entitled to the benefits of the relevant treaty;
(b)   … the ISP is carrying on a business as an ISP, is dealing at arm's length with the taxpayer and does not provide other services to the taxpayer in addition to the hosting arrangement which may give rise to a PE [permanent establishment] of the taxpayer; and

---

4   *Premium Tax Navigator* paragraph 530–210 (CCH, 2006).
5   The 1992 OECD Model Income Tax Convention on Income and Capital, article 5. See also: Australian Taxation Office, *Tax Determination TD 2005/2*, paragraph 5.

(c)   … any income from the sale is covered by the business profits article of the tax treaty and not some other article.[6] (footnotes omitted)

Turning to GST, the first thing to note is that in entirely domestic transactions, GST works the same way online as offline.

EXAMPLE

> Harold and Lou are both Australian citizens residing in Australia. Lou operates an online music shop, hosted in Australia, from which Harold purchases music files. In such a situation, Harold would have to pay GST on the transaction just as if he had purchased the music offline.

While it is clear that GST is to be paid in this scenario, it still raises one question—was the sale for goods or services? Although GST applies to both goods and services, determining the character of the sold product is nevertheless important as it may affect matters such as the time and the place of the transaction. In our example, the sold product was music files. Similar questions arise with things like digital pictures, movie files and software generally. The issue was discussed in Chapter 6 in the context of the applicability of the Sale of Goods Acts and the *Trade Practices Act 1974* (Cth). That discussion is not repeated here. However, a few words must be said about the way this question has been dealt with in the taxation setting. The most relevant statements are found in *GST Ruling* GSTR 2003/8.

CASE EXAMPLE *GST RULING* GSTR 2003/8[7]
AUSTRALIA, AUSTRALIAN TAXATION OFFICE, 2003

This ruling examined the operation of aspects of the GST legislation. What makes it important for our purposes is that it discussed the question of whether software can be categorised as goods:

> We take the view that a supply of 'off-the-shelf' computer software sold embodied in a disk is a supply of goods and therefore excluded from ss 38–190. The fact that a sale of 'off-the-shelf' software on disk is accompanied by a 'shrinkwrap licence'—which may deny users the authority to make backup copies, modify, or resell the software or to

>>

---

6   Australian Taxation Office, *Tax Determination TD 2005/2*, paragraph 2.
7   Available at <http://law.ato.gov.au/pdf/gstr2003-008.pdf>.

>>   decompile the code—does not in itself change the character of the supply to a supply that is made in relation to a right.

Similarly, where computer software is supplied in intangible form—for example by downloading it from the Internet—the inclusion of a 'clickwrap licence' in similar terms to the common form of 'shrinkwrap licence' referred to above will not, in itself, mean that the supply is a supply that is made in relation to rights. Where the software downloaded is standard or 'off-the-shelf' software, what is supplied is the computer program, subject to restrictions on its use. Incidental copyright rights, such as the right to copy for downloading purposes, do not change the essential nature of the supply. Such a supply is not a supply of goods. Nor is it a supply that is made in relation to rights.

However, a supply of the right to use the copyright in the program itself for commercial purposes, which allows the licensee to modify, adapt or copy or otherwise do what would ordinarily be the exclusive right of the copyright owner, is a supply that is made in relation to rights.

Where a one-off solution is developed by a computer programmer for a client, the correct analysis of the supply will depend on all of the facts and circumstances, including the terms of the contract between the programmer and the client. (paragraphs 30–33) (footnote omitted).

Intangibles
Rights that have legal value but are not necessarily related to a physical object; examples include a debt owed, copyright in computer software, and the supply of services rather than goods.

European Union
An international organisation of European countries formed in 1993 to reduce trade barriers and increase cooperation among its members.

Value-added tax (VAT)
A tax levied on the difference between a commodity's price before taxes and its cost of production.

This discussion is arguably even more important in relation to imports. While GST is payable on the import of goods, it is generally not payable on imported **intangibles** like software downloaded from the Internet. This system clearly favours import of intangibles over local businesses supplying the same. Indeed, as GST generally is not paid on exports, exporters as well as importers benefit from the current Australian system.

The EU approach and its impact on Australian e-commerce

The **European Union** (EU) has taken a rather aggressive approach to e-commerce taxation, and Australian businesses engaging in e-commerce may have to take account of the EU's approach.

In contrast to the USA, for example, the European tax systems are largely focused on **value-added tax** (VAT), similar to the Australian GST. While, as seen in the Australian context, income tax can operate rather effectively in the e-commerce environment, VAT and GST cause greater difficulties. That is why some countries relying on VAT are more aggressive in their approach to e-commerce taxation than those states driven by income tax—they simply have more to lose.

Under the EU's VAT scheme, products not classed as goods (for example information products such as downloaded software) are classed as services and are subject to VAT. The EU amendment to the Sixth VAT **Directive**[8] has interesting effects on such services:

> Although technically complex, in summary its effect is to require a non-EU supplier of services to [EU] consumers to register with the tax authorities in the EU jurisdiction of its choice. The supplier is then required to identify the EU country from which each of its consumer customers originates, and to charge them VAT at the rate of their country of residence. [...] The alternative is for the supplier to create an establishment in a chosen EU Member State and to make the supplies from that establishment. [...] In this case, supplies to all EU consumers are made at the VAT rate of the country of establishment, which should, of course, be the EU Member State with the lowest VAT rate.[9]

Directive of the European Union (EU)
A legislative instrument of the European Parliament that compels member states to enact legislation of similar effect.

This system is interesting for several reasons, as is illustrated in the AUSrock example.

EXAMPLE

AUSrock Pty Ltd sells Australian rock music from its website, www.ausrock.com.au. One day, Radim, who resides in the Czech Republic, purchases MP3 files from www.ausrock.com.au. The next day, Konstantinos, who resides in the United Kingdom, purchases MP3 files from the same site.

If AUSrock Pty Ltd has no establishment in any EU Member State, it needs to charge VAT at the rate of the buyer's country of residence (in this example, 19 per cent for Radim, and 17.5 per cent for Konstantinos).

If, on the other hand, we say that AUSrock Pty Ltd has an establishment in an EU Member State, it would have to charge the VAT rate of that country. For example if it had an establishment in Germany, it would only charge 16 per cent VAT.

One fundamental question arising from this approach is, of course, why an Australian company like AUSrock Pty Ltd in our example should care about collecting tax for the European Union. Such collection would make the Australian company's pricing less competitive and would be associated with costs and administrative issues.

The EU clearly recognises these concerns, and the rules about establishment work to assist foreign companies to a degree. Further, the EU has indicated its intention to back up these rules with severe consequences for companies failing to abide by them:

---

8   Council Directive 2002/38/EC of 7 May 2002 amending temporarily Directive 77/388/EEC as regards the value-added tax arrangements applicable to radio and television broadcasting services and certain electronically supplied services, OJ L 128 p 41, 15 May 2002.

9   Chris Reed, *Internet Law: Text and Materials*, 2nd edn, Cambridge University Press, Cambridge, 2004, p 274.

For an operator, even one located outside the EU, to risk exposure to significant and unresolved tax debts in the world's largest marketplace cannot be considered prudent business practice. Neither does the debt lapse over time but continues to hover over the business and even, in certain circumstances, passes on to a subsequent purchaser of the operation. The presence of such a liability is furthermore hardly likely to assist in access to legitimate capital or funding sources. [...] The risk of punitive tax assessments is also high. Moreover, in certain cases, sanctions under civil or criminal law may attach to the managers or owners of the business.[10]

At the same time, the EU recognises that despite all these measures, not all foreign suppliers will comply, and at least one commentator has concluded that as far as non-EU e-commerce businesses are concerned, 'the Directive is effectively a scheme for voluntary submission to taxation'.[11]

OTHER AREAS OF CONTROVERSY

From the discussion above it is clear that e-commerce taxation is a complex and controversial area of law. Here, we will highlight a few additional issues.

To tax or not to tax?

A logical starting point when discussing the controversial areas of taxing e-commerce is to ask whether e-commerce should be taxed at all. Several arguments have been put forward in favour of taxing e-commerce. For example it has been said that as more and more transactions take place online rather than offline, taxing traditional commerce will not generate as much revenue as it previously did. If the government is to receive as much revenue as in the past, it will need either to increase the tax on offline transactions or to tax e-commerce. Increasing the tax on offline transactions would be contrary to the principle of neutrality. Indeed, the very suggestion that e-commerce should not be taxed is contrary to that principle. It has also been suggested that since wealthy and educated people use e-commerce to a much greater extent than poor and uneducated people, taxing offline transactions but not e-commerce transactions works to widen the gap between the rich and the poor in society. Indeed, it has been said that e-commerce usefully can spark a total reform of the tax system. In other words, instead of not taxing e-commerce, the development of suitable approaches to taxing e-commerce should work as a catalyst for a more general tax reform.

Against these arguments it has for example been said that taxation slows down the development of the Internet in general and e-commerce in particular. Further, bearing in mind the complex nature of the international tax system, there is an

---

10 Explanatory Memorandum; see Reed at 274.

11 Chris Reed, *Internet Law: Text and Materials*, 2nd edn, Cambridge University Press, Cambridge, 2004, p 275.

obvious risk of inexperienced traders not complying with the law, due to ignorance. While ignorance of the law is not a defence as such, some assessment of reasonableness may be called for. It has also been suggested that taxation development cannot keep pace with the rapid development of technology, which carries the risk of undesirable results.

It is clear there is a healthy discussion about the legitimacy of taxing e-commerce. However, as has been seen above, Australia is by no means alone in taxing e-commerce activities.

Transfer pricing

Transfer pricing is another troublesome area. E-commerce is an ideal environment for creative company structuring; a business can benefit significantly from dividing its activities among related business enterprises located in different countries. Transfer pricing can be achieved for example 'by attributing more profit to an entity in the lower-tax country and attributing more deductible outgoings to the entity in the higher-tax country'.[12] While tax agencies seek to limit this practice, the anonymity and speed of e-commerce make their task difficult.

Transfer pricing
The practice of reducing the overall tax placed on a company group by strategically distributing profits and deductions among the members of the group.

Tax havens

The problem of **tax havens** is not completely dissimilar to the problem of transfer pricing—both involve tax avoidance based on the structure of the business. Some jurisdictions have no, or very low, taxes. Those places are known as tax havens. With the flexibility of e-commerce, it is relatively easy for a business to base itself in a tax haven, and still target the whole world with its business activities. Thus, while not unique to e-commerce, the use of tax havens is a big issue in e-commerce taxation.

Tax havens
A country that offers very low tax rates.

Transactional anonymity

We have already indicated that **transactional anonymity** may cause enforcement problems. Where the buyer is anonymous—which is common in online transactions—the supplier will normally not know the geographical location of the parties with whom they interact. This has several consequences. For example an Australian company selling products to a consumer in an EU Member State may need to identify the consumer's geographical location in order to ascertain the applicable VAT rate that must be charged.

Transactional anonymity
Where the purchaser of goods or services remains unidentified and anonymous.

---

[12] Paragraph 530–400.

In Chapter 3 we discussed technologies that may be useful in this context. While not 100 per cent accurate, geo-identification may make it possible for e-commerce businesses to identify the geographical location of those who visit their websites. However, such identification comes at a price—the lowering of the degree of anonymity—and, as discussed in Chapter 9, anonymity is an important component in the protection of privacy.

The Information Technology Association of America (ITAA) has commented on the usefulness of geo-identification in the tax context:

> [G]iven the current inability of such technologies [i.e. geo-location technologies] to overcome obstacles presented by corporate networks, anonymizers, AOL users, IPv6 and [...] other issues [...], coupled with their lack of complete certainty as to customer location, they cannot be relied upon for consumption tax purposes.
>
> Moreover, given that the new EU VAT rules base taxation on customer residence, not physical location of a customer at the time of a transaction, geolocation software do [sic] not resolve any of the concerns about being able to independently identify the correct taxation jurisdiction.[13]

The absence of physical records

E-commerce is also associated with verification difficulties as there generally are no physical records of the transactions. In other words, e-commerce does not leave the 'paper trail' left by traditional forms of transactions. This is a problem particularly where both the product and the payment are digital, such as where a person purchases a movie file paying with electronic cash.

The lack of physical exchange of documents also has implications for matters such as when an invoice is 'issued'. In *GST Determination* GSTD 2005/2 it was concluded that where an invoice is issued via a website, it is issued at the time the recipient is informed that the invoice has been made available on the website.

Taxing the technology

In light of the difficulties of applying traditional tax schemes to e-commerce and other online activities, a range of new tax schemes have been suggested. A feature common to all those schemes is that they seek to tax the technology behind the transactions. The best known of these schemes is the proposed '**bit tax**'. Under this scheme, a tax would apply based on the volume of Internet traffic. This tax would be collected by ISPs, and passed on to the government.

Bit tax
A tax on every binary digit of information transmitted across the Internet.

---

13   Information Technology Association of America, *ECommerce Taxation and the Limitations of Geolocation Tools* available at <www.itaa.org/taxfinance/docs/geolocationpaper.pdf> last accessed 26 July 2007.

One obvious problem with such a tax scheme is that some highly valuable commercial activities would be taxed at a very low rate as they do not require the sending of large files, while a person sending photographs of children to their grandparents would be taxed at a comparatively high rate, as photographs are large when measured in bits.

Australia has confirmed that it will not introduce a bit tax.

The customs problem

Traditionally, the customs services have been able to ensure that appropriate tax is paid on imports. However, with the event of cross-border e-commerce, the volume of small-value cross-border transactions has increased tremendously. The customs services face an overwhelming task in trying to maintain control over such imports. Even before the event of e-commerce, governments realised that not all imports are worth taxing—in some cases, the cost of taxing the import is greater than the tax gained. Many countries have set limits so as to ensure that imports under a certain value are exempt from import taxes. As far as Australia is concerned, imports under the amount of $1000 attract no import tax. Many e-commerce consumer transactions will fall within this category.

A related problem flows from the fact that many products sold over the Internet are intangible—the customs services will never see such products crossing the country's borders, and consequently cannot ensure that appropriate taxes are imposed.

Negative impact on developing countries

It has been suggested that the absence of tax on e-commerce transactions risks increasing the existing gap between developed and developing countries. While developed countries may be able to withstand the revenue loss that flows from a lack of e-commerce taxation, developing countries, particularly those relying heavily upon consumption taxes, may not have that ability.

CONCLUDING REMARKS AND FURTHER READING

This chapter has illustrated how tax affects and is affected by e-commerce. The reader has been introduced to the complexities of international taxation, and has been made aware that these complexities are greater, rather than more limited, in the e-commerce context.

Further, it has been demonstrated that the area of e-commerce taxation is far from settled and that different countries have adopted different approaches—all of which potentially affect businesses engaged in e-commerce, as such businesses are likely to come into contact with a considerable number of people from foreign jurisdictions.

Further reading on the topic of taxation in the context of the Internet and e-commerce might include:

Australian Taxation Office <www.ato.gov.au>

Clayton Chan, 'Taxation of Global E-Commerce on the Internet: The Underlying Issues and Proposed Plans' (2000) 9 Minn J Global Trade 233

C Alexiou and D Morrison, 'The Cross-Border Electronic Supply EU–VAT Rules: Lessons for Australian GST' (2004) 14 Revenue L J 119

Yee Fen Lim, *Cyberspace Law: Commentaries and Materials,* 2nd edn, Oxford University Press, Melbourne, 2007

Review questions for this chapter can be found on the book's Online Resource Centre at www.oup.com.au/orc/fordersvantesson.

09

PRIVACY

O Understand how privacy issues affect e-commerce

O Have an understanding of the structure of Australia's privacy regulation

O Be familiar with the most important aspects of that regulation

O See how privacy protection stems from international human rights law

O Recognise the availability of technical means for self-help

WHAT THIS CHAPTER IS ABOUT

This chapter discusses privacy in the context of e-commerce and the Internet. Having noted the international origins of privacy protection, it examines how Australian law protects privacy.

This is an interesting time to examine Australian privacy regulation, as there have been several developments during the past few years. Indeed, several aspects of Australian privacy regulation are currently in a state of flux. This highlights the increasing emphasis society places on privacy regulation. However, it also means that some of what is said in this chapter may be outdated rather quickly and readers are advised to familiarise themselves with the primary materials, such as relevant Acts of Parliament, in addition to what is said in this chapter.

WHAT IS 'PRIVACY'?

While most people have an instinctive understanding of what is meant by the term 'privacy', there is not one single, widely adopted definition. Put very simply, privacy could be said to mean 'the right to be let alone'.[1] Another possible definition is that privacy is 'the interest of a person in sheltering his or her life from unwanted interference or public scrutiny'.[2] An even more sophisticated definition would be to say that privacy relates to '[m]aterial that so closely pertains to a person to his[/her] innermost thoughts, actions and relationships that he[/she] may legitimately claim the prerogative of deciding whether, with whom and under what circumstances he[she] will share it'.[3] None of these definitions could be said to be more correct than the others, but taken together they provide a clear picture of what we mean when we talk about privacy.

Another approach to defining the term 'privacy' is to examine the types of regulation that are said to work towards protecting privacy. As far as Australian law is concerned, this is the approach we take below.

When is privacy a concern?

Before discussing the origins of privacy protection and the current Australian privacy regulation it is illustrative to consider a few examples of situations in which privacy is a concern in our modern society.

While we are mainly concerned with privacy in the context of the Internet and e-commerce, that is by no means the only area in which privacy is a concern. For example the widespread use of mobile phones with built-in cameras, combined with an increased number of cameras present in public spaces, means that large parts of our public lives are, or can be, recorded.

Turning to the Internet and e-commerce context, studies show that privacy is a serious concern, on several levels, for people engaged in online activities.

Perhaps the most suitable starting point is simply to consider what information your web browser (the program used to access websites, such as Netscape or Internet Explorer) sends to servers hosting websites you seek to visit. Most people would probably be surprised to know that in addition to your computer's IP address, which potentially can be used to identify you as an individual, your web browser sends information such as your language settings and the address of the website you visited prior to the current site.[4] With that type of information being transmitted over an open network, it is clear that privacy certainly should not be taken for granted. Other

---

[1]   S Warren and L Brandeis, 'The Right to Privacy' (1890) 4 *Harv L R* 193.

[2]   P Nygh and P Butt, *Butterworths Concise Australian Legal Dictionary*, 2nd edn, Butterworths, Sydney, 1998.

[3]   Australian Law Reform Commission, *Unfair Publication: Defamation and Privacy*, Report No. 11, 1979, p 110.

[4]   For a greater understanding of the types of information transmitted by your web browser, see for example <www.svantesson.org/projects/geo-identification.aspx>.

examples include the practice of leaving so-called cookies on computers used to visit websites. A cookie is a small file stored on your hard drive by websites you visit. When you revisit the same website—or in some cases a related website—the information stored in the cookie is sent to the server hosting the website. That way, cookies can be used to indicate that you have visited the website in question before—and even what content you viewed and what you downloaded.

Cookies do not, in themselves, identify you. However, where a cookie can be linked to identifiable information, which would be the case where you provide your e-mail address or perhaps your name and address on a website, the end result is that a detailed profile of your surfing habits and purchases can be built up.

So far we have been discussing privacy concerns arising from the Internet's structure. But more worrying is that unscrupulous individuals can use the Internet to get access to our personal information. For example by using key-logging programs installed on our computers through viruses or bundled as part of downloaded software applications, hackers can monitor everything we type, thereby getting access to passwords and sensitive personal information.

The origins of privacy regulation

The right of privacy is well established in international human rights law. Already by 1948 the Universal Declaration of Human Rights (UDHR) had recognised such a right. It is therefore only logical that when the UDHR inspired the development of the International Covenant on Civil and Political Rights (ICCPR) in 1966 the right of privacy was included. In article 17 the ICCPR states:

(1) No one shall be subjected to arbitrary or unlawful interference with his privacy, family, home or correspondence, nor to unlawful attacks on his honour and reputation.
(2) Everyone has the right to the protection of the law against such interference or attacks.

Australia is a party to the ICCPR and therefore is bound by article 17, among other provisions. As Australia also is a party to the second optional protocol associated with the ICCPR, Optional Protocol 2, any person under Australian jurisdiction can lodge a petition with the United Nations Human Rights Committee (UNHRC) if Australia does not act in accordance with article 17. Where such a petition is made, the UNHRC will make a non-binding determination that Australia may choose to follow or ignore.

Bearing in mind that the UNHRC's decisions are non-binding, this might seem to be a rather weak system. However, this approach is not strange or unusual in international law, and countries not following the UNHRC's decisions are frequently criticised and subjected to political pressure.

As far as personal information is concerned, a gigantic step was taken in 1980 when the OECD presented its *Guidelines on the Protection of Privacy and Transborder Flows of Personal Data* (1980). These guidelines have been very influential and have affected the approach taken to privacy in many nation states including Australia.

However, for our purposes, the most important aspect of the above discussion is that it shows that the right of privacy is an internationally recognised human right.

An overview of Australian privacy regulation

Australia has taken a patchwork approach to the regulation of privacy. That is logical when we consider the diversity of issues involving privacy. This diversity has led to distinctions being drawn between different forms of privacy. The following partly overlapping categories are typically distinguished:

o   information privacy;
o   personal privacy;
o   communications privacy; and
o   surveillance privacy.

Of these categories, information privacy is by far the most relevant in the context of e-commerce. Consequently, a large part of the discussion below is focused on the *Privacy Act 1988* (Cth), which is the main instrument regulating information privacy.

Personal privacy relates to matters associated with the physical body, such as cavity searches and genetics testing, and is regulated through a patchwork of torts, as well as specific legislation. The more broadly relevant torts are examined briefly below.

Communications privacy is regulated in part by the *Telecommunications Act 1997* (Cth). That Act provides, among other things, privacy rules for a number of organisations participating in the telecommunications industry. However, many such organisations are also regulated by the *Privacy Act*.

The *Telecommunications (Interception) Act 1979* (Cth) illustrates how the four categories outlined above overlap, as it fits within both communications privacy and surveillance privacy. Its main aim is to prevent unlawful interception of communication passing over a telecommunications system, where the parties to the communication are not aware of the interception. In the context of surveillance privacy the *Surveillance Devices Act 1999* (Vic) and the workplace-related Acts (discussed below) must also be mentioned.

Key aspects of Australia's privacy regulation are discussed here. In doing so, focus is placed on federal law, but reference is also made to state law[5] where appropriate.

THE *PRIVACY ACT 1988* (CTH)

When the *Privacy Act 1988* (Cth) was first introduced it regulated only the public sector. However, on 22 December 2001 an amendment took effect that extended the

---

[5]   The states and territories have invoked a wide range of statutes aimed at various privacy-related matters. See, for example: *Privacy and Personal Information Protection Act 1998* (NSW), *Information Privacy Act 2000* (Vic), *Invasion of Privacy Act 1971* (Qld), *Personal Information and Protection Act 2004* (Tas), *Health Records (Privacy and Access) Act 1997* (ACT), and *Information Act 2002* (NT).

Act to parts of the private sector. At the time of writing, the *Privacy Act* is the object of an inquiry by the Australian Law Reform Commission (ALRC). Consequently, it is possible the Act will undergo dramatic changes over the next couple of years. In light of that, it is not useful to focus on the finer details of the Act in place at the time of writing. But we do discuss the main features of the Act and examine the areas that are likely to undergo a change in light of the ALRC's work.

Main features of the Act

The *Privacy Act* contains various provisions dealing with matters such as the role of the Office of the Privacy Commissioner, and Privacy Codes. In addition, it contains eleven Information Privacy Principles (IPPs) and ten National Privacy Principles (NPPs). The IPPs regulate the public sector and the NPPs regulate the private sector. However, it is possible that a future version of the Act will contain a single set of Privacy Principles regulating public and private sectors alike.[6]

We will focus on the NPPs, as private-sector regulation is far more relevant for the scope of this book than public-sector regulation. However, before we examine the ten NPPs, a few observations should be made.

The NPPs only regulate *personal information*, defined as:

> information or an opinion (including information or an opinion forming part of a database), whether true or not, and whether recorded in a material form or not, about an individual whose identity is apparent, or can reasonably be ascertained, from the information or opinion.[7]

This wide definition seems to indicate that the Act is far-reaching. However, while the Act regulates collection of personal information in all circumstances, it only regulates personal information that is held in a record. A *record* is defined to include documents, databases (however kept), and photographs or other pictorial representations of a person, and expressly excludes publications such as magazines, books, newspapers or other publications (however published) that are or will be generally available to members of the public.[8]

This has the interesting consequence that where personal information appears on a publicly available website, its use and disclosure are not regulated by the *Privacy Act*. However, collection of that information is regulated. Thus, any organisation collecting personal information from the website is regulated by the Act. Further, an organisation making personal information available on a website must be able to show that it collected the information in accordance with the Act.

Apart from these limitations, there are several other restrictions on the applicability of the NPPs. For example the NPPs do not apply to the journalism activities of media organisations, registered political parties or organisations subscribing to an

---

[6] Australian Law Reform Commission, *Issues Paper 31—Review of Privacy* (October 2006), pp 183–185.

[7] *Privacy Act 1988* (Cth) s 6.

[8] *Privacy Act 1988* (Cth) s 6.

approved privacy code. Further, only organisations with an annual turnover exceeding $3 000 000 are covered by the Act. Thus, the majority of Australian businesses are not covered. Finally, the NPPs do not apply to employee records.

Presumably because privacy is viewed as a human right, the drafters of the *Privacy Act* opted for a complaint system. That means where a person feels that his privacy rights have been violated he cannot bring an action in the courts. Instead, a complaint must be made to the Privacy Commissioner, who will investigate, and where appropriate decide, the dispute.

We now examine the ten NPPs.

NPP 1: Collection

Collection is defined as gathering, acquiring or obtaining personal information from any source and by any means.[9] Thus, collection includes an organisation keeping personal information it has not sought or has come across by accident. This means that if an organisation receives an e-mail that includes personal information, it has collected that personal information unless it deletes the e-mail from its system within a reasonable time. NPP 1 outlines several rules governing the way collection of personal information is to occur. For example an organisation must collect personal information only 'by lawful and fair means and not in an unreasonably intrusive way'[10] and 'must not collect personal information unless the information is necessary for one or more of its functions or activities'.[11]

Further, where 'it is reasonable and practicable to do so, an organisation must collect personal information about an individual only from that individual'[12] and if personal information is not collected directly from the data subject, the organisation collecting the information must ordinarily make sure the data subject is informed that collection has occurred.[13] In addition, in collecting information, the organisation must take reasonable steps to make the individual aware of:

- 'the identity of the organisation and how to contact it';[14]
- 'the fact that he or she is able to gain access to the information';[15]
- 'the purposes for which the information is collected';[16]
- 'the organisations (or the types of organisations) to which the organisation usually discloses information of that kind';[17]

---

[9]   Office of the Privacy Commissioner, *Guidelines to the National Privacy Principles* (September 2001), p 22, available at <www.privacy.gov.au/publications/nppgl_01.pdf> last accessed 25 February 2007.

[10]   NPP 1.2.

[11]   NPP 1.1.

[12]   NPP 1.4.

[13]   NPP 1.5.

[14]   NPP 1.3(a).

[15]   NPP 1.3(b).

[16]   NPP 1.3(c).

[17]   NPP 1.3(d).

○   'any law that requires the particular information to be collected';[18] and
○   'the main consequences (if any) for the individual if all or part of the information is not provided'.[19]

Several common forms of collecting personal information online are arguably contrary to NPP 1. For example, to the extent that the information can be connected to an identifiable individual, information regarding a person's browsing habits collected using cookies is possibly not in line with NPP 1.

NPP 2: Use and disclosure

NPP 2 regulating use and disclosure of personal information is the most complex of the ten NPPs. Essentially, it provides that an organisation may only use or disclose personal information for the primary purpose for which the information was collected.[20] It then goes on to provide some exceptions to that main rule. For example the organisation may use or disclose personal information for law enforcement purposes[21] or for the purpose of avoiding risks to the health and safety of a particular individual[22] or of the society at large.[23] In addition, the organisation may use or disclose personal information for direct marketing in certain circumstances.[24]

An organisation may use or disclose personal information for a secondary purpose—a purpose other than the primary purpose—provided the secondary purpose is related to the primary purpose and the individual would reasonably expect the organisation to use or disclose the information for the secondary purpose.[25]

Finally, as in many other parts of the Act, the data subject's consent works like a 'miracle cure' to virtually any violation of NPP 2.[26] The term 'consent' is not defined in the Act. The Act simply states that it 'means express consent or implied consent'.[27] Guidelines issued to assist in the interpretation of the Act only add that consent requires 'knowledge of the matter agreed to' and that consent is 'invalid if there is extreme pressure or coercion'.[28]

However, organisations interested in engaging in good privacy practice may wish to take a stricter approach to when consent can validly be given, and avoid not only extreme pressure or coercion but all forms of pressure or coercion. Further, it may be prudent to allow people to vary, or revoke, consent they have given.

---

[18]   NPP 1.3(e).
[19]   NPP 1.3(f).
[20]   NPP 2.1.
[21]   See for example NPP 2.1(f).
[22]   NPP 2.1(e)(i).
[23]   NPP 2.1(e)(ii).
[24]   NPP 2.1(c).
[25]   NPP 2.1(a).
[26]   NPP 2.1(b).
[27]   *Privacy Act 1988* (Cth) s 6.
[28]   Office of the Privacy Commissioner, *Guidelines to the National Privacy Principles* (September 2001), p 22, available at <www.privacy.gov.au/publications/nppgl_01.pdf> last accessed 25 February 2007.

NPP 3: Data quality

NPP 3, which regulates the minimum quality of the personal information organisations process, is largely self-explanatory. It reads: 'An organisation must take reasonable steps to make sure that the personal information it collects, uses or discloses is accurate, complete and up-to-date.'

NPP 4: Data security

Ensuring that personal information is kept in a safe manner is as much a concern for the data subject as it is for the organisation processing the information. In light of that, NPP 4 regulates data security by prescribing that organisations must take 'reasonable steps' to protect the information so as to avoid (1) misuse, (2) loss, and (3) 'unauthorised access, modification or disclosure'.

Further, NPP 4 states that an organisation must take 'reasonable steps' to dispose appropriately of personal information it no longer needs. Appropriate disposal includes the destruction or permanent de-identification of the personal information.

The question of what amounts to reasonable steps will, as always, depend on the circumstances of the individual case. For our purposes it is particularly important to note that simply deleting data from a computer is unlikely to be enough, as data so disposed of can often be recovered.

NPP 5: Openness

After the introduction of the Private Sector Amendment in 2001, there was a dramatic increase in the number of organisations that issued privacy policies. That was partly a result of NPP 5, which states:

> (5.1) An organisation must set out in a document clearly expressed policies on its management of personal information. The organisation must make the document available to anyone who asks for it.
> (5.2) On request by a person, an organisation must take reasonable steps to let the person know, generally, what sort of personal information it holds, for what purposes, and how it collects, holds, uses and discloses that information.

NPP 6: Access and correction

NPP 6 ensures that individuals have the right to access and have corrected personal information held about them. While organisations are entitled to charge a 'not excessive' fee for providing access to the personal information, there are only a few circumstances in which an organisation can refuse to provide access. Access can be denied, for example, where 'providing access would be likely to prejudice an investigation of possible unlawful activity'[29] and where 'the request for access is frivolous or vexatious'.[30]

---

[29]   NPP 6.1(i).
[30]   NPP 6.1(d).

NPP 7: Identifiers

NPP 7 seeks to make sure that organisations do not misuse unique identifiers (such as tax file numbers) assigned to individuals by the Commonwealth Government.

NPP 8: Anonymity

NPP 8 simply states: 'Wherever it is lawful and practicable, individuals must have the option of not identifying themselves when entering transactions with an organisation.' Unfortunately, organisations virtually never abide by this provision and NPP 8 is arguably the most widely ignored of all the NPPs. This can possibly be due to people in general lacking an expectation of anonymity. For example we have grown accustomed to having to provide our personal information to the websites we interact with, even where such interactions could have taken place anonymously.

NPP 9: Transborder data flows

NPP 9 is complex and the exact details of its application are far from clear. It aims at preventing a situation where the privacy protection offered under Australian law is undermined by organisations exporting personal information to other countries without similar protection. As such, it rests on a sound and logical foundation.

Put simply, NPP 9 states that an organisation may only transfer personal information where certain requirements are met. For example such transfer is allowed if:

o   'the organisation reasonably believes that the recipient of the information is subject to a law, binding scheme or contract which effectively upholds principles for fair handling of the information that are substantially similar to the National Privacy Principles';[31] or

o   'the individual consents to the transfer';[32] or

o   'the transfer is necessary for the performance of a contract between the individual and the organisation, or for the implementation of pre-contractual measures taken in response to the individual's request';[33] or

o   'the transfer is necessary for the conclusion or performance of a contract concluded in the interest of the individual between the organisation and a third party';[34] or

o   'the organisation has taken reasonable steps to ensure that the information which it has transferred will not be held, used or disclosed by the recipient of the information inconsistently with the National Privacy Principles'.[35]

---

[31]   NPP 9(a).
[32]   NPP 9(b).
[33]   NPP 9(c).
[34]   NPP 9(d).
[35]   NPP 9(f).

Further, transfer is allowed where all of the following requirements are met:

o   'the transfer is for the benefit of the individual';[36]
o   'it is impracticable to obtain the consent of the individual to that transfer';[37] and
o   'if it were practicable to obtain such consent, the individual would be likely to give it'.[38]

NPP 9 gives rise to a particularly interesting dilemma in the context of e-mail.

A university professor e-mails exam results (amounting to personal information) to a student who uses a free web-based e-mail system like Microsoft's Hotmail. It is commonly the case that such e-mail systems are hosted on servers located in foreign countries. Has the university professor in such a situation transferred personal information to a foreign country? And, if so, has she acted in violation of NPP 9?

EXAMPLE

While it is acknowledged that university professors at public universities would be more likely to be regulated under the IPPs, the example is nevertheless illustrative. Should it be the case that the professor is governed by the NPPs, it would seem undisputable that she has transferred personal information to a foreign country. But perhaps it could be said that the student in our example has consented to such a transfer by making the choice of using that particular kind of e-mail system. If this argument is accepted, the professor has not acted in violation of NPP 9.

NPP 10: Sensitive information

NPP 10 provides particularly strict regulation for the processing of sensitive information. *Sensitive information* is information relating to an individual's (1) political, religious or philosophical beliefs or affiliations, (2) heath and sexuality, (3) racial or ethnic origin, or (4) criminal convictions.[39]

Some areas of controversy

Certain areas of possible reform are of particular interest for our purposes. It has been questioned whether the definition of personal information adopted in the *Privacy Act* is valid in today's technology-driven society. For example under the current definition it is questionable whether a computer's IP address is personal information: are IP addresses 'about an individual whose identity is apparent, or can reasonably be ascertained, from the information'?

Another area of controversy is the very scope of the Act. The exclusion of 'small businesses' has been criticised, as it means that approximately 94 per cent of

---

[36]   NPP 9(e)(i).
[37]   NPP 9(e)(ii).
[38]   NPP 9(e)(iii).
[39]   *Privacy Act 1988* (Cth) s 6.

Australian businesses are exempt from the Act.[40] Many businesses in the e-commerce industry currently fall within this exemption.

A third area of controversy is whether the Act operates effectively in the context of developing technologies such as Radio Frequency Identification (RFID), location detection technologies and Voice over Internet Protocol (VoIP).

Workplace surveillance law

The extent to which employers are allowed to supervise the behaviour of their employees has always been a controversial issue. But never before has that question been more relevant than in today's technologically advanced workplace. The dilemma is that, on one hand, the employer has a legitimate interest in what employees do during work hours. On the other hand, employees' use of e-mail and the Internet may reveal considerable amounts of sensitive personal information about the employee and those with whom the employee corresponds. Further, the fact that employees may need to log on to the computer system using a password may give a false sense of privacy.

As noted above, the *Privacy Act* does not apply in relation to employee records. Therefore, the definition of employee records is crucial when determining what, if any, protection the *Privacy Act* provides in the workplace. Section 6 of the *Privacy Act* states:

> 'Employee record', in relation to an employee, means a record of personal information relating to the employment of the employee. Examples of personal information relating to the employment of the employee are health information about the employee and personal information about all or any of the following:
>
> (a) the engagement, training, disciplining or resignation of the employee;
> (b) the termination of the employment of the employee;
> (c) the terms and conditions of employment of the employee;
> (d) the employee's personal and emergency contact details;
> (e) the employee's performance or conduct;
> (f) the employee's hours of employment;
> (g) the employee's salary or wages;
> (h) the employee's membership of a professional or trade association;
> (i) the employee's trade union membership;
> (j) the employee's recreation, long service, sick, personal, maternity, paternity or other leave;
> (k) the employee's taxation, banking or superannuation affairs.

The *Privacy Act* still applies to workplace e-mails or other communications that contain personal information not classed as an employee record. Thus, for example, the Privacy Commissioner has stated that the *Privacy Act* applies where, as often happens, an employer logs the employees' web browsing activities.[41] Where a workplace communication contains personal information that would be classed as

---

[40] Australian Law Reform Commission, *Issues Paper 31—Review of Privacy* (October 2006), pp 183–243.

[41] Office of the Privacy Commissioner, *Guidelines on Workplace E-mail, Web Browsing and Privacy* (30/3/2000), <www.privacy.gov.au/internet/e-mail/index.html> last accessed 27 July 2007.

an employee record, but is not being used directly in relation to the employment relationship, the employee record exception will not apply.[42]

In addition to this protection provided on a federal level, individual states have enacted relevant legislation such as the *Workplace Surveillance Act 2005* (NSW) and the *Surveillance Devices (Workplace Privacy) Act 2006* (Vic). These are, however, not discussed here.

A TORT OF PRIVACY?

Influenced by an academic article written by Samuel Warren and Louis D Brandeis in 1890,[43] US law has recognised a tort of privacy for many years. In Australia there is currently no such tort, but we appear to be witnessing steps being taken towards one. In 2002 the Australian High Court opened the door for the development of a tort of privacy by making clear that the 1937 decision in *Victoria Park Racing*[44] does not prevent such a development, as had long been thought.[45] Prompted by the High Court's judgment, a Queensland District Court judge, Skoien J, bravely concluded that there was now a tort of privacy in Australian law.[46] While subsequent court decisions have been critical of Skoien J's conclusions,[47] it seems likely that such a tort will develop in Australia, either through common law or under statute.

It will be interesting to see how such a tort is structured once it is put in place. It will also be interesting to see how the availability of such a tort will affect e-commerce and other uses of the Internet.

ALTERNATIVE CAUSES OF ACTION PROTECTING PRIVACY

Causes of action
The legal ground on which a claim is based when going to court.

Apart from the measures discussed above, there are several other legal **causes of action** that, while not put in place to protect privacy, could very well be used for such an aim. Some are discussed in other parts of this book. For example misrepresentation and passing off (discussed in chapters 6 and 14 respectively) can be used to protect against one's picture being used in an advertisement. We say a few words here about other relevant causes of action not discussed elsewhere.

---

42   *Privacy Act 1988* (Cth) s7B(3).
43   S Warren and L Brandeis, 'The Right to Privacy' (1890) 4 *Harv L R* 193.
44   *Victoria Park Racing and Recreation Grounds Co Ltd v Taylor* (1937) 58 CLR 479.
45   *Australian Broadcasting Corporation v Lenah Game Meat Pty Ltd* (2002) 208 CLR 199.
46   *Grosse v Purvis* [2003] QDC 151.
47   *Kalaba v Commonwealth of Australia* [2004] FCA 763; *Giller v Procopets* [2004] VSC 113.

Defamation

The rules of the tort of defamation were harmonised throughout the Australian states from 1 January 2006.[48] The aim of this tort is to protect a person's reputation. Put simply, to establish the tort, the plaintiff has to show:

○ the material in question was defamatory (for example lowered the plaintiff's reputation in the eyes of a third person);

○ the plaintiff was identified as the one the defamatory materials related to; and

○ the defamatory material was published in the sense of entering the mind of a third person.

The connection between the tort of defamation and protection of privacy is rather strong. For example in order to publish something defamatory about a person the publisher may need to collect personal information about the victim. Further, the very publication of the defamatory material may constitute disclosure under the *Privacy Act*.

Trespass

The tort of trespass has a long history. Originally, it was aimed at unlawful interference with land in another person's possession—**trespass to land**. Typically, trespass would occur where a person enters somebody else's land, or remains on someone else's land after having been asked to leave.

This traditional type of trespass has little if anything to do with e-commerce and the Internet. However, a different form of trespass is also recognised: **trespass to a chattel**. In the US a plaintiff has successfully argued that the tort of trespass to chattels has been committed when the defendant sends an unwelcome e-mail to the plaintiff's server, as the e-mail constituted interference with the server.[49] Along the same lines, it has been held that the tort of trespass to a chattel has been committed when someone uses a **web crawler** to map the content on the plaintiff's server.[50] A common feature in both these cases was that the defendants had continued their conduct after having been told by the plaintiffs not to do so.

In this way, it is clear that the tort of trespass to chattels has the potential to be used to protect privacy or related rights. However, it is unclear whether an Australian court would take the same approach as the US courts did in the cases mentioned.

Trespass to land
A cause of action in torts law that involves unlawful interference with land which is in the possession of another.

Trespass to chattels
A cause of action in torts law that involves intentional or negligent interference with another person's possession of movable property (chattels).

Web crawler
An automated computer program which navigates the Internet indexing its content, usually for search engines. Also known as web spiders or robots.

---

48 *Defamation Act 2005* (NSW), *Defamation Act 2005* (Qld), *Defamation Act 2005* (Vic), *Defamation Act 2005* (SA), *Defamation Act 2005* (Tas), *Defamation Act 2005* (WA). Note also *Defamation Act 2006* (NT).
49 *Intel Corp v Hamidi*, 1 Cal, Rptr 3d 32 (Cal, 2003).
50 *eBay, Inc v Bidder's Edge, Inc*, 100 F Supp 2d 1058 (ND Cal, 2000).

Nuisance

Nuisance

A cause of action in torts law that involves unlawful interference with an owner's or occupier's use or enjoyment of land.

The tort of **nuisance** protects against unlawful interference with the enjoyment of land. Thus it shares some features with the tort of trespass to land, and the two overlap to a certain extent.

The law distinguished between two forms of nuisance: public nuisance and private nuisance. The tort of *public nuisance* is committed where the unlawful interference relates to public spaces. For example where a person blocks a public road in order to use it for his own purposes the tort of public nuisance may have been committed. The tort of *private nuisance* is committed where the unlawful interference relates to private spaces. A typical example of private nuisance would be where a person plays loud music late at night so as to make impossible the neighbours' enjoyment of their land. Thus, the tort of nuisance may possibly be used to protect privacy, but would rarely have any real application in the Internet and e-commerce context.

Self-help: technical means for protecting privacy

In addition to taking action, either in the courts or by making a complaint to the Privacy Commissioner, individuals concerned about their online privacy have a range of technical tools at their disposal. It is not the intention of this book to examine these self-help tools in detail. However, it is important that the reader is aware of their existence. As the former Federal Privacy Commissioner, Malcolm Crompton, noted in May 2004: 'It's extraordinarily important that we ensure protection of our own privacy and personal safety, rather than accepting what others want to push on us.'[51]

Anonymiser

An application designed to allow web users to visit websites anonymously, disguising their IP addresses.

The two privacy-enhancing technologies examined here are Freenet[52] and **anonymisers**.

Freenet is a decentralised, encrypted and anonymous Internet application aimed at allowing people to publish and obtain information on the Internet without any risk of censorship. The philosophy behind Freenet is that '[w]ithout anonymity there can never be true freedom of speech, and without decentralization the network will be vulnerable to attack'.[53]

Each user of Freenet gives up some hard-drive space and bandwidth. As all content is encrypted and 'routed' through nodes in the network, users do not know what content they are hosting, or indeed, the location of the content they are accessing. This has significant legal implications. For example, as no person can know what material

---

51 Records Management Association of Australasia, NSW branch, *Technology Issues Report*, July 2004, p 6 <www.rmaa.com.au/docs/branches/nsw/pub/TISreport/2004/TIS200407. pdf> last accessed 27 July 2007.

52 <http://freenetproject.org> last accessed 27 July 2007.

53 <http://freenetproject.org/whatis.html> last accessed 27 July 2007.

is stored on their hard drive, it may be difficult to argue that they are liable if hosting some form of illegal content. Finally, the efficiency of the network is maintained by storing and deleting files according to their popularity.

Anonymisers are applications designed to allow web users to visit websites anonymously.[54] They act as an added layer—a buffer—between the web surfer and the websites visited. When a web surfer uses an anonymiser, his IP address is only transmitted to the provider of the anonymiser. He is then assigned a new IP address by the anonymiser in relation to any websites he visits while applying the anonymiser. Consequently, the websites cannot know the actual IP address of the web surfer.

Finally, we must also mention that by taking care with what sites are visited, and by using appropriate browser settings, a web surfer can minimise the risk of privacy violations, but cannot or course completely eliminate it. A user should also have a good virus protection system and regularly scan the computer for spyware.

CONCLUDING REMARKS AND FURTHER READING

Australia's approach to privacy protection was examined with particular emphasis on privacy protection in the context of e-commerce and the Internet. As has been shown, Australian law takes a patchwork approach, with a wide range of privacy-related law. While there is clear room for improvement, it should be clear that, taken together, this patchwork represents a serious attempt to ensure the protection of privacy.

However, while regulation can help deter people from violating the privacy rights of others, it can do little to prevent 'computer errors' that lead to privacy violations. With its high speed and wide reach, Internet communication is a 'perfect' environment for mistakes that might have severe privacy implications. As has been pointed out by several people, to err is human, but to really foul things up takes a computer.

For further reading on the topic of privacy law, the Internet and e-commerce, see:

ALRC, Privacy, Issues Paper 31 available at <www.austlii.edu.au>

Australian Privacy Foundation <www.privacy.org.au>

Lee A Bygrave, *Data Protection Law: Approaching its Rationale, Logic and Limits*, Kluwer Law International, 2002

Yee Fen Lim, *Cyberspace Law: Commentaries and Materials,* 2nd edn, Oxford University Press, Melbourne, 2007

Office of the Privacy Commissioner <www.privacy.gov.au>

Review questions for this chapter can be found on the book's Online Resource Centre at www.oup.com.au/orc/fordersvantesson.

---

[54]   A range of free anonymisers can be accessed at <www.svantesson.org>.

10

SPAM

OBJECTIVES // BY THE END OF THIS CHAPTER, YOU WILL:

O Understand why spam is a major problem

O Have a solid understanding of how Australia regulates spam

O Be aware of some technical ways in which spam may be addressed

WHAT THIS CHAPTER IS ABOUT

The unfortunate truth is that virtually every person who uses e-mail has received unsolicited—or so-called spam—e-mail. This chapter examines the legal issues associated with such e-mail. Since 2004, spam has been regulated by a specific piece of legislation in Australia. The *Spam Act 2003 (Cth)* will consequently be the focal point for this chapter.

SPAM AND THE INTERNET

Spam e-mails account for approximately 40–80 per cent of the total number of e-mail messages sent on the Internet. While most of us complain about the number of spam e-mails we receive, few can compete with Microsoft's co-founder, Bill Gates. In 2004 news reports indicated that Bill Gates receives approximately 4 million spam e-mails per day!

Spam being sent over the Internet has several negative implications. It:

○   slows down the network;
○   may be offensive;
○   is perceived as annoying;
○   may be sent as part of scams; and
○   costs society enormous amounts in lost productivity.

It has been estimated that each employee in Sweden loses approximately seven seconds of work time for each spam e-mail received; the total cost of spam within the European Union was estimated at $4 500 million per year.[1]

While spam is being sent from virtually all countries connected to the Internet, some countries are worse than others. The USA is by far the biggest producer of spam e-mails; other major 'offenders' include China, Russia, the United Kingdom, and Japan.[2]

THE *SPAM ACT 2003* (CTH)

In Australia, spam is regulated by the *Spam Act 2003 (Cth)* which came into force in 2004. This Act will be examined in detail here. But before doing so, it is important to point out that the sending of spam, and activities associated with the sending of spam (such as the collection of addresses), also may violate the *Privacy Act 1988* (Cth) and other privacy-related Acts. Further, as noted in Chapter 9, the tort of trespass to chattels has been successfully used to combat spam in overseas jurisdictions.

Main features of the Act

The key provision of the *Spam Act* is s 16(1), which makes clear that a person must not send, or cause to be sent, a commercial electronic message that (1) has an Australian link, and (2) is not a designated commercial electronic message. To understand this provision we need to answer the following questions:

○   What is 'a commercial electronic message'?
○   When does a commercial electronic message have an 'Australian link'?
○   When is a commercial electronic message designated?

---

[1]   Anders Lignell, 'Kärleksbrev stoppar skräppost', *Aftonbladet* (19 October 2004).
[2]   See <www.spamhaus.org/statistics/countries.lasso> last accessed 6 March 2007.

The wording of s 16(1) means the *Spam Act* does not focus on bulk e-mail as such. Typically, when thinking of spam, people would tend to think of e-mail sent in large quantities. While it is clear that actions are unlikely to be taken in relation to the sending of just one e-mail, s 16(1) shows that the sending of one single e-mail may constitute spamming.

To get the answer to the first question—the meaning of 'a commercial electronic message'—we have to examine two sections. Section 5(1) provides a definition of what constitutes an electronic message:

> For the purposes of this Act, an electronic message is a message sent:
> (a) using:
>   (i)   an Internet carriage service; or
>   (ii) any other listed carriage service; and
> (b) to an electronic address in connection with:
>   (i)   an e-mail account; or
>   (ii) an instant messaging account; or
>   (iii) a telephone account; or
>   (iv) a similar account.

Section 6 then defines when such an electronic message is commercial. In assessing whether or not an electronic message is a commercial electronic message, regard should be had to the content of the message, how the message is presented, and the content that can be accessed if one follows links or other contact information found in the message.[3] Having outlined the factors to be taken into account, s 6 goes on to outline the types of messages that are regarded as commercial. So, if by taking account of the factors outlined above, it is concluded that the message fits within any of the following categories, it is a commercial electronic message whose purpose is:

○   to offer to supply goods or services;[4] or
○   to advertise or promote goods or services;[5] or
○   to advertise or promote a supplier, or prospective supplier, of goods or services;[6] or
○   to offer to supply land or an interest in land;[7] or
○   to advertise or promote land or an interest in land;[8] or
○   to advertise or promote a supplier, or prospective supplier, of land or an interest in land;[9] or
○   to offer to provide a business opportunity or investment opportunity;[10] or
○   to advertise or promote a business opportunity or investment opportunity;[11] or

---

[3]   *Spam Act 2003* (Cth) s 6(1)(a–c).
[4]   *Spam Act 2003* (Cth) s 6(1)(d).
[5]   *Spam Act 2003* (Cth) s 6(1)(e).
[6]   *Spam Act 2003* (Cth) s 6(1)(f).
[7]   *Spam Act 2003* (Cth) s 6(1)(g).
[8]   *Spam Act 2003* (Cth) s 6(1)(h).
[9]   *Spam Act 2003* (Cth) s 6(1)(i).
[10] *Spam Act 2003* (Cth) s 6(1)(j).
[11] *Spam Act 2003* (Cth) s 6(1)(k).

○ to advertise or promote a provider, or prospective provider, of a business opportunity or investment opportunity;[12] or

○ to assist or enable a person, by a deception, to dishonestly obtain property belonging to another person;[13] or

○ to assist or enable a person, by a deception, to dishonestly obtain a financial advantage from another person;[14] or

○ to assist or enable a person to dishonestly obtain a gain from another person;[15] or

○ a purpose specified in the regulations.[16]

This definition has not been free from criticism. For example while it is clear that it does not cover standard telephone voice messages,[17] it is not immediately clear how messages sent by fax[18] or Voice over Internet Protocol (VoIP)[19] ought to be regulated.

The answer to the second question—the meaning of 'Australian link'—is found in s 7:

> For the purposes of this Act, a commercial electronic message has an Australian link if, and only if:
>
> (a) the message originates in Australia; or
> (b) the individual or organisation who sent the message, or authorised the sending of the message, is:
>   (i) an individual who is physically present in Australia when the message is sent; or
>   (ii) an organisation whose central management and control is in Australia when the message is sent; or
> (c) the computer, server or device that is used to access the message is located in Australia; or
> (d) the relevant electronic account-holder is:
>   (i) an individual who is physically present in Australia when the message is accessed; or
>   (ii) an organisation that carries on business or activities in Australia when the message is accessed; or
> (e) if the message cannot be delivered because the relevant electronic address does not exist—assuming that the electronic address existed, it is reasonably likely that the message would have been accessed using a computer, server or device located in Australia.

12 *Spam Act 2003* (Cth) s 6(1)(l).
13 *Spam Act 2003* (Cth) s 6(1)(m).
14 *Spam Act 2003* (Cth) s 6(1)(n).
15 *Spam Act 2003* (Cth) s 6(1)(o).
16 *Spam Act 2003* (Cth) s 6(1)(p).
17 *Spam Act 2003* (Cth) s 5(5).
18 Department of Communications, Information Technology and the Arts, *Report on the Spam Act 2003 review*, 2006, p 6, available at <www.dcita.gov.au> last accessed 6 March, 2007.
19 Department of Communications, Information Technology and the Arts, *Report on the Spam Act 2003 review*, 2006, pp 45–46 available at <www.dcita.gov.au> last accessed 6 March 2007.

Thus, in talking about an Australian link, the provision is not referring to a link in the sense of hyperlinks. Instead, the Act uses this unique term to determine how closely related the message is to Australia.

This definition can also be criticised for another effect: in some rare circumstances, such as in the example below, the Act will apply in what can be described as 'overseas to overseas' situations.

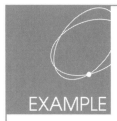

EXAMPLE

Imagine that a person working at the Stockholm office of a large international organisation receives a commercial electronic message. Imagine further that the commercial electronic message is in Swedish, is sent by a Swedish corporation located in Sweden, and relates to a specifically Swedish product or service. Under these circumstances it would be undesirable for Australian spam legislation to be applicable. Yet that is exactly what the result of ss 7(d)(ii) and 7(c) may be in certain circumstances. If the international organisation receiving the commercial electronic message 'carries on business or activities in Australia when the message is accessed', s 7(d)(ii) seems to indicate an 'Australian link'. Further, if the international organisation receiving the commercial electronic message is set up in such a manner that all e-mails are accessed from a mail server located in Australia (perhaps due to the organisation's head office being located here), s 7(c) would seem to indicate an 'Australian link'. The Swedish company sending the commercial electronic message might find some comfort in s 16(3), which states that s 16(1) does not apply where the sender did not, and could not reasonably, know of the Australian link. However, it is still undesirable for the legislation to provide that there may be an Australian link also in pure 'overseas to overseas' situations.

The third question—the meaning of 'a designated commercial electronic message'—is answered in Schedule 1 of the Act. Essentially, it states that a commercial electronic message is classed as 'a designated commercial electronic message' where (a) it contains no more than factual information,[20] (b) the message is sent by, or on behalf of a government body, registered political party, religious organisation, charity, charitable organisation or educational institution,[21] or (c) the regulations provide that the commercial electronic message is classed as a designated commercial electronic message.[22]

In addition to regulating the actual sending of spam, as is done in s 16(1), the *Spam Act* also regulates a range of other aspects of spamming. Section 17 makes clear that commercial electronic messages must contain certain accurate sender information, and s 18 states that such messages must contain a functional unsubscribe facility.

---

[20] *Spam Act 2003* (Cth), Schedule 1, Clause 2.
[21] *Spam Act 2003* (Cth), Schedule 1, Clauses 3 and 4.
[22] *Spam Act 2003* (Cth), Schedule 1, Clause 5.

Like the rules found in s 16(1), the rules in ss 17 and 18 are also limited to commercial electronic messages with an Australian link, and do not apply to designated commercial electronic messages. Further, just like s 16(1), ss 17 and 18 do not apply if the person sending the message did not know, and could not reasonably have known, that the message had an Australian link.[23]

Another feature shared by all the provisions discussed so far is that they do not only regulate the persons directly involved in the sending of spam. They also extend to persons:

- aiding, abetting, counselling or procuring a contravention of the relevant section; or
- inducing, whether by threats or promises or otherwise, a contravention of the relevant section; or
- being in any way, directly or indirectly, knowingly concerned in, or party to, a contravention of the relevant section; or
- conspiring with others to effect a contravention of the relevant section.[24]

Finally, just as in the context of the *Privacy Act 1988* (Cth), consent cures breaches of s 16(1). That means that where a person has consented to receiving spam, no violation of s 16(1) occurs where spam is sent to that person. In contrast, consent has no effect in relation to ss 17 and 18.

Rules about address-harvesting

Part 3 of the *Spam Act* regulates address-harvesting, or more precisely, address-harvesting software and harvested-address lists. The Act defines address-harvesting software as:

software that is specifically designed or marketed for use for:

(a) searching the Internet for electronic addresses; and
(b) collecting, compiling, capturing or otherwise harvesting those electronic addresses.[25]

A harvested-address list is:

(a) a list of electronic addresses; or
(b) a collection of electronic addresses; or
(c) a compilation of electronic addresses;

where the production of the list, collection or compilation is, to any extent, directly or indirectly attributable to the use of address-harvesting software.[26]

The thinking behind the Act seems to be that as long as there are large lists of e-mail addresses that can be used for spamming, or tools for the creation of such lists, there is a risk of spamming. In line with this thinking, the Act regulates the supply, acquisition and use of address-harvesting software and harvested-address lists.

---

[23] *Spam Act 2003* (Cth) ss 16(3), 17(2) and 18(2).
[24] *Spam Act 2003* (Cth) ss 16(9), 17(5) and 18(6).
[25] *Spam Act 2003* (Cth) s4.
[26] *Spam Act 2003* (Cth) s4.

In s 20 the Act states that persons should not supply, or offer to supply, (1) address-harvesting software, (2) harvested-address lists, or (3) licenses to use such software or lists.[27] This rule applies where the supplier or receiver of the software or list is either 'an individual who is physically present in Australia at the time of the supply or offer'[28] or 'a body corporate or partnership that carries on business or activities in Australia at the time of the supply or offer'.[29] This rule does not apply where:

> the supplier had no reason to suspect that the customer, or another person, intended to use the address-harvesting software or the harvested-address list, as the case may be, in connection with sending commercial electronic messages in contravention of section 16.[30]

Further, it does not apply where:

the supplier:
(a) did not know; and
(b) could not, with reasonable diligence, have ascertained;

that the customer was:
(c) an individual who was physically present in Australia at the time of the supply or offer; or
(d) a body corporate or partnership that carried on business or activities in Australia at the time of the supply or offer.[31]

Evidentiary burden
See *Burden of proof.*

Where a person seeks to rely on the latter of these exceptions, she or he bears an **evidentiary burden** in relation to that matter.[32] Furthermore, just as in relation to ss 16, 17 and 18, the harvesting rules are wide enough to also cover people involved in aiding, abetting, inducing (etc) violation of the Act.

Section 21 of the Act regulates the acquiring of address-harvesting software and harvested-address lists. It largely mirrors s 20 but talks about 'acquiring' rather than supplying. Section 22, regulating the use of address-harvesting software and harvested-address lists, is also structured in a manner similar to that of ss 20 and 21. It reads as follows:

(1) A person must not use:
    (a) address-harvesting software; or
    (b) a harvested-address list;
    if the person is:

---

27   *Spam Act 2003* (Cth) s 20(1).
28   *Spam Act 2003* (Cth) s 20(1)(e)(i).
29   *Spam Act 2003* (Cth) s 20(1)(e)(ii).
30   *Spam Act 2003* (Cth) s 20(2).
31   *Spam Act 2003* (Cth) s 20(3).
32   *Spam Act 2003* (Cth) s 20(4).

      (c) an individual who is physically present in Australia at the time of the use; or

      (d) a body corporate or partnership that carries on business or activities in Australia at the time of the use.

(2) Subsection (1) does not apply in relation to the use of address-harvesting software or a harvested-address list, if the use was not in connection with sending commercial electronic messages in contravention of section 16.

(3) A person must not:

      (a) aid, abet, counsel or procure a contravention of subsection (1); or

      (b) induce, whether by threats or promises or otherwise, a contravention of subsection (1); or

      (c) be in any way, directly or indirectly, knowingly concerned in, or party to, a contravention of subsection (1); or

      (d) conspire with others to effect a contravention of subsection (1).

Remedies

The Australian Communications and Media Authority (ACMA) is a statutory authority which, among other things, has responsibility for the *Spam Act*. In carrying out this responsibility, the ACMA has several functions. For example it conducts or commissions research and education programs relating to spam. It also issues formal warnings where it identifies breaches of the Act, and can accept written undertakings by persons who have contravened the Act to modify their behaviour. ACMA can also take action in the courts where it has identified a breach of the Act.

So what are the consequences for those who act in contravention of the *Spam Act 2003* (Cth)? Where the Federal Court finds a person has breached any provisions discussed above, it may order the person to pay a pecuniary (money) penalty to the Commonwealth.[33] Further, the court may make an order to the effect that the offending party compensates a person who received, and suffered damages due to, spam e-mail.[34]

In addition, injunctions can be granted to (1) restrain a person from engaging in contraventions, or (2) force a person to perform a particular act, where failure to do so constitutes a contravention of the Act.

The *Spam Act* applied

Since the commencement of the *Spam Act* on 10 April 2004, there have been a range of matters leading to fines being issued, and businesses providing enforceable undertakings.[35] The first matter brought before the courts came to a conclusion through the Federal Court's judgment handed down on 27 October 2006.

---

33 *Spam Act 2003* (Cth) s 24(1).

34 *Spam Act 2003* (Cth) s 28(1).

35 Philip Argy, 'How Much "Clarity" in the Spam Act?', (2005) 8(6) *Internet Law Bulletin* 90.

CASE EXAMPLE *AUSTRALIAN COMMUNICATIONS AND MEDIA AUTHORITY V CLARITY1 PTY LTD (2006) FCA 1399[36]*

AUSTRALIA, FEDERAL COURT OF AUSTRALIA, 2006

The dispute related to the conduct of the first respondent, Clarity1 Pty Ltd, and the second respondent, Mr Mansfield (who authorised the sending). The respondents were found to have acted in breach of s 16(1) by sending, and authorising the sending of, a large amount of e-mail, and of violating s 22 by using, and authorising the use of, address-harvesting software and harvested-address lists. The Court ordered the first respondent to pay a penalty of $4 500 000, and the second respondent to pay a penalty of $1 000 000. In setting the penalties, the Court noted:

> I [...] accept that it can be reasonably inferred that the respondents' conduct is likely to have resulted in real loss or damage to the recipients of the CEM [commercial electronic message] in the form of direct financial costs associated with purchasing blocking and filtering software; other financial costs in the form of lost time and productivity; and non-financial costs in the form of annoyance and frustration at having received unsolicited CEMs. Such loss or damage is therefore an aggravating factor to be taken into account. (paragraph 31)

> Further, the court granted injunctions restraining the respondents from continuing the sending of spam, and ordered that the respondents pay costs.

This judgment has gained widespread attention, as it illustrates the harsh penalties that can be imposed on spammers. It also signals that the *Spam Act* is much more than a 'toothless tiger', and that it needs to be taken seriously.

TECHNOLOGY AS THE ANSWER

Several technologies have been suggested to address the spam problem. For example it has been suggested that if a small charge applied to each e-mail sent, spamming would become unprofitable. It has also been suggested that as an alternative to a financial cost, the sender could pay with time. In other words, the sending of an e-mail could freeze their Internet connection for a very short time. While the effect of sending one, or a few, e-mails would not be noticeable, the sending of millions of spam e-mails would freeze the system for a considerable period. Both could be described as detrimental technologies—they have a detrimental effect on all e-mail.

---

[36]   Available at <www.austlii.edu.au/au/cases/cth/federal_ct/2006/1399.html>.

The alternative approach is known as curbing technologies—technology, where the aim is not to have a detrimental effect on all e-mail, but curb the sending of spam specifically. The best example is where a blacklist provider monitors the sources of spam and makes available lists of such sources. These blacklists are used by ISPs to block all e-mail coming from those sources. This approach is very efficient and addresses large quantities of spam.

Another form of filtering occurs closer to the end user. Most people use filters in their e-mail systems that try to identify and reject spam. These filters are constantly evolving, but then so is the spammers' level of sophistication. One example illustrating this game of 'cat and mouse' is the spammers' use of '**safe words**' or '**white list words**'. Many modern spam filters are based on Bayes' theorem (named after Thomas Bayes). By studying past e-mails these filters learn to separate spam from legitimate e-mails. One important ingredient in being able to do so is the recognition of words (or phrases) typically associated with spam, and words (or phrases) typically associated with legitimate e-mail. For example words like 'Viagra', 'casino' and 'cash' may typically indicate that the message is spam, while words like 'wireless', 'comment' and 'column' may typically indicate that the message is a legitimate e-mail. As a consequence of this approach to spam filtering, one often sees spam e-mail containing a list of words that have nothing to do with the spammer's message—words inserted into the spam just to fool filters based on this approach.

Safe words
A list of ordinary words, injected by spammers into e-mails, meant to trick spam filters into identifying the message as legitimate.

White list words
See *Safe words*

Another way for spammers to get around spam filters is to change the spelling of typical spam words. For example it is not unusual to get e-mails with headings such as 'Vi@gra' or 'Stöck Inv_est'.

CONCLUDING REMARKS AND FURTHER READING

Spam is a major problem for the Internet and it affects everyone using the Internet. Even if you are one of those rare people who get no spam at all, you are affected by the fact that the network runs more slowly than it would if it did not have to deal with spam.

This chapter has examined the Australian approach to spam regulation, and in addition, discussed some technical approaches for dealing with spam.

For further reading on the topic of spam, the Internet and e-commerce:

Australian Communications and Media Authority <www.acma.gov.au>

Sammy Isreb, 'Can the Spam Act 2003 independently protect the public against spam, or are additional legally sanctioned technology based solutions required?' (2006) 11 *Media and Arts Law Review* 272

Yee Fen Lim, *Cyberspace Law: Commentaries and Materials,* 2nd edn, Oxford University Press, Melbourne, 2007

Review questions for this chapter can be found on the book's Online Resource Centre at www.oup.com.au/orc/fordersvantesson.

11

COPYRIGHT AND COMPUTER SOFTWARE

OBJECTIVES // BY THE END OF THIS CHAPTER, YOU WILL:

○ Have a basic understanding of copyright—what it is and what it protects

○ Understand why copyright was chosen to protect computer software, despite its not being entirely suitable for the purpose

○ Know the situations in which reverse engineering of software is permitted

○ Know how courts approach infringements of 'substantial parts' of computer programs

○ Appreciate some of the difficulties with non-literal elements of computer programs such as menu commands and screen displays, as well as with collections of data in databases

○ Understand the balance the legislature has tried to achieve in regulating devices that circumvent copy protection systems

WHAT THIS CHAPTER IS ABOUT

This is the first of four chapters that explore intellectual property issues. This chapter begins with an explanation of the nature of intellectual property, followed by a brief primer on copyright for those who are new to the topic. The rest of this chapter focuses on the way copyright protects computer software. The following chapter considers some of the important copyright issues raised by the Internet and the Web. The other intellectual property chapters are Chapter 13 on domain names and trade marks and Chapter 14 on patents, confidentiality and passing off.

Computer software is used on stand-alone machines and in consumer devices that have nothing to do with the Internet and e-commerce. A full discussion of the protection of computer software thus goes far beyond our focus on Internet and e-commerce law.

However, the Internet and e-commerce would not operate without software, so the topic is equally relevant for our purposes.

We outline the rocky road followed before computer software gained the protection of copyright law. We explain the development of the reverse engineering exceptions—situations in which it is legitimate to reproduce or decompile software. This is followed by an examination of the copyright approach when only parts of computer programs are copied. We then move on to the longstanding and complex debate over the nature and limits of copyright when dealing with the 'non-literal' elements of software (such as program structure and screen displays). We also explain the different views on when databases should attract copyright protection.

Copying is relatively easy in the digital environment. Many content creators use technological solutions to prevent it. This, in turn, has led to the development of devices that circumvent copy prevention technology. We end the chapter by considering how copyright law discourages the use of circumvention devices.

WHAT IS COPYRIGHT?

Intellectual property

Copyright is one of the topics grouped under the umbrella of intellectual property—a collective term used to describe a number of concepts of a similar nature. It is sometimes used in a narrow sense to include only copyright, patents, trade marks and industrial designs, all of which have been regulated by statute for some time. More often the term is used in a wider sense to cover similar common law concepts and more recent statutes. In this broad sense, intellectual property might include plant breeders' rights, circuit layout rights, business names, commercial goodwill, passing off (sometimes called common law trade marks), trade secrets and confidential information. The approach to intellectual property has not been consistent or uniform because each of these concepts developed separately. What they have in common is that they all describe rights closely connected with information, ideas, or other intangibles—the word 'intellectual' signifies that the subject matter is the product of the intellect.

A major theme running through intellectual property law is that it aims to achieve a suitable balance between the interests of the individual and society. Individuals need to be able to exploit the fruits of their inventions or ideas, otherwise there would be no incentive for these activities. On the other hand, perpetual monopolies would stifle development—society as a whole benefits if inventions and ideas are open and can be improved on by others. Courts are often guided by this balancing act when interpreting legislation or deciding cases.

Many intellectual property rights are regulated by the Federal Parliament—the constitution gives it power over 'copyrights, patents of inventions and designs, and trade marks'.[1] Each of these topics is the subject of a federal statute. Intellectual property rights are generally enforceable by **civil action**, although the statutes do create some criminal offences.

---

[1]   *Commonwealth of Australia Constitution Act* s 51(xviii).

Civil action

Litigation brought by one or more parties protecting their own interests (as opposed to a criminal action, in which someone is prosecuted on behalf of the state).

Works and secondary works

In the context of copyright law, original literary, dramatic, musical and artistic creations are known collectively as works; sound recordings, films, television and sound broadcasts, and published editions of works are also protected—we refer to these as 'secondary works'.

Copyright

In English law, copyright is usually traced to the *Statute of Anne* in 1709,[2] when authors were first given exclusive rights to prevent others from copying their published works. Copyright is still based on this model—it is a bundle of exclusive rights given to authors for a limited time, which enables them to prevent others from dealing with their creations in certain ways. Copyright is not an exhaustive definition of *all* the things you can do with your creation; it is a limited bundle of things you are entitled to stop others from doing.

Copyright is the subject of several international treaties, the best-known of which is the Berne Convention.[3] The broad principles of these treaties are common (and reciprocally recognised) in most countries.[4]

The current Australian Act was passed in 1968.[5] It is lengthy (over 500 pages) and has been added to and amended many times.[6] This partly explains its complexity. To understand the basics, there are three important questions. What does copyright protect? When and how does it arise? Once you have copyright, what can you stop others from doing?[7]

What does copyright protect?

Copyright first developed to protect literary works, but was extended to cover dramatic, musical and other artistic works (collectively known as 'works'). As technology developed, other types of media were added, notably sound recordings, films, television and sound broadcasts, and published editions. We refer to

---

[2]   *Copyright Act 1709*, 8 Anne c 19 (UK).

[3]   *International Convention for the Protection of Literary and Artistic Works*, concluded at Berne on 9 September 1886, current version available at <www.wipo.int/treaties/en/ip/berne/index.html> last accessed 29 July 2007.

[4]   Regulation 4 of the *Copyright (International Protection) Regulations 1969* extends the protection of Australian copyright law to materials from a Berne Convention country, a Rome Convention country, a Universal Copyright Convention country, a WIPO Copyright Treaty country, a WIPO Performances and Phonograms Treaty country or a WTO/TRIPS agreement country in certain circumstances.

[5]   *Copyright Act 1968* (Cth). In this chapter, all references to 'the Act', and all references to section numbers without specifying an Act, refer to this Act.

[6]   The amendments with which we are particularly concerned are: *Copyright Amendment Act 1984; Copyright Amendment (Computer Programs) Act 1999; Copyright Amendment (Digital Agenda) Act 2000; US Free Trade Agreement Implementation Act 2004, Copyright Legislation Amendment Act 2004; and Copyright Amendment Act 2006.*

[7]   A word of caution is appropriate: this treatment of copyright is only intended to summarise basic concepts. Some details are, for the sake of brevity, omitted or glossed over.

these as 'secondary works'.[8] The way in which computer programs came to be treated as literary works is described below.

Copyright is not designed to protect ideas, processes or functions. Thus, with a book, copyright protects the actual words used, but not the plot or broad storyline. It protects the computer code that makes a computer perform functions (such as cut, copy and paste) but does not prevent others from writing their own code to implement the same functions. Copyright only protects the writing or other material form in which the idea is expressed.[9] Shortly we will discuss the implications of this for the protection of various non-literal aspects of computer software.

When and how does copyright arise?

There is no registration system.[10] Copyright exists once the work is made.[11] The copyright notice (for example '© 1997 Jane Smith') is not a legal requirement—it serves only to identify the owner and remind people that the work is protected.

For copyright to arise under Australian law, the subject matter must be made by a 'qualified person' (essentially an Australian citizen or resident), or must have been first published in Australia.[12] There are also provisions that recognise copyright in certain things (such as computer programs) legally made in other 'qualifying countries'.[13] In some situations, ownership of copyright is conferred on persons other than authors.[14] The most common example is that an employer owns the copyright where a work is created as part of a contract of employment.[15] In the case of secondary works like films

---

8   They are in a separate part of the Act (Part IV) because they were seen as being derived from the original works (literary, dramatic, musical and artistic). This has resulted in the rather inelegant collective description of them in the Act as 'subject matter other than works', and the duplication of many of the provisions that apply to works. Where we need to refer to both types of works, we use the phrases 'works and secondary works' or 'copyright materials'.

9   See for example, s 22 as read with the definition of 'material form' in s 10.

10   This is unlike the USA, which had a system of compulsory registration until 1989 when it became a signatory to the Berne Convention. To comply with the Convention, the USA recognises copyright as existing automatically once the work is created, but still encourages registration by (among other things) making it a requirement before being able to enforce one's rights in court. For further information, see US Copyright Office, 'Copyright Basics', Circular 1, <www.copyright.gov/circs/circ1.html> last accessed 21 Feb 2007.

11   *Copyright Act 1968* (Cth) (the Act) s 22, which also describes when some of the secondary works like sound recordings and films are deemed to be made.

12   Section 32.

13   See, for example, in relation to computer programs, s 10AB. 'Qualifying countries' are defined in s 10 to include countries that are party to the Berne Convention or members of the World Trade Organization whose laws are consistent with the Agreement on Trade Related Aspects of Intellectual Property Rights (TRIPS). Reciprocal recognition of copyright generally is dealt with in the *Copyright (International Protection) Regulations 1969*.

14   Section 35.

15   Section 35(6) deals with employment situations.

and television broadcasts, the Act also provides for the resolution of ownership issues between performers, producers and directors.[16] These assumptions about ownership can be changed by agreement between the parties.

Although there is an originality requirement for copyright, it has a low threshold compared with other areas of intellectual property law. Creating a new work that has not itself been copied is generally sufficient.[17] The degree of creativity required is contentious, particularly when applied to databases. We discuss this in more detail later.

Copyright lasts for a limited time, after which the work is released into the public domain. The time period is generally the lifetime of the author plus another 70 years or, if the author is unknown or dead at the time of publication, 70 years after first publication.[18] The same periods apply to secondary works, except for television and sound broadcasts (which last for 50 years after they were broadcast) and published editions of works (which last for 25 years after they were published).[19]

What can you stop others from doing?

In relation to literary, dramatic and musical works, the copyright holder has the exclusive right to:

○　reproduce it in a material form (including turning it into a film or sound recording or converting it to or from a digital form);[20]

○　publish it, perform it in public, or communicate it to the public;[21]

○　make an adaptation of it (including a translation, dramatisation, or rewriting of code in another language);[22] and

○　in the case of a computer program or a sound recording of other literary, dramatic or musical works, enter into a commercial rental arrangement.[23]

For artistic works the list is simpler. The copyright holder has the exclusive right to reproduce it, publish it and communicate it to the public.[24] Reproduction includes making a two-dimensional copy of a three-dimensional artistic work, and vice versa.[25]

The exclusive rights given to the copyright holder of secondary works are:[26]

○　with sound recordings, to make a copy, cause it to be heard in public or communicate it to the public, and enter into a commercial rental arrangement;

○　with films (which, in this context, includes a video), to make a copy, cause it to be seen or heard in public, and communicate it to the public;

---

[16]　See ss 97–100.

[17]　Section 32.

[18]　Sections 33 and 34. Until recently the period was 50 years, but was amended by the *US Free Trade Agreement Implementation Act 2004* (Cth) to be consistent with US law.

[19]　Sections 93–96.

[20]　Section 31(1)(a)(i) as read with s 21(1) and (1A).

[21]　Section 31(1)(a)(ii)–(iv).

[22]　Section 31(1)(a)(v) as read with the definition of 'adaptation' in s 10.

[23]　Section 31(1)(c) and (d), and see the definition of 'commercial rental arrangement' in s 10.

[24]　Section 31(1)(b).

[25]　Section 21(3).

[26]　Sections 85–92.

o   with a television or sound broadcast, to re-broadcast it or communicate it to
         the public; with the visual images from a television broadcast, to make a film
         of them; and with sounds from a television or sound broadcast, to make a
         recording of them; and

o   with published editions of works, to copy them.

An 'infringement' occurs where a person, without permission from the owner,
breaches any of the owner's exclusive rights, or authorises others to breach them.[27]
Unauthorised importation, selling or the exhibition of infringing copies are also
infringements[28]—sometimes described as secondary infringements.

Individual creators of works and films—not companies or other entities—also
have personal rights of association with their creations.[29] These 'moral rights' include
the attribution right (to be identified as the author when certain things are done
with the work); the right not to have the work falsely attributed to others; and the
integrity right (not to have the work treated in a derogatory way). These rights cannot
be transferred or assigned to others, although creators can consent to their works
being treated in a way which infringes them.

Apart from these moral rights, copyright can be sold and transferred like any
other property. However, it is more common, at least in the information technology
world, for use of the work to be licensed. This enables the owner to grant multiple
licenses, while retaining ownership of the copyright. Licenses can grant permission
to use all or only some of the exclusive rights; and can also be granted with time or
geographical limits and conditions.

The Act contains several defences, some of which are discussed in more detail
below. There is an important difference between US law, which has a general defence
of 'fair use', and Australian law, which specifies particular limited defences known as
'fair dealing'. The US provision enables courts to adjudicate on new or unanticipated
situations, balancing the interests of the parties. The Australian approach does not.
It only covers fair dealing for the purposes of research or study, criticism or review,
parody or satire, the reporting of news, and for judicial proceedings or the giving of
legal advice.[30] Recent Australian amendments also allow recording from television and
radio for later private viewing (known as time shifting); recording of music for private
use on alternative devices (space shifting); and copying certain materials from one
form to another (format shifting).[31]

The advent of computers and digital technology has provoked a period of
intense debate and development of copyright concepts. We turn to examine some of
these developments.

---

[27]   Sections 36 and 101, as read with s 13.
[28]   Sections 37–38 and 102–103.
[29]   See Part IX (sections 189–195AZO).
[30]   *Copyright Act 1968* (Cth) ss 40, 41, 41A (added in 2006), 42 and 43. Sections 44–83 also
        clarify the position with certain types of works and in particular industries.
[31]   *Copyright Amendment Act 2006*, introducing new ss 109A and 110AA into the *Copyright Act
        1968* (Cth).

COPYRIGHT PROTECTION FOR SOFTWARE

Source code
A set of computer instructions expressed in a high-level programming language, which can be read and amended by humans. See also *Object code*.

Object code
A set of machine-readable instructions usually generated by compiling or assembling source code.

World Intellectual Property Organization (WIPO)
A specialised agency of the United Nations with headquarters in Geneva, established in 1967 to promote the protection of intellectual property throughout the world.

As computers developed through the 1960s and 1970s there was speculation about whether copyright would apply to computer software. There were no specific provisions in the 1968 Act, and protection would have had to be on the basis that a computer program was a literary work. A computer program, at least when written in **source code**, is similar to other literary works, at least in the sense that it is an idea expressed in a material form. But there are also a number of important differences. The literary, dramatic, musical and artistic works traditionally protected by copyright are generally designed to appeal to the human senses as an experience. Computer programs are designed to perform functions; the source code does not appeal to the senses in the same way as other copyright works. Computer programs are generally distributed in machine-readable form (**object code**), and are not designed to be read or understood by most humans. Given these differences, it is questionable whether copyright is a suitable vehicle for protecting computer software.[32]

In 1978 the **World Intellectual Property Organization (WIPO)** produced a report that concluded, despite these difficulties, that copyright was still the best method of protection.[33] The report considered patent law inappropriate because the logical steps or algorithms in computer programs were not generally patentable, and software was not itself a mechanical device or sufficiently inventive to warrant a patent.[34] It also considered introducing a new species of intellectual property for computer programs (known as *sui generis* protection)[35] but concluded that international agreement would be essential and, even if achievable, would take too long. The advantage of copyright, on the other hand, was that it was already recognised and in place around the world.

In Australia the issue was brought to the fore in 1983. Apple Computers sued Computer Edge Pty Ltd in the Federal Court for infringing its copyright by producing chips that duplicated the ROM code in the Apple II computer.[36] The trial judge, Beaumont J, held that neither source code nor object code was a literary work because they did not afford information, pleasure or instruction, but merely drove a machine

---

[32]   See for example W R Cornish, *Intellectual Property: Patents, Copyright, Trade Marks and Allied Rights*, 3rd edn, Sweet & Maxwell, London, 1996, pp 181–182; D S Karjala, 'A Coherent Theory for the Copyright Protection of Computer Software and Recent Judicial Interpretations' (1997) 66 U Cin L R 53, 56–66, cited by the High Court in *Data Access Corporation v Powerflex Services Pty Ltd* [1999] HCA 49, [25].

[33]   *Model Provisions for the Protection of Intellectual Property Rights in Computer Software*, WIPO Publication No. 814, Geneva, 1978.

[34]   See Chapter 14 for more detailed discussion of software patents.

[35]   From the Latin phrase meaning 'of its own kind'.

[36]   *Apple Computer Inc v Computer Edge Pty Ltd* (1983) ATPR 40–421.

(a function). This led to a National Symposium on the Legal Protection of Computer Software in March 1984, and the *Copyright Act* was amended.[37] The amendments made it clear that literary works included computer programs; computer programs included source and object code; and material form included any form of storage (visible or not) from which the work could be reproduced.

Debate about the appropriateness of copyright for the protection of computer software continued. In 1995 the Federal Government's Copyright Law Review Committee gave a detailed report in which it rejected the idea that patents or a *sui generis* regime would be better. Since then there have been a number of refinements to the treatment of computer programs under the *Copyright Act*. We will deal with the important ones in their context throughout this and the next chapter.

Before moving on to some of the difficult issues, we outline the more important identifiable phases during the development of software. Referring back to these phases will help in understanding the issues.

EXPLANATION SOFTWARE DEVELOPMENT

Developing a software program generally involves:

1   Having an idea about a broad function (or functions) to be performed.
2   Deciding on the specifications and features needed to perform those functions, including how the user will interact with the program (menus, commands, screen display).
3   Breaking the task down into functions and sub-functions, and planning and designing how they will be implemented (the structure, sequence and organisation of the various functions and sub-functions).
4   Working out in some detail the logical steps required for each function and capturing these steps in algorithms or **pseudocode**.
5   Writing the source code that implements these steps.
6   Compiling the source code into object code, testing it, and, if necessary, fixing any problems with it.

Pseudocode
A high-level description of a computer program. The description generally uses natural language explanations (e.g. English) of the steps to be taken, but does not contain actual program code.

These broad steps are usually identifiable, but there is often overlap and a degree of reiteration—they can be seen as a continuum, moving from the abstract idea at the outset to the detailed implementation or expression of the idea at the end.

---

[37]   *Copyright Amendment Act 1984* (Cth). The amendments were made before the final appeal in *Apple Computer Inc v Computer Edge Pty Ltd*, so the result of the appeal is of academic interest. For the record, the Federal Appeal Court subsequently held that source code was a literary work and object code was an adaptation of it, so they were both entitled to protection. The majority in the High Court agreed that source code was a literary work, but held that object code in ROM was not, because it was not in a material form, and was not perceptible or intelligible.

The source and object code produced at the end of this process are specifically protected as a result of the 1984 amendments (mentioned above). It is logical that both should be protected. They are both versions of the final form of expression of the initial idea. The only difference between them is that a special software program (a compiler) translates human-readable source code to machine-readable object code. The process is very similar to a machine translating one language into another. As with languages, object code can also be translated back into source code (using a decompiler).[38] Because it is easy enough to translate both ways, if copyright is to exist in the one form, it should equally exist in the other.

We turn to consider why limited exceptions were introduced in 1999.

The reverse engineering exceptions

Given that source and object code cannot be reproduced without permission, can you write your own version of someone else's program? Can you buy a copy of their program, use it for a while to see what it does, and then write your own source code to do the same thing?[39] The simple answer here is that you have not copied their source or object code—you have merely used your own code to reproduce the functions performed by the computer. Functions are not protected by copyright.[40] Any similarities in the code are incidental; your code is original in the sense that it was created by you without directly copying anyone else's work. Section 47B(3) reinforces this conclusion. It makes it clear that a reproduction automatically made (for example in a computer's RAM) while running a licensed copy of the program to study its ideas and functions, is not an infringement.

The problem is that just using a program does not tell you a lot about how it works. Can you decompile a program to see how the source code works, and then write your own code to do the same thing? Taking something apart to see how it works so you can build your own version is known as reverse engineering. In the mechanical and industrial world, it is perfectly acceptable. A car manufacturer can take a competitor's car apart to see how it works, and can (in the absence of a patent) build a similar car. The time this would take is considered to be sufficient market advantage

---

[38]   The source code produced might not be exactly the same as the original. In most programming languages there are several ways of instructing the computer to perform the same task—the exact phrases or syntax selected in the decompiler might not be the same as those used by the original programmer. This would be similar to translating English into a foreign language, and then someone else translating it back into English—there would be minor differences of expression.

[39]   We consider separately below what would happen if you were to produce something that looked and felt the same, or which had a menu system or screen display that was the same.

[40]   See *Admar Computers Pty Ltd v Ezy Systems Pty Ltd and Ors* [1997] 853 FCA (29 August 1997); *Coogi Australia Pty Ltd v Hysport International Pty Ltd and Ors* [1998] FCA 1059 (21 August 1998); *Data Access v Powerflex* [1999] HCA 49.

for the original manufacturer; the benefit to society of having competitors being able to improve on the original is seen as paramount. However, there are added concerns in the digital world. The time taken by the reverse engineering of software is minimal, the exposed source code can be directly copied very easily (an infringement), and it would be difficult to detect and prove an infringement by looking at the finished product.[41] For these reasons, copyright regimes tend to treat decompilation of software as an infringement, whether the exposed source code is subsequently copied or not.[42]

The initial prohibition on all decompiling raised problems of its own. Imagine you bought software from a developer who later disappeared or went out of business. If you subsequently discovered there were crucial errors in the software, shouldn't you be able to decompile it to fix the errors? US courts recognised that decompiling in some circumstances was a 'fair use' of the software.[43] The EU came to a similar conclusion.[44] Following the recommendations of a review, the Australian Federal Parliament implemented three exceptions in 1999.[45] The first is where you want to make another independent program connect to or operate with the original program (the 'interoperability' provision).[46] The second is where you want to correct errors that prevent the original program from operating properly.[47] The third is where you want to test the security of or investigate a flaw or vulnerability in the original program.[48] All require you to be working from a legitimate copy of the software; not to decompile more than reasonably necessary; and not to be able to get what is needed from another source within a reasonable time. In other words, decompilation must be a last resort.

A section was also inserted to clarify that the making of backup copies by legitimate owners or licensees of software is not an infringement. The section does not permit decompiling software, or modifying the program to get around a copy prevention system, to make the backup copy.[49]

These exceptions are absolute—none can be excluded by a provision in a software licence.[50]

---

[41] See discussion of the non-literal elements below, and particularly *Admar Computers Pty Ltd v Ezy Systems Pty Ltd and Ors* [1997] 853 FCA (29 August 1997).

[42] See s 21(5)(b). Compilation of someone's source code into object code without permission is also an infringement—see s 21(5)(a).

[43] *Atari Games Corporation v Nintendo Inc*, 975 F 2d 832 (Fed Cir, 1992) and *Sega Enterprises Ltd v Accolade Inc*, 977 F 2d 1510 (9th Cir, 1992).

[44] *The Legal Protection of Computer Programs*, Council Directive 91/250/EEC of 14 May 1991, article 6.

[45] The *Copyright Amendment (Computer Programs) Act 1999* (Cth) inserted Div 4A (sections 47AB–47H), implementing the recommendations of the Copyright Law Review Committee's 1995 report on *Computer Software Protection*.

[46] See s 47D.

[47] See s 47E.

[48] See s 47F.

[49] See s 47C.

[50] Section 47H.

Copying parts of software

How much needs to be copied before infringement occurs? The Australian Act follows the UK approach in providing that it is still an infringement if the activity involves a 'substantial part' of the copyright material.[51] What is a substantial part?

CASE EXAMPLE *AUTODESK INC V DYASON (NO. 2)* (1993) 25 IPR 33
AUSTRALIA, HIGH COURT OF AUSTRALIA, 1993

Autodesk Inc sold a computer-assisted drafting package (AutoCAD) for about $5200. To deter piracy they included a hardware device (the 'AutoCAD lock'), without which the software would not run. The lock had to be plugged into the printer port on the computer. A single lock was supplied with the software and could not be purchased separately. The lock did not prevent users from making illicit copies, but with only one lock, the purchaser could run only one copy of the software at a time. Dyason designed an alternative lock (the 'Auto Key lock') which performed the same function, and sold it for about $500.

The technical evidence was that the software made regular challenges to the AutoCAD lock. The lock used a pseudo random number generator to give up to 127 responses. The software had a 'look-up table' containing the 127 legitimate responses. If no response or an incorrect response was received from the AutoCAD lock when compared with the look-up table, the software would shut down. Dyason used an oscilloscope to view the electronic transitions (changes in voltage) between the computer and the AutoCAD lock. By doing this he was able to work out the responses and use his own method to send them from his Auto Key lock.

Autodesk alleged there had been a breach of copyright in its computer program, part of which was in the AutoCAD lock. Dyason argued that what was in the AutoCAD lock was not a computer program or, if it was, that it was not a substantial part of the AutoCAD program.

The High Court held Dyason had breached copyright. It concluded he had indirectly copied the look-up table, and that this was a substantial part of a literary work. In reaching this conclusion, the Court said if something was essential, it must be a substantial part, even if it was only a small part in terms of quantity—one has to look at the significance of the contribution of the part to the whole.

This conclusion—that an essential part of a program must be a substantial part—was quite contentious. An English judge pointed out that it would result in

---

[51] Section 14(1). In the USA and Canada, the test is merely whether there is a substantial similarity between the original and copied material.

'any part of any computer program' being regarded as substantial, because, without that part, the program would not work.[52] The High Court reconsidered its approach some years later in *Powerflex*,[53] which we deal with more fully when considering look and feel issues (below). It agreed with the reasoning in *Autodesk* that a data table within a computer program is not itself a computer program, but that even if it were not a computer program, it could still attract copyright protection, either as a substantial part of a computer program or as a literary work in its own right. However, the Court overruled one aspect of the *Autodesk* decision. It held that an unoriginal part of a program, which would not itself attract copyright protection, could not be a substantial part.[54] In *Powerflex*, this enabled the court to decide that the collection of command words—which were not sufficiently original to attract copyright protection on their own—could not be a substantial part of the program merely because of their importance to its operation. On this reasoning, the look-up table in *Autodesk* should only have attracted copyright if it was sufficiently original.[55]

The court in *Powerflex* recognised a problem with this, but suggested it could only be addressed by legislation.[56] If a data table is original enough, it cannot be reproduced because it is a *literary work*. An exception to the reproduction right, as we saw earlier, is that *computer programs* can be reproduced (this includes decompiling) to achieve interoperability.[57] But if the data table is a literary work rather than a computer program it would not be covered by this exception. A determined programmer could prevent the interoperability exception from being effective, by inserting a sufficiently original data table on which the operation of the program depended. Such a table could not be decompiled under s 47D. As suggested by the High Court, the legislature soon remedied this. Section 47AB was introduced. It says that, for the purposes of ss 47A to 47H (the part of the Act dealing with the reverse engineering exceptions, including interoperability):

> 'computer program' includes any literary work that is:
>
> (a) incorporated in, or associated with, a computer program; and
>
> (b) essential to the effective operation of a function of that computer program.

The data table (which would not normally be treated as a computer program) would thus be part of the computer program for the purposes of reproducing or decompiling it to achieve interoperability, correct errors or test security.

---

[52] Pumfrey J in *Cantor Fitzgerald International v Tradition (UK) Ltd*, Unreported, High Court of Justice, Chancery Division, 15 April 1999, [75], quoted in *Data Access v Powerflex* [1999] HCA 49, [82].

[53] *Data Access v Powerflex* [1999] HCA 49.

[54] At [84–86], per Gleeson CJ, McHugh, Gummow and Hayne JJ (Gaudron J dissenting on this issue).

[55] *Data Access v Powerflex* [1999] HCA 49, [87]. As to the originality requirement, see the discussion below under the topic of databases.

[56] *Data Access v Powerflex* [1999] HCA 49, [125]. The Court did not spell out the difficulty in as much detail as we explain it here.

[57] Section 47D. See the discussion above.

IDEAS AND THEIR EXPRESSION

We explained earlier that copyright does not protect ideas.[58] It protects the material form in which the idea is expressed. We have seen how this is achieved by protecting both source and object code, and we have seen the balance that is struck by allowing the limited reverse engineering exceptions. From the source code, going backwards in time through the development process we described above, one can see that the expression of the idea becomes more abstract the further back we go. At what stage should copyright protection cease because it would merely be protecting the idea?[59]

In the IT environment, the difficulties with this dichotomy between ideas and their expression can be divided into three broad categories: pseudocode, design (the structure, sequence and organisation), and look and feel (the interface, consisting of screen displays—the 'look', and menus and commands—the 'feel').

Pseudocode

As the name suggests, pseudocode is not really code, but resembles it. It consists of generalised statements in a natural language (English, for example) of the algorithms that will be necessary to program the computer. It shows the structure of the planned program and indicates the statements that will be needed, but omits the detailed syntax and rules required by a particular programming language. Human intervention and a degree of skill and effort are still required to write the necessary source code in a programming language. Since pseudocode cannot actually make a computer perform any functions, it does not satisfy the definition of a 'computer program' in s 10.[60] Can it be protected as a literary work in its own right?

The law on this issue is a little unclear. In *Admar's* case,[61] an employee had left and formed another company which produced a competing wine management program. The source code was written in a different database programming language, so was clearly not a direct reproduction. In trying to prove that it was an adaptation of their source code, Admar led evidence from computer experts who had generalised

---

[58]   Some Copyright Acts expressly state this. For example the USA Act says it does not protect any 'idea, procedure, process, system, method of operation, concept, principle or discovery' (*US Copyright Act 1976*, 17 USCS § 102(b)). The Australian Act does not, but the sentiment is often expressed in case law. For example, see the discussion of *Data Access v Powerflex Services* [1999] HCA 49 below.

[59]   US courts dealt with this issue long before computer programs arrived on the scene. For example, in *Nichols v Universal Pictures Corp*, 45 F 2d 119, 121 (2d Cir, 1930), Learned Hand J suggested a play could be described in increasing levels of abstraction with more and more of the detail left out, perhaps ultimately getting to the title alone. He surmised there must be a point at which copyright ceases to exist, since otherwise copyright would prevent use of the idea. This is known as the merger doctrine.

[60]   The High Court in *Data Access v Powerflex Services* [1999] HCA 49, [48] to [52] came to a similar conclusion. Although it was based on an earlier definition of computer program, the current definition does not appear to affect this reasoning.

[61]   *Admar Computers Pty Ltd v Ezy Systems Pty Ltd and Ors* [1997] 853 FCA (29 August 1997).

the two programs into pseudocode, and then compared the pseudocode. Goldberg J decided this evidence was irrelevant in proving an infringement relating to the source code. All it would prove was that the general structure and methods of the two programs were the same, but this did not prove anything about whether the source code had been illegitimately adapted.[62]

One should be wary of interpreting this case as suggesting that pseudocode is not protected by copyright.[63] The case was not about whether there had been an infringement of copyright in the pseudocode, but whether copyright in source code had been infringed. There seems little doubt that a written document containing pseudocode would be a literary work, provided it was sufficiently detailed to be more than just an idea, and that it satisfied the originality requirement.[64] Making a direct or literal copy would be an infringement. If you were to obtain someone else's pseudocode in a written form, and place it on the Internet for others to see, this would be an infringement of the reproduction right and of the right to communicate it to the public. The difficulty arises when there is an indirect reproduction, in the sense that someone who has seen the original pseudocode writes their own pseudocode that does the same things. The issue here comes down to whether there has been a reproduction of the particular form of expression in the original, or just a reproduction of the ideas and functions, now expressed in their own original form. Similar issues arise in relation to software design.

Design (structure, sequence and organisation)

Many decisions in other jurisdictions have dealt with similar facts to *Admar*. They do not focus on the narrow issue of whether a pseudocode analysis can be used to prove copyright infringement of a computer program. They deal more generally with whether a competing program, which uses the same (or a similar) design to perform the same functions as the original program, infringes copyright.

Before tackling this controversial issue, we need to clarify a few points. First, design, in this sense, refers to the structure of the code, the sequence of and inter-relationship between the sub-functions or modules, and the way the code and its sub-functions are organised. (Sequence, structure and organisation are often abbreviated as SSO.) Second, the owner of the original program cannot complain about a competitor's program performing the same functions, since copyright does not protect ideas or functions.[65] Third, if the competitor has reproduced the same functions without

---

62   The case also involved an allegation of misuse of confidential information, and Goldberg J accepted that the pseudocode analysis would be relevant in addressing this issue.

63   This seems to be the conclusion drawn by some commentators—see for example Rhys Bollen, 'Copyright in the Digital Domain' (2001) 8(2) MurUEJL 11, [38].

64   This statement is justified when considering examples of other documents held to attract copyright. Examples include football betting coupons (*Ladbroke (Football) Ltd v William Hill (Football) Ltd* [1964] 1 WLR 73) and instructions on a herbicide label (*Elanco v Mandrops* [1979] FSR 46).

65   See discussion above.

having any access to the source code, pseudocode or SSO (for example by using the program to study its functions and then implementing the same functions)[66] there is no infringement. Fourth, if the competitor has access to the source code of the original program, and has directly reproduced or adapted it, there is an obvious infringement, and the question of whether there is copyright in the SSO need not be asked.[67] To exclude this possibility, let us assume the competitor's program, like that in *Admar*, has been written in a different programming language, and the actual lines of code show no obvious connection with each other. There can only be an infringement in this situation if the owner of the original program has copyright in the SSO.

In 1987 a US court accepted that the SSO can be protected by copyright.[68] Later cases agreed, although different tests were proposed and developed. The most widely accepted test in the USA is now the three-step abstraction–filtration–comparison test.[69] Starting with the source code, the court will:

1   Abstract the two programs to the level at which they are alleged to show similarity—in other words, extract the SSO at comparable levels.
2   Filter out those aspects for which there is no copyright. This includes such things as ideas, procedures, methods of operation, concepts or principles, since these are expressly excluded by the US Act.[70] This step involves an application of the merger doctrine: if there is only one or a limited number of efficient ways of implementing an idea, then the idea and its expression are said to have merged. Once they have merged, there can no longer be copyright in the expression of the idea, since protecting it would effectively prevent others from using the idea. The court would also exclude elements of the SSO that were taken from the public domain or dictated by external factors (such as things required by the specifications of the computer or operating system, or required for compatibility with similar programs).
3   Compare the remaining elements (the 'core of protectability') between the two programs to see if there is substantial similarity.

This test should be treated with caution. It has supporters[71] and detractors.[72] It is based on at least two important differences between US and Australian law: the filtration step is required because of the express exclusion of ideas in the US statute;[73] and the

---

[66]   See the earlier discussion of this under 'The reverse engineering exceptions'.
[67]   This was recognised by the court in *Lotus Development Corp v Borland International*, 49 F 3d 807 (1st Cir, 1995) when commenting on the *Altai* test discussed below.
[68]   *Whelan Associates v Jaslow Dental Laboratory*, 797 F 2d 1222 (3d Cir Court of Appeals, 1986).
[69]   Proposed in *Computer Associates v Altai*, 982 F 2d 693 (2d Cir Court of Appeals, 1992) and known as the *Altai* test; approved in *Lotus Development Corp v Borland International*, 49 F 3d 807 (1st Cir, 1995) and *Sega Enterprises v Accolade Inc*, 977 F 2d 1510 (9th Cir Court of Appeals 1993).
[70]   US *Copyright Act 1976*, 17 USCS § 102(b).
[71]   See, for example, Julian Velasco, 'The Copyrightability of Non-literal Elements of Computer Programs' (1994) 94(1) Col L R 242.
[72]   See, for example, William F Patry, 'Copyright and Computer Programs: A Failed Experiment and a Solution to a Dilemma' (2003) 46(1–2) NYLS LR 201.
[73]   US *Copyright Act 1976*, 17 USCS s 102(b). The Australian Act has no equivalent.

comparison step focuses on the US requirement that there be 'substantial similarity' between the two things being compared.[74] UK law is more like Australian law in these respects. Cases in the United Kingdom generally agree that the SSO can be protected, although there are some differences over the relevance of the US authorities.[75]

Australian courts have not dealt directly with this question, but it appears they are less inclined to recognise copyright in the SSO. Apart from the *Admar* case— which, as we saw earlier, had a narrower focus—this is evident in the High Court's judgment in *Powerflex*.[76] The main issues raised were about the interface, rather than the SSO, so we deal with the facts and the court's reasoning more fully in the next section. However, one aspect is relevant here. The trial court upheld the argument that copyright in three macros had been infringed by the respondent writing his own code to implement the same functions. The judge held this was an adaptation of the original because the source code, although in a different language, displayed strong objective similarities. The High Court rejected this conclusion. It interpreted the definition of adaptation narrowly, stating: 'In accordance with the fundamental principle that copyright protects expression and not ideas, this [an infringement by adaptation] must relate to the copying of the code ... rather than a copying of the idea or function underlying the code.'[77] The implication seems to be: (1) if you do not have access to the original code, writing your own code that replicates the same functions is unlikely to be an infringement, no matter how similar the SSO might be; and (2) if you do have access to the original code, and have implemented it in a different language, then the question is whether you have reproduced or adapted the original code, not whether you have reproduced or adapted the SSO.

Look and feel (the interface)

Early US cases held that copyright protected menu structures and command interfaces,[78] as well as screen displays (even where generated by different code).[79] A series of cases involving Lotus Development Corporation's spreadsheet program (Lotus 1-2-3) illustrate how these attitudes changed in US courts. The judge who granted copyright protection to the command interface in the *Paperback* case (in 1990), also heard the trial in the *Borland* case (in 1992).[80] Relying largely on the *Whelan* decision,[81] he reasoned that if a programmer had many

---

[74] The Australian Act does not mention 'substantial similarity'. The relevant question is whether there is a reproduction or adaptation of a substantial part of the material.

[75] See, for example, *John Richardson Computers v Flanders* [1993] FSR 497, which approves the *Altai* test, and *Ibcos Computers v Barclays Finance* [1994] FSR 275 which finds the US approach unhelpful.

[76] *Data Access v Powerflex Services* [1999] HCA 49 (30 September 1999). We dealt with the court's comments on the meaning of a 'substantial part' earlier.

[77] Per Gleeson CJ, McHugh, Gummow and Hayne JJ at [110].

[78] *Lotus Development Corp v Paperback Software*, 740 F Supp 37 (D Mass, 1990).

[79] *Stern Electronics v Kaufman*, 669 F 2d 852 (2d Cir, 1982); and in the sequence and general behaviour of interlinked screens, *Borderbund Software v Unison World Inc*, 648 F Supp 1125 (ND Cal, 1986).

different command structures to choose from, the original command structure must be protected because there was no merger of the idea with its expression.

By the time the appeal in *Borland* got to the First Circuit (in 1995),[82] the court was more inclined to take the interests of users into account. It focused on the need for interoperability, saying it was in the interests of users that Borland's program was compatible, so those who were familiar with Lotus 1-2-3 would be able to switch without having to learn new commands or rewrite their Lotus macros. The First Circuit held that Lotus did not have copyright in its command structure, since it was a method of operation. A similar conclusion was reached when Apple claimed that Microsoft infringed copyright in its user interface (a combination of menus and displays).[83] The prevailing US view thus appears to be that there is no protection for the look and feel of a program.

In 1999, the Australian High Court was faced with issues very similar to the Lotus cases.

 **CASE EXAMPLE** *DATA ACCESS V POWERFLEX SERVICES (1999) HCA 49 (30 SEPTEMBER 1999)*
AUSTRALIA, HIGH COURT OF AUSTRALIA, 1999

Data Access owned the copyright in Dataflex, a suite of computer programs that enabled a user to develop a customised database. A programmer, who had become familiar with Dataflex, decided to create a compatible system. By studying the documentation and operation of Dataflex, he was able to write his own source code for a competing system known as Powerflex. Data Access alleged three similarities between the programs infringed copyright: Powerflex had the same command words, implemented certain macros to perform the same functions as Dataflex macros, and used a Dataflex compression table to achieve the same file structures. We discussed the court's treatment of the macros earlier (in the section on SSO). Here we deal with the command words.

Two hundred and twenty-five command words were common to both programs. The trial court held 169 of these infringed copyright. Some were unique words made up by Dataflex, but many were English words or combinations, such as 'BOX', 'CHART' and 'PAGEBREAK'. Use of these command words ensured that Powerflex had the same look and feel, and was easy to use by anyone familiar with Dataflex. Data Access relied on four arguments: >>

80   *Lotus Development Corp v Borland International Inc*, 799 F Supp 203 (D Mass, 1992) was also heard by Judge Keeton.
81   *Whelan Associates v Jaslow Dental Laboratory*, 797 F 2d 1222 (3d Cir Ct App, 1986).
82   *Lotus Development Corp v Borland International Inc*, 49 F 3d 807 (1st Cir, 1995).
83   *Apple Computer, Inc v Microsoft Corp*, 35 F 3d 1435 (9th Cir, 1994), although arguably much of this decision turned on the interpretation of an early licence agreement between Apple and Microsoft.

>> 1   That each of the command words was a computer program and protected by copyright. On this issue, the trial judge had followed *Lotus Development Corp v Paperback Software*, 740 F Supp 37 (D Mass, 1990), holding that there was more than one way of expressing the idea behind each word, so the words could attract copyright because the merger doctrine did not apply. The High Court preferred to follow the Full Federal Court's approach, restricting itself to an interpretation of the Act. It concluded that each word did not satisfy the definition of computer program because, while it might be a single instruction, it was not a set of instructions. It suggested that what was protected by copyright was the code invoked by the command word, and this had not been reproduced.

2   That the 'collocation' (special arrangement) of command words was a computer program and protected by copyright. The court held that, although the list of command words together formed a set of instructions, the set did not cause the computer to perform a particular function. The collocation was therefore also not a computer program.

3   That the collocation of command words was a substantial part of the whole Dataflex system, which was protected by copyright as a literary work. The court said that what was taken from the original program had to be original. Here the court acknowledged that the choice of commands and their structure and sequence would be relevant when compared 'at the same level of abstraction'. But it held that, since each of the command words here lacked sufficient originality on its own, and could easily be replaced, the command words were irrelevant to the choice of commands, structure and sequence, and were not a substantial part of the literary work.

4   That the table of command words printed in the Dataflex User Guide was a compilation that attracted copyright. As before, the court held that these words lacked sufficient originality in their own right, and the arrangement of them in alphabetical order in a table did not involve sufficient skill and labour to make it original.

The result in *Powerflex* was that the High Court denied copyright protection for the command words—a similar result to the Lotus litigation in the USA. In doing so, it ignored the merger doctrine and the abstraction–filtration–comparison test. It would be premature, however, to conclude that these tests are irrelevant in Australian law, since *Powerflex* was argued on the basis of the qualities of the command words, rather than on whether the overall look and feel of the program had been reproduced.

There is one other possibility when considering screen displays. In 1996, the Australian Federal Court held that an animated screen display in an interactive video game was a film for copyright purposes.[84] The Full Court agreed, dismissing the appeal.[85] However, it is unlikely that a normal software interface would be animated enough to be likened to a film, so it is doubtful it would be treated in the same way.

---

[84]   *Sega Enterprises Ltd and Anor v Galaxy Electronics Pty Ltd and Anor* [1996] 761 FCA 1 (28 August 1996).

[85]   *Galaxy Electronics Pty Ltd and Anor v Sega Enterprises Ltd and Anor* [1997] 403 FCA (23 May 1997).

COPYRIGHT IN DATABASES

Copyright does not exist in an idea, nor in factual information such as one's name or address. But there is some protection for a *collection* of factual information, such as a database of names and addresses. The definition of 'literary work' specifically mentions a table or compilation, but protection will depend on whether the compilation is sufficiently original.

When is it sufficiently original? There are two views. The US Supreme Court[86] came to the conclusion in 1991 that there was no copyright in the telephone white pages, since no creativity had been required or displayed in arranging an alphabetical listing of the data collected by the telephone company. But it said that where the selection and arrangement of the data showed originality—in the sense of a creative spark—there would be protection. This is known as the *Feist* creativity test. An example of a compilation that shows this sort of originality might be a collection of clever or famous quotations. There may or may not be copyright in each quotation, but the compilation would involve careful selection, and would therefore be creative and sufficiently original to attract copyright protection of its own.

In 2002 the full Australian Federal Court had to decide whether Telstra had copyright in the telephone directory it produced on a CD.[87] The court preferred the 'sweat of the brow' test to the *Feist* creativity test, and held there was sufficient originality in the database. The sweat of the brow test asks whether there has been sufficient work, effort or expense in gathering the information, even if no creativity was involved in its selection or arrangement. It is thus a lower test for originality than the creativity test—it protects databases merely because of the investment in time and effort. One interesting aspect of this case was that Desktop Marketing admitted taking all the listed data from Telstra's white pages, but alleged that because there was no copyright in the data, and it was presented in a different way on their CD, it could no longer be seen as a copy. The court rejected this argument, saying that once the database attracted copyright, a resemblance in the form of publication was not required for the reproduction to be an infringement.

In Australian law, one can still copy individual entries from the database, unless they are protected in their own right. However, if the sweat of the brow test means the whole database is protected, then reproducing a substantial part would also infringe copyright.[88] As with computer programs, whether the part taken is substantial will presumably depend on its quality or importance as much as its quantity.[89]

---

[86]　*Feist v Rural Telephone Service Co, Inc,* 499 US 340 (1991).

[87]　*Desktop Marketing Systems Pty Ltd v Telstra Corporation Limited* [2002] FCAFC 112 (15 May 2002).

[88]　Section 14(1), discussed above in relation to computer programs.

[89]　See the earlier discussion of *Autodesk Inc v Dyason* (No. 2) (1993) 25 IPR 33. It is unclear how the High Court's observation in *Data Access v Powerflex* [1999] HCA 49 (that an important part can not attract copyright as a substantial part if it is unoriginal) would apply to unoriginal facts in a database.

Both the EU Database Directive and the WIPO Copyright Treaty addressed these issues.[90] They both reaffirm the traditional view that copyright in a database exists where the selection or arrangement of material is the author's own creation. This wording tends to support the *Feist* creativity test.[91] The EU Database Directive also recognises a *sui generis* right (over and above copyright) that prohibits the unauthorised extraction from, or utilisation of, a non-original database in which there has been substantial investment in obtaining, verifying or presenting the data. There is some debate about whether such a right is necessary or appropriate.[92]

CIRCUMVENTION DEVICES AND RIGHTS MANAGEMENT

Among other things, the Digital Agenda amendments implemented two reforms suggested by the WIPO Copyright Treaty (1996). The first discourages circumvention of copy protection measures. The second helps owners assert and prove their rights. We describe each in turn.

Circumvention of technological protection measures

The provisions regarding circumvention devices have been controversial. The original section[93] listed a number of things a person could not do if copyright material was protected by a technological protection measure (TPM). The list involved dealing with a circumvention device in various ways, such as making, selling or promoting them. (Interestingly, it did not prohibit the *use* of a circumvention device.) A circumvention device was defined as something that had little purpose other than circumventing a TPM. The crucial definition was of a TPM, which was defined as:

> A device or product ... designed, in the ordinary course of its operation, to prevent or inhibit the infringement of copyright ... by either ...
>
> (a) ensuring that access ... is available solely by use of an (authorised) access code or process; (or)
> (b) through a copy control mechanism.

The provisions were tested as part of Sony's worldwide action to crack down on piracy of its PlayStation games.

---

90 Directive 96/9/EC of the European Parliament and of the Council of 11 March 1996 on the legal protection of databases; WIPO Copyright Treaty 1996, CRNR/DC/94.

91 See, for example, Daniel J Gervais, 'Feist Goes Global: A Comparative Analysis of the Notion of Originality in Copyright Law' (Summer 2002) 49 J Co pr Socy 949.

92 Hasan A Deveci, 'Databases: Is *Sui Generis* a Stronger Bet than Copyright?'(2004) 12(2) IJL & IT 178.

93 Section 116A as introduced by the *Copyright Amendment (Digital Agenda) Act 2000*.

CASE EXAMPLE *STEVENS V KABUSHIKI KAISHA SONY COMPUTER* (2005) HCA 58 (6 OCT 2005)

AUSTRALIA, HIGH COURT OF AUSTRALIA, 2005

Sony's games were manufactured with a Regional Access Code (RAC) embedded in a special track on the CD. The RAC could not be transferred to a new disk when copying the CD. When a CD was inserted into a PlayStation console, the Boot ROM chip in the console's circuit board attempted to read the RAC, and, if it could not find a valid RAC, the game would terminate. Two purposes were served by this. By using different RACs, Sony was able to divide its market into regions, ensuring that CDs bought in one region could not be played on machines bought in another. It also discouraged illicit copying, since copied disks could not be played without a valid RAC embedded in them.

A market soon developed for modifications ('mod chips') that could be fitted to the PlayStation console, overriding the RAC look-up process. Sony took action against Eddie Stevens, who sold mod chips in Sydney. The Australian Competition and Consumer Commission (ACCC) joined the litigation, objecting to the use of regional codes to prevent legitimate owners of games purchased in one region from playing them in another. The High Court held that the Boot ROM/RAC system was not a TPM, and the mod chips were thus not circumvention devices. Its judgment focused on the phrase 'prevent or inhibit' in the definition of TPM. The court agreed that the system did not prevent copying—it only prevented playing CDs after they were copied. As to whether the system 'inhibited' infringements of copyright, the court noted that it also prevented the playing of region-coded CDs after they had been legally obtained. It reasoned that giving the word 'inhibit' a wide interpretation covering this situation would effectively allow Sony to use copyright law to create a new market segmentation right that it would not otherwise have. It thus favoured a narrow interpretation of the word 'inhibit' to mean that the conduct being inhibited must be infringing conduct—the device must make the *actual infringing act* more difficult. Since this system only inhibited the playing of the CD afterwards, it was not covered by the definition of TPM.[94]

Before the High Court handed down its decision, the 2004 Australia–US Free Trade Agreement (AUSFTA) was signed.[95] It required legislation dealing with circumvention of technological measures that 'control access' to protected material.[96] This induced

---

[94] See paragraphs [38]–[47] and [56]. Sony's second argument was that the playing of the copied CD involved a reproduction in the console's RAM, and the Boot ROM/RAC system prevented this infringing act from occurring. We will deal with the High Court's view of this argument in the next chapter.

[95] Australia–United States Free Trade Agreement (AUSFTA), signed Washington DC, 8 February 2004, text and guide available at <www.dfat.gov.au/trade/negotiations/us.html> last accessed 22 February 2007.

[96] Article 17.4.7.

speculation whether Parliament would have to override the effect of the *Stevens v Sony* judgment. In February 2006 an Australian parliamentary committee reported this would not be necessary.[97] It reasoned that the relevant article in the agreement dealt only with copyright, so, in the context, technological measures controlling access for other purposes (such as restricting competition) were not covered.

The *Copyright Amendment Act 2006* (Cth) replaced s 116A with several more detailed provisions. They prohibit use as well as supply of a circumvention device, then enumerate certain exceptions (for example to achieve interoperability).[98] As expected, the definition of TPM was replaced, implementing several changes. The main change is that it now includes a second type of TPM, known as an 'access control technological protection measure', which is separately defined. This fulfils the AUSFTA obligation, but there are two parts of the definitions that try to retain the effect of the *Stevens v Sony* judgment. The first is that the definitions of both a TPM and an access control TPM specifically do not apply to films, computer programs and computer games 'to the extent that [the protection device] controls geographic market segmentation by preventing the playback in Australia of a non infringing copy'.[99] The second is a more general method. The definition of an access control TPM requires that the protection device be used 'in connection with the exercise of the copyright'.[100] This would exclude a device that protected rights other than copyright. Whether these provisions will be successful in retaining the effect of the *Stevens v Sony* judgment, for example where a single access control system has two functions, one of which inhibits copyright infringements and one of which has some other function, remains to be seen.

Electronic rights management information

The protection of **electronic rights management information (ERMI)** has not been as controversial as the anti-circumvention provisions. Removal or alteration of ERMI where the person knew (or ought reasonably to have known) that it would induce, enable, facilitate or conceal a copyright infringement gives the copyright owner a right to take civil action as well as being a criminal offence.[101] The same applies to the distribution, importation or communication to the public of a copy of the altered work or secondary work.[102]

Electronic rights management information (ERMI)
Electronic information attached to copyright material disclosing the name of the copyright owner and the terms under which the material can be used.

---

[97] House of Representatives Standing Committee on Legal and Constitutional Affairs, *Review of Technological Protection Measures Exceptions*, February 2006, <www.aph.gov.au/house/committee/laca/protection/report.htm> last accessed 22 February 2007.

[98] Sections 116AK to 116AQ (rights to take civil action) and 132APA–132APE (criminal provisions).

[99] See paragraph (c) of each definition in s 10(1).

[100] See paragraph (a)(ii) of the definition of 'access control technological protection measure' in s 10(1).

[101] Sections 116B and 132AQ.

[102] Sections 116C and 132AR.

CONCLUDING REMARKS AND FURTHER READING

The protection of computer software has presented several interesting challenges, not the least of which is whether copyright is a suitable vehicle in the first place. Computer programs are generally designed to perform functions; copyright is not well-suited to protecting functions. This chapter has illustrated how copyright initially gained wide protection against reverse engineering, but the protection has gradually been relaxed by the introduction of reverse engineering exceptions in the Act, and by courts interpreting the Act narrowly when faced with alleged infringements involving non-literal elements. In other areas we have seen the balance shifting towards owners of intellectual property: the protection of databases—already quite wide by copyright standards—may grow in line with the EU's *sui generis* extraction right, and new anti-circumvention provisions have been introduced.

If one theme runs through this chapter, it is the continual ebb and flow in the balance between the interests of content creators and society as a whole. In the next chapter we examine attempts to find this balance when dealing with some of the issues raised by Internet and web technology (such as the sharing of media files on peer-to-peer networks).

For further reading on the topics covered in this chapter:

Yee Fen Lim, Ch 9, 'Copyright on the Internet', in *Cyberspace Law: Commentaries and Materials,* 2nd edn, Oxford University Press, Melbourne, 2007

On the development of protection for computer software

D Rowland and E Macdonald, Ch 2, 'Protecting and Exploiting Rights in Software— Intellectual Property Rights', in *Information Technology Law*, 2nd edn, Routledge-Cavendish, Oxford, 2000

On the *Powerflex* decision and its ramifications

R Evenden, 'Copyright Protection of Computer Programs in Australia' (2001) 43 *Journal of the NSW Society for Computers and the Law*

Review questions for this chapter can be found on the book's Online Resource Centre at www.oup.com.au/orc/fordersvantesson.

COPYRIGHT AND THE INTERNET

OBJECTIVES // BY THE END OF THIS CHAPTER, YOU WILL:

○ Know about the right of communication to the public

○ Understand the arguments about copies made while transmitting data over the Internet and while using software in the normal way

○ Recognise copyright issues raised by web technology, including web pages, hyperlinking, framing and search engines

○ Appreciate the challenges created by peer-to-peer file sharing technology and know how the law is developing in response

WHAT THIS CHAPTER IS ABOUT

This is the second of four chapters that explore intellectual property issues. The previous chapter introduced copyright and explored the protection of computer software. In this chapter we focus on the copyright challenges raised by the Internet and the Web. The following two chapters deal with domain names and trade marks (Chapter 13), and patents, confidentiality and passing off (Chapter 14).

We noted in the previous chapter that copyright consists of a bundle of exclusive rights and that the owner can stop others from making use of these rights without permission. Of the exclusive rights, the reproduction and communication rights are the most relevant when dealing with computers and the Internet. The reproduction right (which we dealt with fairly extensively in the previous chapter) is fairly easy to understand—most people know you cannot copy literary, artistic and other similar works without permission. The communication right is a little less straightforward, so we start the chapter with an explanation of this right.

Our enquiry then moves on to discuss the various copies made during communication over the Internet and during the use of computer products—copies in RAM, routers and caches. We deal with legislative attempts to clarify when they infringe copyright, and the difficulties interpreting these provisions.

The remainder of the chapter is devoted to issues raised by web technology and the way it is used. We discuss the copyright implications of web pages, hyperlinks, frames, and search engines. We end the chapter with the copyright challenges raised by file-sharing technology.

COMMUNICATION TO THE PUBLIC

The right to communicate copyright material to the public was introduced in 2001 as part of the government response to issues raised by digital technology.[1] Previously, there were only two similar rights: to broadcast material and to transmit it to subscribers to a diffusion service (for example by cable). The right of communication to the public replaced these two rights. It is a broad technology-neutral right which gives copyright owners greater control over the way their material is distributed.

'Communicate' in this context is restricted to electronic communication—material in other formats is covered by the publishing right. But communicate does not only mean sending something (actively transmitting it); it also covers making it available online (passive communication or 'uploading' it).[2] The 'public' includes the public within and outside Australia.[3] Unauthorised uploading onto a server in Australia therefore infringes copyright, even if the website is only available overseas.

The Act does not define 'public' in any more detail. In 1997 the High Court had to decide whether playing music to customers while they were on hold on a business telephone line was 'to the public'.[4] The court concluded that it was, even though there might only be one customer hearing the music at a time—'to the public' did not require a gathering of people simultaneously accessing the work. The court also approved earlier cases which held that, when interpreting the term, the distinction between commercial and private use was important. For example in 1992 the Federal Court held that playing 25 seconds of music on a 14-minute training video shown to 11 staff members in a voluntary training session was performing the music in public, largely because of the commercial nature of the use.[5]

---

[1]   *Copyright Amendment (Digital Agenda) Act 2000* (Cth), effective 4 March 2001, amending ss 31(1)(a)(iv) (for works), 85(1)(c) (sound recordings), 86(c) (films), and 87(c) (television and sound broadcasts) of the *Copyright Act 1968* (Cth).

[2]   *Copyright Act 1968* (Cth) s 10(1) definition of 'communicate'.

[3]   *Copyright Act 1968* (Cth) s 10(1) definition of 'to the pubic'.

[4]   *Telstra Corporation Limited v Australasian Performing Right Association Limited* (APRA) [1997] HCA 41 (14 August 1997). This was for the purpose of the previous diffusion right, but the reasoning would apply to the same phrase used in relation to the communication right.

[5]   *Australasian Performing Right Association Limited v Commonwealth Bank of Australia* (1992) 40 FCR 59.

We discuss infringements of this communication right, and the more straightforward reproduction right, throughout the remainder of this chapter. Our next topic is whether the numerous copies made while downloading and using Internet material might infringe these rights.

DOWNLOADING AND USING INTERNET MATERIAL

In the digital environment, copies seem to abound. To download something from the Internet, a copy passes through various routers, and will normally be kept for a while in their caches. If a proxy server is used, a copy will pass through the server's active memory (RAM) while it is processed, and possibly be stored in its cache. Once the file reaches the user who requested it, a copy has to be loaded into RAM so the computer can process it, and whatever is seen on the screen is generated by a copy in the display's memory. Are all these copies legitimate?

Non-visible or inaccessible copies

We need to deal first with the argument that copies hidden inside machines do not count. As discussed in the previous chapter, in 1984 the High Court held that object code in computer memory was not a literary work because it was imperceptible or unreadable.[6] Legislation was introduced to change this. It defined 'material form' to include 'any form (whether visible or not) of storage from which the work ... can be reproduced'.[7]

This took care of the objection that RAM copies are 'hidden'. However, both the Federal and High Courts subsequently held that RAM copies were still not necessarily covered by this definition.[8] They held that the phrase 'from which the work ... can be reproduced' meant the work had to be accessible by humans. The courts concluded that the devices they were considering (a DVD player and a Sony PlayStation respectively) would have had to be modified in some way for humans to be able to access what was in RAM.

---

[6] *Computer Edge Pty Ltd v Apple Computer Inc* [1986] HCA 19 (6 May 1986); see discussion in Chapter 11.

[7] The definition of material form introduced by the *Copyright Amendment Act 1984* (Cth).

[8] The Federal Court in *Australian Video Retailers Association Ltd v Warner Home Video Pty Ltd* [2001] FCA 1719 (7 December 2001), [103] (Emmett J); and in *Kabushiki Kaisha Sony Computer Entertainment v Stevens* [2002] FCA 906 (26 July 2002), [126]–[150] (Sackville J). The Full Court of the Federal Court agreed with Sackville J by a majority of 2:1 on this point in *Kabushiki Kaisha Sony Computer Entertainment v Stevens* [2003] FCAFC 157 (30 July 2003) and the High Court agreed in *Stevens v Kabushiki Kaisha Sony Computer Entertainment* [2005] HCA 58 (6 October 2005), [62]–[79] (majority judgement); but compare *Microsoft Corp v Business Boost* (2000) 49 IPR 573 where Tamberlin J held that launching a program into RAM and loading onto hard disk are reproductions in material form.

Once again the legislature intervened. The definition of 'material form' was amended to 'any form (whether visible or not) of storage ... (whether or not the work ... can be reproduced)'.[9]

The legislative intention is clearly that RAM copies, and other similar digital copies inside machines, are to be treated as reproductions in a material form—it does not matter that they might be relatively inaccessible or unreadable by humans. Are they non-infringing reproductions?

Express and implied licences

Even without legislation, copies made during downloading and use would arguably be covered by express or implied licences—provided the activity involves a non-infringing initial copy and is an authorised download. If I buy software over the Internet from a legitimate site by paying for it and downloading it to my hard disk, it will normally be subject to an end-user licence.[10] The licence would normally expressly give me the right to install the product on my hard disk and use it.

Even if there is no express end-user licence, permission would be implied from the fact that I am permitted to download the material. It must also be implied that the copies in RAM and in my display's memory while I am using the product in the normal way are made with permission. The same would be true of the copies that were automatically created in the routers and caches on the Internet when I downloaded the product. On the other hand, if I were to buy software from a site distributing infringing copies, none of the copies made while downloading or using the software would be made with the owner's express or implied permission.

Legislative clarification

For the avoidance of doubt, provisions have been inserted in the Act to reassure service providers handling downloads as well as people using material in the normal way. Section 43A deals with copies of works made *during communication* (and s 111A has the same exemption for secondary works). It says:

> 43A Temporary reproductions made in the course of communication
>   (1) The copyright in a work, or an adaptation of a work, is not infringed by making a temporary reproduction of the work or adaptation as part of the technical process of making or receiving a communication.

Subsection (2) makes it clear this exemption does not apply if the work being communicated is an infringing copy. Section 43A therefore appears to reach the same conclusion as if there is an implied licence protecting temporary router and cache copies made during the downloading of non-infringing material.

---

[9]   *US Free Trade Agreement Implementation Act 2004* (Cth) s 186. The High Court appeal was heard after the amendments had been introduced.

[10]   As to whether these licences are likely to be binding, see the discussion of clickwrap agreements in Chapter 4.

Copies made during *normal use* of products are covered by general provisions dealing with all types of material, as well as a more specific section dealing with computer programs. The general provision allows

> the making of a temporary reproduction of the work if the reproduction is incidentally made as a necessary part of a technical process of using a copy of the work.[11]

The more specific provision dealing with computer programs allows reproductions

> incidentally and automatically made as part of the technical process of running a copy of the program for the purposes for which the program was designed.[12]

Again, the exemptions only apply to a non-infringing use of the product.[13]

Difficulties with the provisions

There are still some grey areas. It is not clear that cache copies are always covered by these exceptions. Nor is there clarity about what amounts to a 'temporary' copy. Before explaining these concerns, we need to ensure a basic understanding of caches.

A cache is a temporary storage area where frequently used data can be kept for ease of access some time later. In the Internet environment, local cache copies make communications more efficient because they save time and bandwidth usage—a request for a file is serviced by the nearest cache copy instead of having to go out on the Internet to find the original again. Caches exist on individual web users' machines (look for a folder named 'Temporary Internet Files'). Cache copies stored on proxy servers and routers are accessed by multiple users.

At first glance it is difficult to see why anyone would object to cache copies. There are three reasons. If a website owner updates their site, remote cached pages may not be replaced immediately and may contain information that is no longer accurate. Second, a website owner might remove data from their site, intending to withdraw permission for it to be reproduced or communicated to the public. Cached copies would then be infringing copyright. Third, accessing local cache copies might not be reflected in the usage statistics collected by 'hit counters' on original sites, and the lower number of hits might affect advertising revenue.

Meaning of 'part of the process of communication'

Given that there are valid reasons for objecting to cache copies, the issue is whether copyright law can be used as the basis of an objection. Most caches are automatic and operate behind the scenes. Once space is allocated to them, they fill up automatically, replacing older files with more recent ones. But they *can* be turned on or off at will—

---

[11]   *Copyright Act 1968* (Cth) s 43B; and see s 111B for secondary works.
[12]   *Copyright Act 1968* (Cth) s 47B.
[13]   *Copyright Act 1968* (Cth) ss 43B(2), 111B(2) and, for computer programs, 47B(1)(b) and (2).

they are not strictly *required* for a successful communication. So are they 'part of the technical process of making or receiving a communication'? The 'normal use' exceptions (s 43B and 111B) use the phrase 'as a *necessary* part ... of the process of using a copy' (emphasis added). Compare this with the 'during communication' exceptions (s 43A and 111A), which do not use the word 'necessary'. Does this imply that reproductions made during communication do not have to be *necessary* to warrant protection?

This seems quite a strong argument, and would lead to the conclusion that it does not matter that cache copies made during downloading are not strictly required—they are still covered by the section. But there is still doubt about the limits of the protection. Some ISPs actively manage the contents of their cache to anticipate demand.

EXAMPLE

Magnum Internet Services Pty Ltd is an Internet service provider in the Hunter Valley, a well-known wine-growing region in New South Wales. Most of its customers are involved in the wine trade in some way. Magnum spends some time finding wine-related websites from around the world and ensuring that copies are stored in its server's cache. This saves time and money, since requests for these sites by Magnum customers are served by the local cache copies instead of using international Internet bandwidth.

It is unclear whether these copies will be regarded as 'part of the technical process of making or receiving a communication'. We will see shortly that the 'safe harbour' provisions suggest they are not protected copies.

Meaning of 'temporary copy'

Both the *'during communication'* and general *'normal use'* provisions apply to temporary copies.[14] If an ISP actively ensures that cache copies persist for a long time, at what stage will they lose the protection? Even with automatic caches, if the space allocated is large, or traffic is light, copies may persist for long periods. It is unclear where the line is to be drawn between what is temporary and what is not.

In 2004, as a result of the Australia–US Free Trade Agreement (AUSFTA), a limited defence for ISPs was introduced—known as the 'safe harbour' scheme.[15]

---

14   *Copyright Act 1968* (Cth) ss 43A/111A and 43B/111B respectively. The provision applying to normal use of computer programs (s 47B) does not require that the copy be temporary—merely that it be incidentally and automatically made.

15   *Copyright Act 1968* (Cth) *Division 2AA—Limitation on remedies available against carriage service providers* (s 116AA–116AJ) inserted by the *US Free Trade Agreement Implementation Act 2004*. It is similar to the scheme in the USA. Note that in the USA, the fair use doctrine may also give an ISP a complete defence as well.

Safe harbour protection for transmitting and caching

The safe harbour is not a total defence—it merely limits the remedies that might be claimable. Provided all the conditions are met, a court is not permitted to award damages or other monetary awards against the ISP. Likely remedies are an order that the ISP should remove or disable access to the infringing material, or 'some other less burdensome but comparably effective non-monetary order'.[16]

The safe harbour covers four different types of activity. We give a brief overview of the relevant transmission and caching provisions here (known as category A and B activities). We leave the other safe harbour provisions until the discussion of hyperlinking.

Category A activity involves the provision of facilities or services for transmitting, routing or providing connections for copyright material, and includes 'intermediate and transient storage' during these activities.[17] Presumably the term 'intermediate and transient' is meant to indicate something even more fleeting than 'temporary copies' in cache, since caching is covered by Category B. Interestingly, the definition of caching in this part of the Act does not refer to 'necessary' or 'temporary' copies—just that there must be a reproduction in response to an action by a user, done to facilitate efficient access.[18] However, it must be an automatic process.[19] Manually selecting cached material falls outside the scope of the safe harbour—Magnum Internet Services Pty Ltd, our ISP in the wine-growing region, would not be protected. The fact that the safe harbour only covers automatic caching implies that manual caching does not deserve protection—and this could be taken to indicate that the *during communication* exclusions we discussed earlier do not cover manual caching either.

Several conditions must be met.[20] For example an ISP must 'expeditiously remove' cached material upon notification that the material has been removed at the originating site; and must not make substantive modifications to the cached material. The scheme obviously takes the sting out of complaints by ISPs that they feel exposed to copyright infringement claims when operating a cache.

We move on next to discuss a number of copyright issues raised by web technology.

---

[16] *Copyright Act 1968* (Cth) ss 116AG(2) and 116G(4).
[17] *Copyright Act 1968* (Cth) s 116AC.
[18] *Copyright Act 1968* (Cth) s 116AD, describing category B activity, as read with the definition of 'caching' (for the purposes of this part of the Act only) in s 116AB.
[19] *Copyright Act 1968* (Cth) s 116AD.
[20] *Copyright Act 1968* (Cth) s 116AH(1), Items 1 and 3.

WEB TECHNOLOGY

HTML

Hyper Text Markup Language. HTML is the authoring language most commonly used to create Web documents.

Web pages

The basic idea behind the Web is that it is an open forum, where information is shared. In keeping with this philosophy, the **html** code that displays a web page on a browser's screen is generally easy to see.[21] Viewing the techniques used in other web pages is an accepted way of learning how to create your own pages. Are there circumstances in which one could claim copyright is being infringed?

One argument would be that html source code is a computer program. It seems to be covered by the definition:

> *computer program* means a set of statements or instructions to be used directly or indirectly in a computer in order to bring about a certain result.[22]

Html consists of a set of instructions because it tells the browser's machine what to display and how to display it. The result it brings about is a display on the user's screen. It does this indirectly, because the set of instructions has to be interpreted into relevant binary or machine code by the browser software and operating system. Even if the source code is not a computer program, it could still be protected as an original literary work. If protected (either as a computer program or a literary work), reproducing someone else's code without permission on your own web page would be infringing the reproduction right; uploading it to your own website would also be infringing the communication right.

This raises issues discussed in the previous chapter, but it is worthwhile highlighting the arguments here. There might be an argument that what was taken was not protected by copyright, because it was already in the public domain; or because the code was the only way to achieve the particular function, so the merger doctrine applies.[23] If only part of the code was taken, the issue would be whether it was a substantial part.[24] There might also be an argument that, by making the web page (including its code) available for others to see, the owner is granting an implied licence to view and copy the code. This argument has not been tested in court. It would probably be easier to make out in the USA under their fair use doctrine.

Could the author of a web page argue that the page is made up of a number of other media—text, images, animations, video clips—and, whether or not each individual element is protected, there is copyright in the whole as a compilation? The definition of literary work includes a table or compilation.[25] We dealt with the

---

[21] In Internet Explorer, for example, using the View/Source menu causes the html to be displayed in a text editor.

[22] *Copyright Act 1968* (Cth) s 10(1). This definition was discussed more fully in the previous chapter.

[23] See the discussion under 'Ideas and their expression' in the previous chapter.

[24] See the discussion under 'Copying parts of software' in the previous chapter.

[25] *Copyright Act 1968* (Cth) s 10(1), definition of literary work.

application of this definition when considering the protection of databases in the previous chapter. As with a database, the success of this argument will depend on the originality of the compilation.

Could the author of the web page argue that there is copyright in the screen display as an artistic work?[26] We await a decisive Australian case, but it is interesting to note that the argument has been upheld in a Canadian case involving a website. During an industrial dispute an employees' union organised a website that mocked the employer. Although the content was different, the union site used exactly the same shape, structure, colour scheme, borders, navigation bars and layout as the employer's site. The judge held that the arrangement of these commonplace elements can result in an original work, and that the sole question was whether, on a qualitative basis (as opposed to a simply quantitative basis) there had been substantial copying of the design of the site, which was protected as an artistic work. On these facts, he held that there had been substantial copying which infringed copyright.[27]

We move on next to the various issues that arise with the Web's linking technology.

Hyperlinks

Hyperlinking is the ability to make text or images act like buttons that link to other web pages or resources. It is the foundation of the hypertext transfer protocol (http) which brings clickable ease of use to the web. Content creators are generally delighted when others link to their sites—it proves the information is useful. The more links there are, the more web traffic there is likely to be, and this increases the potential for advertising revenue. This explains why web etiquette does not generally require permission before creating a link to someone else's site. Does this mean one can always link to other pages without worrying about legal consequences? Can someone complain if one of your links points to infringing content?[28]

Understanding the way hyperlinks work is important. A hyperlink can point at another page within the same website (a local link) or at a page on another server (a remote link). We are more concerned with remote links here.[29] The link could be to another web page, an image file, a music file or video clip. Publishing the web page containing the link (uploading it) does not create a copy of the linked resource immediately. It is only when a user clicks the link that the targeted resource is copied from its remote host server directly to the user's machine. It does not pass through the site of the person who created the link.

---

[26] See the discussion of screen displays under 'Look and feel' in the previous chapter.

[27] *British Columbia Automobile Association (BCAA) v Office and Professional Employees' International Union*, Local 378, [2001] BCSC 156 (26 Jan 2001) available at <www.courts. gov.bc.ca> last accessed 27 April 2007.

[28] See J Forder, 'Permission to Hyperlink?' (2000) 19 *CCH Law and Technology*, discussing a number of linking cases, including *Ticketmaster Corp v Microsoft Corp*, Complaint CV 97–3055 RAP (CD Cal, 28 April 1997) and *International Reserve Inc v Utah Lighthouse Ministry Inc*, 75 F Supp 2d 1290 (D Utah, 1999).

[29] If the link is to a local file that infringes copyright, it would make more sense to complain to the website owner about the presence of the file itself than about the hyperlink.

Creators of links thus do not directly copy the target resource or communicate it to the public. They facilitate access to the resource by others. When might one be indirectly liable for doing this?

Authorisation liability for providing hyperlinks

Under the Australian Act, liability arises in this situation if you authorise an infringement. It is useful to start with an illustrative factual scenario.

CASE EXAMPLE —THE FACTS

COOPER V UNIVERSAL MUSIC AUSTRALIA PTY LTD (2006) FCAFC 187 (18 DECEMBER 2006)

AUSTRALIA, FEDERAL COURT OF AUSTRALIA, FULL COURT, 2006

Cooper operated the 'mp3s4free.net' website. The site contained hyperlinks to MP3 files on remote servers all over the world. None of the files were hosted on Cooper's site—it was just a structured collection of links. Remote users who were willing to share their files would submit details to Cooper's site, and the details would be converted into a link and displayed on the site. The process was apparently automated, but the trial judge's explanation did not give any details.[30] Cooper conceded that most of the hyperlinked MP3 files were infringing copies. The site had disclaimers, saying, for example:

> Links to third-party websites ... are not necessarily under MP3s4FREE's control ... and [do not] imply MP3s4FREE's sponsorship or endorsement thereof.

And:

> When you download a song, you take full responsibility for doing so.

Many other aspects of the site encouraged free downloading. Cooper clearly had an interest in high usage, since his revenue stream was from advertising on the site.

Universal Music and other copyright owners sued Cooper and his ISP, E-Talk (among others) for authorising copyright infringements.

We turn to the relevant law. The bundle of exclusive rights that constitute copyright 'includes the exclusive right to authorize a person to do [the] act'.[31] Copyright is infringed 'by a person who, not being the owner ... and without the licence of the owner ... authorizes the doing in Australia of any act comprised in the copyright'.[32]

---

[30]   See *Universal Music Australia Pty Ltd v Cooper* [2005] FCA 972 (14 July 2005), [22].

[31]   *Copyright Act 1968* (Cth) s 13(2).

[32]   *Copyright Act 1968* (Cth) ss 36(1) (for works) and 101(1) for secondary works.

Courts have interpreted 'authorize' quite widely. In *University of New South Wales (UNSW) v Moorhouse*,[33] the High Court held that UNSW had authorised infringements by making photocopiers freely available in their library alongside books and other materials that could be copied, without any control or supervision. The judges agreed that the term was wide enough to cover situations where you 'sanction', 'approve', 'countenance' or 'permit' infringements without taking reasonable action to prevent them.[34]

Despite this wide interpretation, ISPs still felt they would be able to rely on the 'Betamax' defence to avoid authorisation liability. The defence arose from the well-known US Supreme Court decision involving Sony's Betamax Video Cassette Recorder.[35] The Supreme Court held that sale of the recorders did not indirectly infringe copyright, even though they were bound to be used for some infringing activities.[36] Using the terminology of the Australian Act,[37] the reasoning was that, in the absence of any control over the way the equipment was used, if it *could* be used for substantial non-infringing purposes, then making it available could not be assumed to be authorising its use for infringing purposes.

The Betamax defence was called into doubt in 1997 when the Australian High Court found that Telstra had authorised infringements by distributing a telephone that enabled owners to copy music into its 'music on hold' facility.[38] In an attempt to reassure ISPs, sections were inserted in the Act to give guidance on authorisation liability.[39] They provide that three things must be taken into account when deciding whether a person has authorised the infringing activity:

1 The extent (if any) of the person's power to prevent the infringement;
2 The nature of any relationship between the person and the infringer;
3 Whether the person took any reasonable steps to prevent or avoid the infringement, including whether the person complied with any relevant industry codes of practice.

Carrier

An entity (like Telstra) that owns telecommunications facilities, and uses them to supply telecommunications services to other entities or the public. Carriers must be licensed by the Australian Communications and Media Authority (ACMA).

Carriage service provider (CSP)

An entity that uses a *carrier's* facilities to supply telecommunications services to the public. An *Internet service provider (ISP)* is a type of CSP.

---

33 [1975] HCA 26 (1 August 1975).
34 Ibid [10] (Gibbs J) and [9] (Jacobs J, with whom McTiernan J agreed).
35 *Sony Corporation of America v Universal City Studios, Inc*, 464 US 417 (1984).
36 The same reasoning was applied in the Australian High Court in *Australian Tape Manufacturers Association Ltd v Commonwealth of Australia* (1993) 176 CLR 480; and in the UK's House of Lords in *CBS Songs Ltd v Amstrad Consumer Electronics plc* [1988] 1 AC 1013.
37 As noted above, the US Act does not deal with authorisation liability in the same way as the Australian Act.
38 *Telstra Corporation Ltd v APRA* [1997] HCA 41 (14 August 1997).
39 *Copyright Amendment (Digital Agenda) Act 2000* (Cth) ss 36(1A) and 101(1A).

Section 39B (and s 112E for audio-visual items, but not for all secondary works) also protects blameless ISPs by making it clear that:

> a person (including a carrier or carriage service provider) who provides facilities for making, or facilitating the making of, a communication is not taken to have authorised any infringement of copyright in a work merely because another person uses the facilities so provided [to infringe copyright].

In deciding *Cooper's* case, the full Federal Court considered the effect of these provisions.

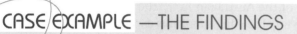

CASE EXAMPLE —THE FINDINGS

COOPER V UNIVERSAL MUSIC AUSTRALIA PTY LTD (2006) FCAFC 187 (18 DECEMBER 2006)

Separate judgments were delivered by Branson and Kenny JJ. French J agreed with the reasons given by both. Considering the three factors to be taken into account, the court found:

1   Cooper had the power to control how the links were added, and to remove them if necessary. He thus had the power to prevent the infringements that occurred through the use of his hyperlinks. E-Talk had the power to stop hosting Cooper's website.

2   Cooper had a relationship with people who used his website. He deliberately attracted users, and benefited financially from their use through advertising revenue. E-Talk's relationship with users of Cooper's website was of little or no relevance.

3   Cooper's disclaimers were cosmetic and misleading, and he took no other reasonable steps to prevent the infringements. E-Talk knew of the copyright problems with Cooper's website, and took no effective steps to put pressure on Cooper to stop the infringements taking place. E-Talk actually took steps to benefit from the volume of traffic, by advertising on Cooper's site in return for hosting the site for free.

In these circumstances the court concluded both Cooper and E-Talk had done more than just facilitating the making of a communication, so the protection of s 112E did not apply. Knowing of the infringing activity, they had actively encouraged and benefited from it, without taking reasonable steps to prevent it.

Kenny J, in discussing authorisation generally, said

> mere inactivity or indifference will be insufficient, especially where there is no knowledge or reason to suspect that the infringement might occur. On the other hand, inactivity or indifference, coupled with other factors, may support an inference of authorization.[40]

---

40   *Cooper v Universal Music Australia Pty Ltd* [2006] FCAFC 187, [145].

Because the case involved an ISP who was found to have actively encouraged or benefited from the infringing activity, it did not answer the fundamental question—could ISPs be liable just by hosting websites that contained links to infringing material? Once told that infringements were taking place, would ISPs be obliged to take action to remove or prevent them? ISPs feared they would become copyright police, with over-zealous copyright owners notifying them of alleged infringing activity, thus forcing them to take action—or at least requiring them to get legal advice on whether the allegations of infringement were justified.

Deep links

Designers of websites often intend that one page (the home page) will be the entry point. When viewed as a hierarchical structure, the home page is at the top, and all other pages fall below it. A link to a page somewhere below the home page is thus known as a 'deep' link. In some situations, website owners object to others creating deep links from other sites. Reasons might include the following:

o   When visitors avoid your entry point, you lose the opportunity to present them with other information, such as conditions of use, the structure of your site, or advertising.

o   If you record visits to your home page but not to every page in your site, you might have no record of their visit, resulting in false statistics and the loss of advertising revenue.

o   If a user does not pay attention to the URL when they click on the link to your site, they might not notice that they are on your site, and this might result in confusion and a lost opportunity to develop goodwill.

Objections to deep links based on allegations of copyright infringement[41] have not yet been tested in a senior court. Most cases in other jurisdictions have been settled before final decision.[42] The best-known judicial statement is from a District Court in the USA:

> Hyperlinking does not itself involve a violation of the *Copyright Act* ... since no copying is involved. The customer is automatically transferred to the particular genuine web page of the original author ... This is analogous to using a library's card index to get reference to particular items, albeit faster and more efficiently.[43]

If this is to be followed, deep linking is unlikely to be an infringement of copyright, since it merely accesses and displays material in the way it was intended to be viewed. However, commercial interests persuaded another recent US District Court

---

41   There may be better reasons for objecting, such as passing off or misleading conduct under s 52 of the *Trade Practices Act 1974* (Cth).

42   *Shetland Times Ltd v Wills* [1997] SLT 669 (Sess Cas 1996, Scot), *Ticketmaster Corp v Microsoft Corp,* Complaint CV 97–3055 RAP (CD Cal, 28 April 1997), *eBay Inc v Bidders Edge Inc,* Case No. C-99–21200 RMW (ND Cal, 14 April, 2000).

43   *Ticketmaster Corp v Tickets.com,* Case No. 99–7654 (CD Cal, Los Angeles, 27 March 2000, Judge Hupp).

to reach the opposite conclusion,[44] and the best that can be said is that there is no clarity on the issue.

We move on next to issues concerning inline links and frames. They are slightly different from normal hyperlinks because they do not display the targeted data or web page exactly as the author intended.

Inline links and frames

Inline links and frames instruct browser software to get the targeted resource and display it on the screen with other information. They make it easy for others to gather material from your website and display it with their information.

Inline links are usually used to position graphic images among text on the page. In the html environment, graphic images are stored in separate files; the inline link enables the image to be displayed 'in line' with the text on a web page. The image file may be held locally, that is, in the same folder as the web page itself;[45] or it may be anywhere else on the web—a remote file.[46] The user who has accessed the page would not know where the image file came from unless they looked at the html code.

Framing is the ability to divide a screen display into several distinct rectangular areas or frames, and treat each as though it is a separate web page. This means someone can display the whole of your web page in a frame next to theirs, or surround your web page with frames containing their logos and advertising. Browser software only displays the URL of the original page that created the frames; the URLs of content in individual frames are not displayed. The user does not know where the information in the frames has come from, and will not be able to bookmark those sections of the page individually, unless they look at the html code.

We consider the activity of the three parties involved—the creator of the page, the browser or user of the page, and the service provider hosting the page.

Liability of the creator of the page

To create a *local* inline link using someone else's image (or other material), a page creator would have to copy the image to the web server that is to host it. If this is done without permission, it would be an unauthorised reproduction, and would also infringe the owner's right of communication to the public.

To create a *remote* inline link using someone else's image (or other material), a page creator would not have to copy the original file. The html code in their page would merely contain a link to the image, so there is no direct infringement.[47] This is

---

[44] *Live Nation Motor Sports, Inc v Davis,* Not reported in F Supp 2d, 2006 WL 3616983 (ND Tex, 2006). See also OUT-LAW.COM, 'Texas court bans deep linking', *The Register,* 23 January 2007, available at <www.theregister.co.uk> last accessed 27 April 2007.

[45] A link to a photograph named 'photo_01.jpg' held locally would look like this: <IMG Src='photo_01.jpg'>.

[46] A link to a photograph on Apple's website might look like this: <IMG Src='www.apple.com/photo_01.jpg'>.

similar to what happens with the creation of a hyperlink, and the same authorisation issues would arise—the page creator would be authorising the infringing reproductions that occur when users access the page.

The same arguments would apply equally to creators of pages that frame material belonging to others.

Liability of the user

When a user accesses a web page containing an inline link or a frame, the html code triggers a request for the target of the link so it can be displayed on the user's machine. The user is unlikely to know the target is being obtained and displayed without permission. Could the innocent user be liable for unknowing infringement? The Act covers this situation in relation to the communication right, but is silent regarding the reproduction right.

Recall that a person infringes the communication right if they transmit or make something available electronically *and* are responsible for determining the content of the communication.[48] To find the innocent user liable, a court would have to hold that, by clicking on the link and accessing the material, the user has 'determined the content' of the ensuing transmission. While this is a rather tortured interpretation, the legislature saw fit to make clear that it is not an infringement. Section 22(6A) was introduced in 2006 'to avoid doubt'. It provides that a person who merely gains access to someone else's online content, or receives a transmission, is not responsible for determining the content.

As for the reproduction right, there is no equivalent protection. By accessing the page, the innocent user has certainly caused a reproduction to be made without the permission of the owner. Knowledge of the tainted nature of the activity is not a requirement for copyright infringement. Presumably a court faced with this situation would make an order that took account of the innocent and technical nature of the infringement. It might for example refuse any claim for damages against the user.

Liability of service providers

When we discussed the exemptions for temporary copies made during the downloading process earlier, we noted that they did not apply to infringing copies. Accessing pages containing unauthorised inline links or frames will create infringing copies. Service providers through whose equipment these copies pass during transmission would also

---

[47] *Perfect10 v Google Inc*, Case No. CV 04–9484 AHM (SHx) (CD Cal, February 2006)—but note a few words of caution: this was only a preliminary injunction in a US District Court, not a final decision; and US decisions on inline images should be treated with caution, since the USA *Copyright Act* is different in several material respects (the equivalent of our authorisation liability is covered by several different concepts such as indirect, contributory and vicarious infringements; and the USA has a broad 'fair use' defence).

[48] *Copyright Act 1968* (Cth) s 10(1) definition of communicate, and s 22(6).

be infringing copyright. Like the users of the content, though, these are technical infringements. In addition, service providers are protected by the safe harbour provisions discussed earlier, which means damages cannot be awarded against them if they comply with the safe harbour requirements.[49]

Search engines and fair use

Web search engines raise some of the most problematic issues. They use automatic 'crawlers' or 'spiders' to gather and index information about every web page they can find. In response to a user's search, they present links to the relevant material. Given the vast resources on the Web, they perform a vital function. The difficulty is that the links they return sometimes point at dubious material—not only as a result of copyright infringement, but also material that is fraudulent, defamatory, racist or pornographic. If they were obliged to constantly filter this information, not only would they have difficult decisions to make, but their search systems would be slower, more expensive and less comprehensive.

Google, perhaps the best known and most widely used search engine, has a reputation for developing useful services that sometimes push the boundaries of what is legal. It is involved in copyright litigation relating to inline links and thumbnail images;[50] hyperlinks to newspaper headlines;[51] keeping archives or cache copies;[52] and digitisation of various library holdings to make searchable indexes for its Global Print Library project.[53] To a large extent, Google relies on the US fair use doctrine to justify these activities.[54] Without such a doctrine in Australia, there is less scope for a full defence.[55] However, the safe harbour's category D activities might provide some protection.

---

[49]   See the earlier discussion on safe harbour requirements.

[50]   *Perfect10 v Google Inc,* Case No. CV 04–9484 AHM (SHx) (CD Cal, February 2006), referred to above in relation to inline images. The court granted a preliminary injunction against Google on the basis that the thumbnail images it created were arguably infringing copyright, distinguishing *Kelly v Arriba Soft Corp,* 336 F 3d 811 (9th Cir, 2003) on this issue.

[51]   *Agence France-Presse v Google Inc,* Case No. 05-0046 (DC Cir, 21 March 2005).

[52]   *Field v Google Inc,* 412 F Supp 2d 1106 (D Nev, 2006); and in Belgium, see *CopiePresse v Google Inc,* Case No. 06/10.928/C (Tribunal de premiere instance de Bruxelles). Google calls its archives 'cache' copies, but they are not temporary copies made as part of the communication process, so do not get the protection of sections 43A and 111A.

[53]   *The Authors Guild v Google Inc,* Case No. 05-CV8136 2005 WL 2463899 (SD NY, 2005).

[54]   An analysis of the USA fair use doctrine is beyond the scope of this book. For useful comments on these cases and the doctrine, see C W Westin, 'Is *Kelly* Shifting under Google's Feet? New Ninth Circuit Impact on the Google Library Project Litigation' (2007) *Duke L and Tech Rev* 0002 available at <www.law.duke.edu/journals> last accessed 31 July 2007.

[55]   See the comment by Branson J in *Cooper v Universal Music Australia Pty Ltd* [2006] FCAFC 187 (18 December 2006) at [40] that the 'assumption that Google's activities in Australia do not result in infringements ... is untested'.

The safe harbour protection for storing and linking

We discussed the safe harbour protection for copies made during transmission and caching of messages (Categories A and B activity) earlier in the chapter. Category C activity consists of carriage service providers 'storing material on systems at the direction of a user';[56] and Category D consists of 'referring users to an online location using information location tools or technology'.[57] You will recall that the safe harbour does not exempt ISPs from liability—it merely means they will not be liable for damages.

To qualify for protection in these categories, certain conditions have to be met. They include:

1   The service provider must not receive a direct financial benefit from the infringing activity if they have the right and ability to control the activity.[58]
2   The service provider must expeditiously remove, or disable access to, the infringing material, or a link to infringing material, if the material has been found to be infringing by a court.[59]
3   If a service provider becomes aware that the material on its system, or to which a link on its system refers, is infringing (or is likely to be infringing) it must remove or disable access to the material or link expeditiously.[60]

The section also makes it clear that the service provider is not required to monitor its service or actively seek infringing activity.[61] These provisions are likely to reassure ISPs who provide search engines or similar collections of links. They will be protected as long as they are not benefiting financially from the primary infringements, and they are prepared to remove or disable links to infringing material once they know of them.

FILE SHARING AND PEER-TO-PEER NETWORKS

Digitisation and the Internet have changed the marketplace for the music, video and film industries. Their well-established distribution channels are challenged by the extraordinary ease with which people can copy and share media. Before the Internet, the industry paid little attention to the small volume of illicit copying for private use. It concentrated on commercial pirates who copied large volumes for resale. With the rise of peer-to-peer networks in the last decade, the industries feel that illicit file sharing is reaching volumes that can no longer be ignored. We start by explaining the basic architecture of peer-to-peer networks. We then describe the copyright infringements

---

[56]   *Copyright Act 1968* (Cth) s 116AE, Category C activity.
[57]   *Copyright Act 1968* (Cth) s 116AF, Category D activity.
[58]   Section 116AH(1), Items 4 and 5, condition 1.
[59]   Section 116AH(1), Items 4 and 5, condition 2.
[60]   Section 116AH(1), Items 4 and 5, condition 2A. There is a prescribed procedure in regulations for removing or disabling material and links.
[61]   Section 116AH(2).

likely to be taking place and why it is difficult to pursue the primary infringers. We end this section with a discussion of the circumstances in which other participants in the sharing activity—software authors, suppliers and content hosts—might be held liable.

Client–server and peer-to-peer architecture

In Chapter 2 we described the client–server model for delivering data—the model initially used for most web activity. It involves a central server responding to requests from clients. A peer-to-peer network uses a variation of this model: numerous machines (called nodes), act simultaneously as a client and a server. Each makes requests for data and responds to requests from others. The model makes it easy for a number of people to share files between themselves.

The first popular implementation of this model was Napster, a music file-sharing system released in June 1999. Napster, however, is not regarded as a pure peer-to-peer system because some functions were still handled by a central server. While the peers—remote users' machines—hosted the music files and made them available to the other peers, Napster kept a database on its central server with information about what was available on the peers, and responded to requests for that information. As we will see, this hybrid or centralised peer-to-peer model made it a relatively easy target for the media industry.

With pure peer-to-peer systems, there is no central server or router managing the traffic. The FastTrack/KaZaa system,[62] for example, organises user machines into nodes and supernodes. When a user accesses the network, their machine may be designated as a supernode if it is faster than the other machines on the network at the time. Every minute, supernodes gather or update information about available files from the nodes in their location. Any requests are directed to and handled by the supernodes, which pass them on to the relevant nodes in their location or to other supernodes. There is no central machine; the supernodes change dynamically, depending on what machines are connected at a particular time.

The primary copyright infringements

Some Internet file-sharing sites take care to ensure their activities are done with the permission of copyright owners.[63] But for most file-sharers, the ease and convenience of using the vast array of free (but infringing) copies is far too attractive. How do these copies get on the Internet, and why do they infringe copyright?

The original source of most infringing copies is usually a legitimate copy. Someone (the purchaser) buys a sound recording or video for their own use. The licence (expressly or impliedly) gives the purchaser the right to listen to or view the content.

---

[62] See the description by Wilcox J in *Universal Music Australia Pty Ltd v Sharman License Holdings Ltd* [2005] FCA 1242 (5 September 2005), [59]—[66].

[63] Apple's iTunes store, for example, was one of the first to embrace this new method of commercially distributing files that complied with copyright by using technological protection measures known as digital rights management (DRM). See <www.apple.com/itunes/store> last accessed 22 Feb 2007.

The purchaser can also share the listening or viewing with a private circle of friends or relatives. Certain reproductions, such as during normal use, are permitted by the Act.[64] For example the time, space and format shifting provisions introduced in 2006[65] would allow the copying of content onto another device (for example CD to iPod) or the making of a digital copy from a tape, as long as it was for private and domestic use.

As soon as purchasers make copies with the intention of sharing them on the Internet, they are acting outside the scope of these limited exceptions. Making files available to others on a sharing system or uploading them onto a server also infringes the right of communication to the public. Once the file is made available online, other users who download it and play or copy it would also be infringing the reproduction right.

The difficulty for the music and film or video industries is that these primary offenders are usually difficult to track down. The time and expense is seldom worthwhile, particularly because the infringers are unlikely to be wealthy enough to pay large compensation claims. There are also difficult privacy issues when copyright owners try to pursue primary infringers. The only realistic way to discover who they are is by obtaining records from an ISP. One Australian case received considerable attention in the media when copyright owners sought the names and contact details of infringers from a number of universities. Limited orders were made against the universities, requiring them to make certain computer logs available to the applicants for inspection in return for undertakings of confidentiality.[66] But this process is expensive and time-consuming—the industries have understandably turned their attention to bigger and wealthier players in the file-sharing system.

Authorisation liability

Other potential defendants include authors who produce the file-sharing software, ISPs who facilitate distribution of the software, and, with hybrid systems, ISPs who host infringing copies of the files or provide links to them. The argument against each is that by providing the software and the network facilities, they are authorising others to infringe copyright.

Our earlier discussion of authorisation liability is equally relevant here—but, instead of applying the legal principles to the hosting of hyperlinks, we are here considering their application to the distribution of peer-to-peer file sharing software. We need only add that in 2001 the US Supreme Court upheld a claim against Napster, the hybrid peer-to-peer system.[67] Napster's servers hosted collections of links to files available for sharing. The Supreme Court held this active involvement—maintaining the databases, knowing that most of the activity involved infringing copies—was sufficient to render Napster liable. It was not long before pure peer-to-peer software developed, avoiding any role for a central agent in handling the files.

---

[64]   *Copyright Act 1968* (Cth) ss 43B and 111B, discussed earlier.

[65]   *Copyright Amendment Act 2006*, introducing new ss 109A and 110AA.

[66]   *Sony Music Entertainment (Australia) Limited v University of Tasmania* [2003] FCA 724 (18 July 2003).

[67]   *A & M Records v Napster, Inc*, 239 F3d 1004 (CA 9, Cal, 2001).

There has been litigation against the distributors of these systems in both the USA[68] and Australia.[69] We will consider the Australian Federal Court case.[70]

CASE EXAMPLE *UNIVERSAL MUSIC AUSTRALIA LTD V SHARMAN LICENSE HOLDINGS LTD (2005) FCA 1242 (5 SEPTEMBER 2005)*

AUSTRALIA, FEDERAL COURT OF AUSTRALIA, 2005

THE FACTS[71]

Sharman was the distributor of the Kazaa peer-to-peer file sharing software (based on the FastTrack network protocol—see the description given earlier). It enabled users to share their music files (called blue files). A search across the system returned clickable links directly to these files, which, when downloaded, were then saved in the user's shared folder and made available to other network users.

A user's search across the system would return a maximum of 200 results. Some results might link to gold files—non-infringing files hosted on a separate server run by an associated company (Altnet). Users choosing to download gold files might have had to enter a licence agreement and pay a fee, unless the gold file was available on a free trial basis.

THE DECISION

Wilcox J agreed that s 112E[72] would protect Sharman if it were merely providing facilities that were being used to infringe. However, he held that Sharman had done more than just provide facilities. This finding was based on these facts:

O   Sharman knew that a high level of infringing activity was taking place;
O   it was in Sharman's financial interests that there be ever-increasing file-sharing activity; and

>>

---

68   *MGM Studios Inc v Grokster Ltd*, 125 S Ct 2764 (US, 2005).

69   *Universal Music Australia Ltd v Sharman License Holdings Ltd* [2005] FCA 1242 (5 September 2005). A second case between Music Industry Piracy Investigations and Perth-based ISP Swiftel was settled after the judgment in *Sharman*. See S Deare, 'Music industry settles BitTorrent case', *ZDNet Australia*, 14 October 2005, available at <www.zdnet.com.au/news> last accessed 29 April 2007.

70   The US Supreme Court's decision in *MGM Studios Inc v Grokster Ltd*, 125 S Ct 2764 (US, 2005), although effectively adverse to the continued distribution of Grokster software, was based on differently expressed provisions in the USA *Copyright Act*, and is beyond the scope of our enquiry here.

71   There were numerous parties involved in this case, both as plaintiffs and defendants, and the facts were a lot more complicated than our simplified summary. For a more detailed discussion, see R Giblin-Chen and M Davison, 'Kazaa Goes the Way of Grokster? Authorisation of Copyright Infringement via Peer-to-Peer Networks in Australia' (2006) 17 *AIPJ* 53.

72   See earlier discussion of this section when dealing with *Cooper v Universal Music Australia Pty Ltd* [2006] FCAFC 187 (18 December 2006).

>> O   Sharman actively encouraged infringing file-sharing activity by (a) promoting a 'Join the Revolution' movement that scorned the attitude of the large media companies; and (b) designing the software so it gave network priority to users who made the most music available to others when compared with their downloads.

Regarding the three factors to be taken into account when deciding authorisation liability,[73] Wilcox J found:

1   Sharman had the power to prevent or at least control the infringements by implementing a keyword filtering system in their software, or by flooding the 200 results with links to gold files before blue files.

2   Sharman's provision of facilities to infringing users established a relationship with them, since, without Sharman's role, they would have been unable to use the software to infringe;

3   Sharman's website notice (in small print) stating it did not condone breaches of copyright, and its licence agreement stating that it was not to be used for infringement, were token efforts.

The court granted an injunction against Sharman, effectively requiring them to modify the software to implement keyword filtering or the flooding of results with links to gold files.

The worrying effect of this decision is that it leaves the *Betamax* defence in doubt. It is unclear what degree of encouragement—or even blatant acquiescence—will be sufficient to justify the granting of injunctions and damages. An overly strict legal approach might discourage research and investment in a technology which, if the number of users is anything to go by, could play an important role in sharing resources and information.

CONCLUDING REMARKS AND FURTHER READING

After this discussion, you should have some idea of the breadth of the challenges to copyright law posed by the Internet and digital technology. They have provoked important amendments to the *Copyright Act* in the last decade. The challenges will continue to mount,[74] and copyright law will need to keep adapting. Is it achieving the right balance? Some suggest not. There is concern, for example, about the recent 'strict liability' criminal provisions introduced in 2006, because they make criminals out of unsuspecting ordinary

---

[73]   See earlier discussion of *Copyright Amendment (Digital Agenda) Act 2000* (Cth) ss 36(1A) and 101(1A). These sections do little more than restate the principles enunciated in *UNSW v Moorehouse* [1975] HCA 26.

[74]   In addition to the issues mentioned in relation to Google's activities earlier, concerns have been raised about copyright infringements on communal facilities like YouTube <www.youtube.com> and MySpace <www.myspace.com>.

users.[75] The cases we have studied appear to work against new and innovative technology, interpreting the Act narrowly in favour of copyright owners and large media companies.

Perhaps the sheer weight of technological innovation will gradually force these attitudes to change. Consider these recent snippets:

○   Contrary to the claims of the recording industry, a new study has found that illegal music downloads have had no noticeable effect on the sale of music.[76]

○   EMI will be the first large media company to allow music from its entire digital repertoire to be sold on the Internet as high quality MP3s without any copyright protection, initially through Apple's iTunes online store.[77]

○   Sharman Networks has reportedly settled the Grokster and Kazaa litigation by signing deals with the music industry to legitimately distribute their music[78] (which they had been asking the industry to do for years). An anonymous music industry official commented: 'We had to spend a considerable amount of money and energy to force [Sharman] to take the deal they always asked for.'

We leave you to consider the implications. Our suggestions for further reading on the topics covered in this chapter are:

Yee Fen Lim, Ch 9, 'Copyright on the Internet', in *Cyberspace Law: Commentaries and Materials*, 2nd edn, Oxford University Press, Melbourne, 2007

R Giblin-Chen and M Davison, 'Kazaa Goes the Way of Grokster? Authorisation of Copyright Infringement via Peer-to-Peer Networks in Australia' (2006) 17 AIPJ 53

M Jackson and M Shelley, 'Black Hats and White Hats: Authorisation of Copyright Infringement in Australia and the United States' (2005) 14(1) IJL & IT 28

Review questions for this chapter can be found on the book's Online Resource Centre at www.oup.com.au/orc/fordersvantesson.

---

[75]   See for example Internet Industry Association, 'New Copyright Laws Risk Criminalising Everyday Australians', News Release, 8 November 2006 <www.iia.net.au/index.php?option=com_content&task=view&id=517&Itemid=32> last accessed 27 April 2007.

[76]   F Oberholzer-Gee and K Strumpf, 'The Effect of File Sharing on Record Sales: An Empirical Analysis' (2007) 115 *Journal of Political Economy* 1 available at <www.journals.uchicago.edu> last accessed 29 April 2007.

[77]   EMI Group Ltd, 'EMI Music launches DRM-free superior sound quality downloads across its entire digital repertoire', Media Release, 2 April 2007 <www.emigroup.com/Press/2007/press18.htm> last accessed 27 April 2007.

[78]   Sharman Networks, 'Content Industries and Sharman Networks Settle All Global Litigation', News Release (undated) <www.sharmannetworks.com/content/view/full/321> last accessed 27 April 2007.

DOMAIN NAMES AND TRADE MARKS

OBJECTIVES // BY THE END OF THIS CHAPTER, YOU WILL:

O Understand how trade marks are regulated and be familiar with the issues they raise in the Internet environment

O Know how the domain name system evolved

O Recognise a number of legal issues associated with the use of domain names including their conflict with trade marks

O Know how domain name disputes are dealt with under ICANN's dispute resolution system

WHAT THIS CHAPTER IS ABOUT

Domain names are a crucial component in the efficient operation of the Internet—leaving aside search engines, they are the signposts that enable people to find what they are looking for. Being 'found' is obviously of great importance for any website operator, and consequently, a good domain name may also be extremely valuable.

This chapter describes how the domain name system has evolved. It goes on to discuss the legal issues that are associated with domain names. Its main focus, however, is analysing how domain name disputes are dealt with under the system put in place by the Internet Corporation for Assigned Names and Numbers (ICANN).

To understand domain name disputes, you will need a basic understanding of trade mark law. Many of the disputes involve some form of conflict between domain names and trade marks. The chapter thus starts with an introduction to trade mark law.

TRADE MARK LAW

Names are of great importance. The law recognises this, and protects names in several different ways. We have, for example, already mentioned that the *Trade Practices Act 1974* (Cth) seeks to prevent companies from engaging in conduct that is misleading or deceptive, or that constitutes a misrepresentation (see Chapter 6). Those rules are clearly relevant where one company is untruthfully making it appear that it has an association with another company by using the same or a similar name. The tort of passing off (discussed in the next chapter) is also relevant.

The area of law most associated with names is trade mark law. Trade marks are regulated by the *Trade Marks Act 1995* (Cth). Section 17 states that a trade mark is a sign that is used, or is intended to be used, to distinguish a person's goods or services from the goods or services of other persons. 'Sign' is defined in s 6:

> *sign* includes the following or any combination of the following, namely, any letter, word, name, signature, numeral, device, brand, heading, label, ticket, aspect of packaging, shape, colour, sound or scent.

In contrast to copyright, trade marks must be registered before they gain the protection of the Act. Registration requires a fee, and if the registrant does not use the mark for three years, the mark may be removed from the register.[1]

From the date of filing the trade mark application, the trade mark is the personal property of the registrant, who has the exclusive right to use the mark for commercial purposes. However, there are several limitations to this right.

First, in registering a trade mark, the registrant needs to identify the class for which the trade mark is sought. The Australian Trade Marks Register is divided into 45 separate classes (34 relating to goods and 11 relating to services). For example class number 25 is titled 'Clothing, footwear, headgear', class number 15 is titled 'Musical instruments', and class number 38 is titled 'Telecommunications'.

Second, the protection of trade marks is typically limited to the geographical area where the registration took place. In other words, where a trade mark is registered in Australia, it is protected only in Australia.

For these reasons, two or more companies may have the same trade mark, either due to their operating in different geographical areas, or due to their operating within different classes.

To obtain a geographically wider protection, the trade mark holder would have to register the trade mark in all of the jurisdictions in which he or she wishes to have the trade mark protected. This raises problems in relation to a communications medium such as the Internet, where information flows across borders (see the discussion of *Ward Group Pty Ltd v Brodie & Stone Plc* [2005] FCA 471 in Chapter 14).

Following the introduction of the *Protocol Relating to the Madrid Agreement Concerning the International Registration of Marks*, it is now possible to register a trade mark in more than one country at a time. There are currently 80 member states of the Madrid Union.[2] Thus, an application can be lodged for trade mark protection in all of these countries simultaneously.

---

[1]   *Trade Marks Act 1995* (Cth) s 92.

So what constitutes a violation of a trade mark? The answer is found in s 120 of the *Trade Marks Act 1995* (Cth), which regulates trade mark violations:

(1) A person infringes a registered trade mark if the person uses as a trade mark a sign that is substantially identical with, or deceptively similar to, the trade mark in relation to goods or services in respect of which the trade mark is registered.

(2) A person infringes a registered trade mark if the person uses as a trade mark a sign that is substantially identical with, or deceptively similar to, the trade mark in relation to:

    (a) goods of the same description as that of goods (registered goods) in respect of which the trade mark is registered; or

    (b) services that are closely related to registered goods; or

    (c) services of the same description as that of services (registered services) in respect of which the trade mark is registered; or

    (d) goods that are closely related to registered services.

However, the person is not taken to have infringed the trade mark if the person establishes that using the sign as the person did is not likely to deceive or cause confusion.

(3) A person infringes a registered trade mark if:

    (a) the trade mark is well known in Australia; and

    (b) the person uses as a trade mark a sign that is substantially identical with, or deceptively similar to, the trade mark in relation to:

        (i) goods (unrelated goods) that are not of the same description as that of the goods in respect of which the trade mark is registered (registered goods) or are not closely related to services in respect of which the trade mark is registered (registered services); or

        (ii) services (unrelated services) that are not of the same description as that of the registered services or are not closely related to registered goods; and

    (c) because the trade mark is well known, the sign would be likely to be taken as indicating a connection between the unrelated goods or services and the registered owner of the trade mark; and

    (d) for that reason, the interests of the registered owner are likely to be adversely affected.

(4) In deciding, for the purposes of paragraph (3)(a), whether a trade mark is well known in Australia, one must take account of the extent to which the trade mark is known within the relevant sector of the public, whether as a result of the promotion of the trade mark or for any other reason.

Traditional trade mark disputes—where a person uses a mark that is deceptively similar to a registered trade mark—can arise in the context of online activities.[3] However, the most interesting aspect of the Internet to which trade mark law is relevant is in relation to domain names.

---

[2]   For the latest membership status see <www.wipo.int/madrid/en/members>.

[3]   See for example *Ward Group Pty Ltd v Brodie & Stone Plc* [2005] FCA 471.

THE DOMAIN NAME SYSTEM

Background and development

Each device on a network requires a unique identifier so that other devices can communicate with it. The protocol underpinning the Internet uses numbers. An Internet Protocol (IP) number consists of four fields, separated by full stops (periods or dots). Each field can contain up to three digits, so an IP number looks like this: *123.231.78.91.*

It soon became apparent that IP numbers were not the best solution—humans find it far easier to recognise and remember names than numbers. This led to the development of the domain name system.[4] A domain name is a computer's location or address on the Internet in words rather than numbers. The words (known as labels) are also separated by full stops. Each label can be up to 63 characters, and the whole name can be up to 255 characters long.[5] A typical domain name looks like this: *bond. edu.au.*

Domain names do not replace IP numbers. If you enter a device's number, communication takes place directly, using the number. But if you enter a domain name, the system has to look up the relevant IP number—the domain name system overlays the number system. The lookup process is unnoticeable—it takes place in fractions of a second without the user being aware of it. Databases containing the lookup information are continually updated and copied to a number of servers around the world.[6]

Top level domain (TLD)
The last or right-most part of a domain name. It may be a country code top level domain (ccTLD), arranged by a two-letter country code, such as .au; or a generic top level domain (gTLD) arranged by type of organisation, such as .com or .edu.

There were originally seven general or worldwide categories, including the now-familiar *.com* (for corporations), *.org* (for non-profit organisations), and *.edu* (for educational organisations).[7] These are known as generic **top level domains** (abbreviated gTLDs)—the top level is the last or right-most label. New gTLDs have since been added, including *.biz*, *.info*, *.name*, and *.travel*. Each country also has its own domain space, using a two-character code—known as a country code top level domain (abbreviated ccTLD).[8] Most administrators of ccTLDs created

---

[4]   The core idea of a DNS was published in November 1983. See Paul Mockapetris, *Domain Names—Concepts And Facilities*, RFC 882, available at <http://rfc.sunsite.dk/rfc/rfc882. html> last accessed 27 April 2007.

[5]   Paul Mockapetris, *Domain Names—Implementation And Specification*, November 1987, RFC 1035, available at <http://rfc.sunsite.dk/rfc/rfc1035.html> last accessed 27 April 2007.

[6]   For a useful general description of the way the 13 root servers are used to 'resolve' a domain name, see InterNIC's FAQ, 'The Domain Name System: A Non-Technical Explanation—Why Universal Resolvability Is Important', at <www.internic.net/faqs/ authoritative-dns.html> last accessed 27 April 2007.

[7]   Proposed in October 1984 (see RFC 920, available at <http://rfc.sunsite.dk/rfc/rfc920. html> last accessed 27 April 2007) but only implemented in January 1986 after a meeting of representatives of the major participating networks.

CHAPTER THIRTEEN // DOMAIN NAMES AND TRADE MARKS 189

subdivisions within their domains that reflected the gTLD categories. In Australia, for example, we have second level domains that include *.com.au, .org.au, .edu.au*.[9]

Someone wanting a domain name decides first in which top level domain they wish to register. For a gTLD, they then apply through an appropriate registrar[10] to register a unique word (a second level name) to use within that category. The chosen name is most likely to be related to their company, activity or trade mark—an example would be *ibm.com*. The owner of the name can also create lower level names within their domain. Thus IBM could allocate the name *www.ibm.com* to their web server, and *mail.ibm.com* to their mail server. The only difference for a ccTLD is that in most countries, one also has to decide on a second level category—so the chosen name will be at the third level. An example would be *ibm.com.au*.

The Domain Name System (DNS) was originally administered by the University of Southern California's Information Sciences Institute. Administration of the country code domains was delegated (usually to academics) in each country. In 1993, a private organisation named Network Solutions Inc (NSI) signed an agreement with the US government-sponsored National Science Foundation undertaking to manage the DNS until September 1998. NSI looked after the central database underpinning the system (known as WHOIS), and had a monopoly on registering names in the lucrative *.com*, *.org*. and *.net* categories.

NSI
Network Solutions Inc, a private organisation originally licensed by the US Department of Commerce to administer the .com, .org and .net generic top level domain names. This function was eventually handed over to ICANN, and NSI now operates as a registrar of domain names.

Early policies and conflicts

Early registration policies in the gTLD space were based on a 'first come, first served' approach. Apart from banning objectionable swear words, authorities did not examine the merits of an application. This was understandable—an open, easy, cheap and non-bureaucratic process was desirable. However, it opened the door to '**cybersquatting**'.

An amusing early example involved a journalist, who, while doing an article on domain names in 1994, discovered that the name *mcdonalds.com* was still available. After

Cybersquatting
Registering a domain name without intending to use it in the long term, but with the intention of making a profit by selling it to someone who already has an interest in using that name but who has failed to register it themselves..

---

8   The ccTLDs were also proposed in October 1984 (see RFC 920, above) and implemented in January 1986. For a list of gTLDs, including their introduction dates and official registries, see ICANN's website at <www.icann.org/registries/listing.html> last accessed 27 April 2007. For all TLDs, including cc TLDs, see <www.iana.org/root-whois/index.html> last accessed 27 April 2007.

9   For the second level domains in the .au space, see <www.auda.org.au/domains/au-domains> last accessed 27 April 2007. Some administrators did not use exactly the same categories. The UK and South Africa, for example, use .co.uk and .co.za as their second level for corporations.

10   The official list of registrars is available at <www.internic.net/regist.html> last accessed 27 April 2007.

contacting the fast food company's headquarters for comment, and being brushed aside, he registered *mcdonalds.com* and used the e-mail address 'ronald@mcdonalds.com' to publicise their lack of foresight. Having made his point, the journalist offered the name back to McDonald's if they would buy Internet equipment for a local school. McDonald's ignored the offer and threatened to sue NSI if they did not revoke the name. NSI gave notice that they would withdraw the name, but later changed their minds. McDonald's eventually agreed to donate $3500 in return for their name, but the aftermath of the incident was that NSI decided it had to change its policy to avoid being sued. What followed was a series of adjustments to the domain name registration policy that seemed to upset everyone.[11]

By the end of 1996, a number of important organisations had formed a voluntary coalition to suggest reforms.[12] It released a memorandum of understanding in February 1997.[13] Although eighty organisations had signed it by May 1997, critics said the proposals did not protect individuals and small businesses, and did not include sufficient international governance structures. NSI resisted the proposals, threatening to protect its investment in the domain name system by refusing to hand over the WHOIS database. For a while it looked as though the dispute could bring the Internet to a halt.[14] In January 1998 the US Department of Commerce (which was still indirectly funding the DNS through the National Science Foundation) stepped in. It issued a discussion paper, and, after receiving feedback, called for a new international non-profit organisation to be formed to take over the DNS. By November 1998 the Internet Corporation for Assigned Names and Numbers (ICANN) had been formed, and it has since looked after Internet names and numbers.

Domain name disputes

The remainder of the chapter will focus on the role played by ICANN, and on how its system for handling domain name disputes works. Before we move to these issues, it is useful to first consider why domain name disputes arise.

As mentioned in the introduction, domain names may carry great commercial value. According to the *Guinness Book of World Records*, the most expensive domain name ever sold is *business.com*, which sold at a price of 7.5 million US dollars in 1999.

---

11   For a useful account, see A Orange, 'Developments in the Domain Name System: For Better or for Worse?' 1993 (3) JILT, available at <www2.warwick.ac.uk/fac/soc/law/elj/jilt/1999_3/orange> last accessed 31 July 2007.

12   The Internet International Ad Hoc Committee (IAHC) included ISOC, IANA, ITU and WIPO. Its historical website can still be seen at <www.iahc.org> last accessed 27 April 2007.

13   The gTLD-MoU, the website for which is also still available at <www.gtld-mou.org> last accessed 27 April 2007.

14   See J Forder, 'Could the Internet be Brought to a Standstill? The Internet Governance Fight and How it Could Affect You' (1998) 10 *CCH Law and Technology Newsletter* 2; also available at Bond University epublications, <http://epublications.bond.edu.au> last accessed 31 July 2007.

Another indication of the commercial value of popular domain names is that, within one hour, the European Registry for Internet Domain Names (EURid) received twenty-three applications for the *sex.eu* domain when it opened the registry for the .eu TLD to anyone within the EU claiming prior rights to a certain domain name.

The issue of cybersquatting was introduced above. In some cases where the domain name corresponds with a trade mark, the trade mark owner has taken action in the courts seeking to gain control over the domain name.

CASE EXAMPLE MARKS AND SPENCER PLC (OTHERS) V ONE IN A MILLION LTD (1998) FSR 265

UNITED KINGDOM, HIGH COURT OF JUSTICE—CHANCERY DIVISION, 1998

The defendant in this case (One in a Million Ltd) had registered a range of domain names of well-known businesses and organisations such as *marksandspencer.co.uk*, *ladbrokes.com* and *spicegirls.com*. It then approached those businesses and organisations seeking to sell the relevant domain names.

The organisations who had trade mark rights in the relevant names took action in the courts, arguing that the defendant's conduct had violated their trade mark rights and amounted to the tort of passing off.

As far as the trade mark issue is concerned, focus was placed on s 10(3) of the *Trade Marks Act 1994* (UK). The function of that section is identical to the function of s 120(3) of the Australian *Trade Marks Act 1995* (Cth). The Court ruled in the trade mark owners' favour, stating:

> There is no requirement under s 10(3) that the goods or services should be similar to those for which the trade mark is registered. It is beyond argument that the trade mark Marks & Spencer has a reputation in the United Kingdom. It seems to me to be equally clear that the defendants' use of it is detrimental to the trade mark, if only by damaging the plaintiff's exclusivity.[15]

And:

> Use 'in the course of trade' means use by way of business. It does not mean use as a trade mark [...]. The use of a trade mark in the course of the business of a professional dealer for the purpose of making domain names more valuable and extracting money from the trade mark owner is a use in the course of trade.[16]

---

[15] *Marks and Spencer PLC (Others) v One in a Million Ltd* [1998] FSR 265.
[16] *Marks and Spencer PLC (Others) v One in a Million Ltd* [1998] FSR 265.

While this case illustrates that successful actions can be brought in the courts, these days, most such disputes are dealt with under the Uniform Domain Name Dispute Resolution Policy discussed below.

The *McDonalds* case mentioned above is a good illustration of the dilemma of domain name allocation. If a person wishes to visit the fast-food company's website, they can either search for it using a search engine like Google or Altavista, or simply type in the domain name likely to be associated with McDonalds. Consequently, McDonald's has a strong interest in having the domain name *mcdonalds.com*, and possible national variations of that name, such as *mcdonalds.com.au*. Indeed, it could be argued that it is in the public's interest that the fast-food giant gets this name, as the majority of people may expect to get to the McDonald's website by visiting the mentioned domain names.

Against this argument it can be argued that the journalist registered the name fairly on a first come, first served basis. Further, what if the journalist's surname had been McDonald? A person whose surname is McDonald may undeniably have a strong interest in registering the domain name *mcdonalds.com*.

Another typical situation in which domain name disputes occur is where two companies have the same trade mark and both wish to get the domain name corresponding to their trade mark. As discussed above, two or more companies can have the same trade mark either because they operate in different geographical areas, or because they operate in different fields. However, there is no way two or more entities can have the same domain name, unless they are sharing it. An example may be illustrative.

EXAMPLE

Based in Australia, Donny's Rubber Pty Ltd sells tyres and has registered the name Donny's Rubber in the relevant trade mark category. A company called Donny's Rubber Pty Ltd also exists in New Zealand. It sells rubber hoses of various kinds. Imagine that both these companies wanted to register the domain name *donnysrubber.com*.

Given the way the domain name system works, it is impossible for both companies to be assigned the sought domain name individually. However, if these two companies act rationally, it will be clear to them that they do not compete. In light of that, a sensible solution may be to share the domain name, so that when a person visits *donnysrubber.com* she is asked whether she wishes to go to the Australia-based Donny's Rubber Pty Ltd that sells tyres, or the New Zealand-based Donny's Rubber Pty Ltd that sells rubber hoses.

The cooperative approach outlined in the example is rare. However, examples can be found.[17] More often, a scenario such as that outlined in the example would be resolved by one company registering the domain before the other and thereby getting the right to keep it (see below).

---

17   See for example <www.winterthur.ch>.

ICANN FUNCTIONS AND DISPUTE RESOLUTION

As alluded to above, ICANN is an international organisation in control of the IP address space allocation, protocol parameter assignment, domain name system management, and **root server system management** functions. It has developed a Uniform Domain Name Dispute Resolution Policy (UDRP), which was adopted in 1999. When registering a domain name, the registrant must commit to following this policy. In other words, one cannot register a domain name without becoming bound by the policy.

> **Root server system management**
> An important function carried out by the Internet governing body, ICANN, to update and maintain the primary Domain Name Servers, which are essential to the Internet's lookup functionality.

As we discussed above, the responsibility for domain name registrations has been delegated so as to create a hierarchical system. Within this system, different domain name registrars have slightly different rules. For example, as is discussed below, the Australian Domain Name Administration has adopted its own .au Dispute Resolution Policy (auDRP). However, all of these various policies are based on, and virtually identical with, ICANN's Uniform Domain Name Dispute Resolution Policy.

While ICANN developed the UDRP, it is not engaged in the task of deciding domain name disputes. Instead, where disputes arise, there are several authorised dispute resolution providers that can decide the matter. The most important provider is the World Intellectual Property Organisation (WIPO). The determinations made by such dispute resolution providers do not prevent the parties litigating the domain name dispute in the courts.[18]

One important aspect of the UDRP is that it contains a mandatory administrative proceeding for settling domain name disputes. The key provision is paragraph 4(a):

> You are required to submit to a mandatory administrative proceeding in the event that a third party (a 'complainant') asserts to the applicable Provider, in compliance with the Rules of Procedure, that
>
> (i)   your domain name is identical or confusingly similar to a trade mark or service mark in which the complainant has rights; and
> (ii) you have no rights or legitimate interests in respect of the domain name; and
> (iii) your domain name has been registered and is being used in bad faith.
>
> In the administrative proceeding, the complainant must prove that each of these three elements are [sic] present.

This provision makes clear that a person who has registered a domain name must submit to the mandatory administrative proceeding where a complainant seeks to assert the right to the domain name in question. It also makes clear that it is for the claimant to prove the presence of the three elements. We will now consider these three elements in more detail.

---

18   See for example Internet Corporation for Assigned Names and Numbers, *Uniform Domain Name Dispute Resolution Policy*, paragraph 4(k), available at <www.icann.orf/dndr/udrp/policy.htm> accessed 31 July 2007, and Australian Domain Name Administration, *.au Dispute Resolution Policy*, paragraph 2.3, available at <www.auda.org.au/policies/auda-2002-22> last accessed 31 July 2007.

Similarity to trade mark

Trade mark rights were discussed earlier in this chapter. In some countries a distinction is drawn between trade marks (used for products) and service marks (used for services). Australian law does not draw such a distinction and the reference to service marks is thus not relevant for Australian conditions.

Paragraph 4(a)(i) makes clear that only those who hold an interest in a trade mark can become complainants. This is of fundamental importance, as it excludes a wide range of claims. However, this limitation is not as strict as one might first think:

> The UDRP [...] does not require that a complainant must hold rights specifically in a *registered* trade mark or service mark. Instead, it provides only that there must be 'a trade mark or service mark in which the complainant has rights', without specifying how these rights are acquired. With this distinction in mind, many decisions under the UDRP have therefore determined that common law or unregistered trade mark rights may be asserted by a complainant and will satisfy the first condition of the UDRP.[19]

In light of this, even personal names, not registered as trade marks, have been seen to meet the requirements of paragraph 4(a)(i).

CASE EXAMPLE *JULIA FIONA ROBERTS V RUSSEL BOYD WIPO D2000–0210*[20]

WIPO ARBITRATION AND MEDIATION CENTER, ADMINISTRATIVE PANEL DECISION, 2000

This dispute related to the domain name *juliaroberts.com*. The complainant was well-known actress Julia Roberts. The respondent (Russel Boyd) had registered the relevant domain name in 1998, and was offering it for sale on the commercial auction website eBay. He had also registered a large number of other domain names corresponding with the names of well-known people.

The Panel held the name Julia Roberts had 'sufficient secondary association with Complainant that common law trademark rights do exist under United States trademark law'.[21] Having reached this conclusion, it was not difficult for the Panel to find that the domain name was identical or confusingly similar to the established common law trademark.

As the respondent had no legitimate interest in the name and had registered it in bad faith, the panel ordered that the domain name be transferred to the Complainant.

---

[19]   WIPO, *Report of the Second WIPO Internet Domain Name Process, 'The Recognition of Rights and the Use of Names in the Internet Domain Name System'* (2001), paragraph 182.

[20]   Available at <www.wipo.int/amc/en/domains/decisions/html/2000/d2000–0210.html>.

[21]   *Julia Fiona Roberts v Russel Boyd* WIPO D2000–0210.

Another important question that arises from paragraph 4(a)(i) is whether the complainant needs to have a registered trade mark or service mark in which the complainant has rights, at the time the domain name is registered. In its very useful overview of Panel Views on Selected UDRP Questions, WIPO states:

> Registration of a domain name before a complainant acquires trademark rights in a name does not prevent a finding of identity or confusing similarity. The UDRP makes no specific reference to the date of which the owner of the trade or service mark acquired rights. However it can be difficult to prove that the domain name was registered in bad faith as it is difficult to show that the domain name was registered with a future trademark in mind.[22]

Legitimate interest

While paragraph 4(a) makes clear that the **burden of proof** rests on the complainant, the UDRP encourages the domain name holder to prepare a response to the claim. Valuable assistance for doing so is found in paragraph 4(c):

> Any of the following circumstances, in particular but without limitation, if found by the Panel to be proved based on its evaluation of all evidence presented, shall demonstrate your rights or legitimate interests to the domain name for purposes of Paragraph 4(a)(ii):

(i)   before any notice to you of the dispute, your use of, or demonstrable preparations to use, the domain name or a name corresponding to the domain name in connection with a bona fide offering of goods or services; or

(ii) you (as an individual, business, or other organization) have been commonly known by the domain name, even if you have acquired no trademark or service mark rights; or

(iii) you are making a legitimate noncommercial or fair use of the domain name, without intent for commercial gain to misleadingly divert consumers or to tarnish the trademark or service mark at issue.

Burden of proof
A party bears the burden of proof in a court case if it is their responsibility to adduce sufficient evidence to prove the fact alleged.

As noted above, the burden of proof lies on the complainant. However, that has the consequence of requiring the complainant to prove the absence of legitimate interests. Acknowledging the difficulty of proving a negative, WIPO has adopted the following approach:

> [A] complainant is required to make out an initial *prima facie* case that the respondent lacks rights or legitimate interests. Once such *prima facie* case is made, respondent carries the burden of demonstrating rights or legitimate interests in the domain name. If the respondent fails to do so, a complainant is deemed to have satisfied paragraph 4(a)(ii) of the UDRP.[23]

---

[22]   WIPO, *Overview of WIPO Panel Views on Selected UDRP Questions*, Question 1.4. <www.wipo. int/amc/en/domains/search/overview/index.html>.

[23]   WIPO, *Overview of WIPO Panel Views on Selected UDRP Questions*, Question 2.1. <www.wipo. int/amc/en/domains/search/overview/index.html>.

The question of whether using a website for criticism, or for a fan club, gives the registrant a legitimate interest in the name has arisen in several cases. However, no consistent approach has developed as to how this question should be answered. In some instances panels have concluded such use of a domain name does not give the registrant a legitimate interest.[24] In other instances panels have concluded such use of a domain name does gives the registrant a legitimate interest.[25]

Bad faith

Paragraph 4(b) outlines indications of registration and use in bad faith:

> For the purposes of Paragraph 4(a)(iii), the following circumstances, in particular but without limitation, if found by the Panel to be present, shall be evidence of the registration and use of a domain name in bad faith:
>
> (i) circumstances indicating that you have registered or you have acquired the domain name primarily for the purpose of selling, renting, or otherwise transferring the domain name registration to the complainant who is the owner of the trademark or service mark or to a competitor of that complainant, for valuable consideration in excess of your documented out-of-pocket costs directly related to the domain name; or
>
> (ii) you have registered the domain name in order to prevent the owner of the trademark or service mark from reflecting the mark in a corresponding domain name, provided that you have engaged in a pattern of such conduct; or
>
> (iii) you have registered the domain name primarily for the purpose of disrupting the business of a competitor; or
>
> (iv) by using the domain name, you have intentionally attempted to attract, for commercial gain, Internet users to your web site or other online location, by creating a likelihood of confusion with the complainant's mark as to the source, sponsorship, affiliation, or endorsement of your web site or location or of a product or service on your web site or location.

What evidence is admissible to prove the bad faith of a registrant who is trying to make a profit? WIPO has shed some light on this question.

> Evidence of offers to sell the domain name in settlement discussions is admissible under the UDRP, and is often used to show bad faith. This is because many cybersquatters often wait until a trademark owner launches a complaint before asking for payment and because panels are competent to decide whether settlement discussions represent a good faith effort to compromise or a bad faith

---

[24]   See for example *Myer Stores Limited v Mr David John Singh* D2001–0763, available at <www.wipo.int> and *Galatasaray Spor Kulubu Dernegi, Galatasaray Pazarlama AS* and *Galatasaray Sportif Sinai Ve Ticari Yatirimlar AS v Maksimum Iletisim AS* D2002–0726, available at <www.wipo.int>.

[25]   See for example *Howard Jarvis Taxpayers Association v Paul McCauley* D2004–0014, available at <www.wipo.int> and *Estate of Gary Jennings and Joyce O Servis v Submachine and Joe Ross* D2001–1042, available at <www.wipo.int>.

effort to extort. Also the legal criteria for showing bad faith directly specifies [sic] that an offer for sale can be evidence of bad faith.[26]

AUSTRALIAN DOMAIN NAME ADMINISTRATION

As mentioned, the Australian Domain Name Administration has introduced its own .au Dispute Resolution Policy. However, as this scheme did not come into force until 1 August 2002, some domain names in the .au domain are still regulated under ICANN's UDRP.[27] The applicable scheme is determined based on factors such as the type of domain name, where the domain name was registered, when the domain name was registered and when the domain name was last renewed.[28]

At a first glance the auDRP is virtually identical to the UDRP. However, when examining the details at least five important differences can be noted.

First, while paragraph 4(a)(iii) of the UDRP talks of the domain name being registered *and* used in bad faith, paragraph 4(a)(iii) of the auDRP merely requires that the 'domain name has been registered *or* subsequently used in bad faith' (emphasis added). This difference may be of great importance where a domain name is registered in good faith, but subsequently used in bad faith.

Second, paragraph 4(b)(i) of the UDRP is limited to situations where the registrant has registered a domain name to sell, rent or otherwise transfer it 'to the complainant who is the owner of the trademark or service mark or to a competitor of that complainant, for valuable consideration in excess of your documented out-of-pocket costs directly related to the domain name'. In contrast, paragraph 4(b)(i) of the auDRP takes a broader approach to the issue of bad faith and refers to:

> [C]ircumstances indicating that you have registered or you have acquired the domain name primarily for the purpose of selling, renting, or otherwise transferring the domain name registration *to another person* for valuable consideration in excess of your documented out-of-pocket costs directly related to the domain name. (emphasis added)

Somewhat similarly, paragraph 4(b)(iii) of the auDRP talks of bad faith where the registrant has 'registered the domain name primarily for the purpose of disrupting the business or activities of another person', while paragraph 4(b)(iii) of the UDRP is limited to such conduct towards 'a competitor'.

Third, paragraph 4(b)(ii) of the UDRP lists as an indication of bad faith the registration of a domain name 'to prevent the owner of the trademark or service mark

---

[26]   WIPO, *Overview of WIPO Panel Views on Selected UDRP Questions*, Question 3.6, available at <www.wipo.int/amc/en/domains/search/overview/index.html>.

[27]   Australian Domain Name Administration, *.au Dispute Resolution Policy*, paragraph 2.1.

[28]   Australian Domain Name Administration, *.au Dispute Resolution Policy*, paragraph 2.1.

from reflecting the mark in a corresponding domain name, provided that you have engaged in a pattern of such conduct'. In contrast, paragraph 4(b)(ii) of the auDRP does not demand that such conduct be part of a pattern.

Fourth, paragraph 4(b)(iv) of the auDRP lists as an indication of bad faith:

> [B]y using the domain name, you have intentionally attempted to attract, for commercial gain, Internet users to a web site or other online location, by creating a likelihood of confusion with the complainant's name or mark as to the source, sponsorship, affiliation, or endorsement of that web site or location or of a product or service on that web site or location.

In contrast, paragraph 4(b)(iv) of the UDRP requires that the registrant has attempted to attract Internet users to *its own* website. Further, paragraph 4(b)(iv) of the UDRP only speaks of 'likelihood of confusion with the complainant's mark', rather than 'likelihood of confusion with the complainant's *name or* mark' (emphasis added) as is the case with paragraph 4(b)(iv) of the auDRP.

Fifth, paragraph 4(c)(i) of the auDRP reads as follows:

> [B]efore any notice to you of the subject matter of the dispute, your bona fide use of, or demonstrable preparations to use, the domain name or a name corresponding to the domain name in connection with an offering of goods or services (not being the offering of domain names that you have acquired for the purpose of selling, renting or otherwise transferring).

In contrast, paragraph 4(c)(i) of the UDRP reads as follows:

> [B]efore any notice to you of the dispute, your use of, or demonstrable preparations to use, the domain name or a name corresponding to the domain name in connection with a bona fide offering of goods or services.

Consequently, as far as paragraph 4(c)(i) is concerned, there are two differences between the UDRP and the auDRP: (1) under the auDRP the registrant need not have taken notice of the dispute, but need only have taken notice of the subject-matter of the dispute, and (2) the auDRP makes clear that the 'offering of domain names that you have acquired for the purpose of selling, renting or otherwise transferring' cannot be a bona fide offering of goods or services.

CONCLUDING REMARKS AND FURTHER READING

From the above discussion it is clear that domain names play a central role in the operation of the Internet. It is also clear that a good domain name is a valuable asset—an asset valuable enough to fight for in the courts or through the system outlined in the UDRP.

In this chapter we have focused on legal issues associated with domain names, with particular emphasis on the UDRP and trade mark law. However, there are several other areas of law such as passing off (Chapter 14), consumer protection law (Chapter 6) and even defamation (Chapter 9) that may be used to protect a domain name.

For further reading on the topic of domain names, see:

.auDA Dispute Resolution Policy <www.auda.org.au/policies/auda-2002–22>

ICANN's Uniform Domain Name Dispute Resolution Policy <www.icann.org/dndr/udrp/policy.htm>

IP Australia <www.ipaustralia.gov.au/trademarks>

Yee Fen Lim, *Cyberspace Law: Commentaries and Materials,* 2nd edn, Oxford University Press, Melbourne, 2007

WIPO UDRP Panel Decisions Index <www.wipo.int/amc/en/domains/index.html>

Review questions for this chapter can be found on the book's Online Resource Centre at www.oup.com.au/orc/fordersvantesson.

14

PATENTS, CONFIDENTIALITY AND PASSING OFF

OBJECTIVES // BY THE END OF THIS CHAPTER, YOU WILL:

O Have an understanding of how patent law affects, and is affected by, the Internet and e-commerce

O Have gained an insight into how the law of confidentiality works to protect trade secrets and other confidential information

O Have developed an understanding of the fundamentals of the tort of passing off, and how that tort can be used in the Internet context, particularly to protect Intellectual Property (IP) rights

WHAT THIS CHAPTER IS ABOUT

In this chapter we discuss the role patents play in the Internet and e-commerce context. It is made clear that patent law affects several aspects of the Internet and of e-commerce.

We also discuss two other IP legal issues—confidentiality and the tort of passing off—that are not strictly limited to the IP context. The reason we discuss trade secrets and confidential information here is that such issues frequently arise where one party is misusing another party's IP rights. Imagine for example a situation where an employee is leaving one company to start her own company to compete with her employer. In such a situation, the employer may seek to ensure that the employee does not use confidential information about how the company operates to gain a competitive advantage.

The importance of the tort of passing off for the IP context is clear from the number of cases where passing off is argued alongside violations of IP rights. Several such cases, relating to e-commerce, are discussed in this chapter.

PATENTS

What is a patent?

In England in the mid-1500s the Crown began to give 'letters patent' (monopoly rights) to manufacturers and importers. Abuse of this system led to the *Statute of Monopolies* in 1623, which banned all monopolies except for a fourteen-year monopoly for a 'manner of new manufacture'. This is still the basis of the patent system we know today.

There is some uniformity in patent law around the world. The 1883 Paris Convention aimed to achieve reciprocal treatment between countries.[1] In 1970, WIPO member states agreed on a *Patent Cooperation Treaty* (PCT).[2] Most recently, WTO member states that signed the TRIPS Agreement[3] undertook to have minimum standards in their patent laws.

The most recent Australian Act was passed in 1990.[4] Patent applications are handled by the Patents Office. Each application has to contain a full description of the subject-matter of the patent. The description is a public record—the patent system does not allow inventors to keep their inventions secret.[5]

There are three types of patent under the Australian system. Two of them only give protection within Australia: a standard patent gives a twenty-year monopoly; and an innovation patent gives an eight-year monopoly. The third type is an international patent, recognised by all WIPO member countries (of which Australia is one) under the 1970 *Patent Cooperation Treaty* (PCT). Applications for PCT patents are administered by each member country's national patent office, although they can also be made to WIPO's International Bureau in Geneva. To get protection in a specific foreign country, one needs to apply to that country's patent office under its national laws.

---

[1] *Paris Convention for the Protection of Industrial Property*, 20 March 1883, available at <www.wipo.int/treaties/en/ip/paris> last accessed 13 June 2007.

[2] *Patent Cooperation Treaty*, 19 June 1970, available at <www.wipo.int/treaties/en/registration/pct> last accessed 31 July 2007.

[3] *Agreement on Trade-Related Aspects of Intellectual Property Rights* (TRIPS), Annex 1C to Final Act, Uruguay Round of Negotiations, signed at Marrakesh April 1994, available at <www.wto.org> last accessed 13 June 2007

[4] *The Patents Act 1990* (Cth) replaced a 1952 Act of the same name.

[5] If secrecy is important, one would rely on other IP rights, such as the duty of confidentiality (which we discuss shortly), rather than a patent.

Under the Australian Act, to be granted a standard patent for an invention, it:[6]

○ Must be a 'manner of manufacture' (from the wording used in the *Statute of Monopolies* of 1623). As we shall see, this requirement is not interpreted literally. It has developed over the years to include such things as devices, substances, methods and processes.

○ Must be novel compared with the 'prior art' (that which existed before). This requirement used to mean that you could not disclose the invention in public in any form before making the application. A 2002 amendment now allows a period of grace, permitting application up to twelve months after public disclosure.[7]

○ Must involve an inventive step compared with the prior art. This means it must not have been obvious to someone skilled in the area.[8]

○ Must be useful. This generally means it must have an industrial or commercial application.

○ Must not have been used 'secretly' before. This means it must not have been secretly used for trade or commerce before, although use during a trial or experiment or when disclosed in confidence is acceptable.[9]

The date of an application establishes a priority date. It allows for the grant of a provisional patent while the Patent Office examines the application thoroughly, establishing the patentability of the invention and comparing it with the prior art.

The requirements for an innovation patent are the same as for a standard patent, except that instead of an inventive step, all that is required is an innovative step—a lower threshold. The idea of an innovation patent is that it gives protection for minor and incremental innovations which would otherwise be unprotected. It is relatively inexpensive and simple to obtain—the patent is granted after it passes an initial check concerned with formalities. No more is done until someone challenges it—a third party or the Commissioner can require a full examination at any stage. Innovation patents must also be fully examined and certified before legal proceedings can be taken to enforce them against infringers.

For standard patents, the Act expressly excludes the patenting of human beings, or biological processes for their generation.[10] It also gives the Commissioner power to refuse a patent for food or medicine (from known ingredients).[11] For innovation patents, the Act also excludes plants and animals, and biological processes for their generation (unless it is a microbiological process).[12] Case law has also regarded certain categories as being in the public domain because no one should have a monopoly over them. They include such things as abstract ideas, plans, schemes, logic, algorithms, methods of calculation or mathematical formulae, and scientific discoveries or theories.[13]

---

[6] Section 18(1).

[7] Regulations 2.2(1A) and 2.3(1A), *Patents Regulations 1991* (Cth), inserted by *Patents Amendment Regulations 2002* (No. 1).

[8] Section 7(2).

[9] Section 9.

[10] Section 18(2).

[11] Section 50(1)(b).

[12] Section 18(3) and (4).

The development of patents in software

Like copyright,[14] use of the patent system to protect computer software has been controversial. This is because computer programs are based on logic or algorithms, which are not generally patentable. Hardware inventions, on the other hand, are patentable (provided they satisfy the statutory requirements). Circuit layouts also have their own *sui generis* protection.[15] Our consideration of the difficulties with software starts with the term 'manner of manufacture'.

In the *NRDC* case[16] in 1959 the High Court agreed that 'manner of manufacture' had a broad and dynamic meaning that had developed over the years, and should not be restricted to a literal interpretation of the word 'manufacture'. In dealing with an application for a weed killer that combined known chemicals in a way that gave them a new use, the court rejected objections that the invention was a process, not a 'manner of manufacture'; that it lacked novelty; and that the chemical reaction was a discovery of the laws of nature. The court concluded that 'manner of manufacture' does not require that something physical or tangible be produced; it included an observable physical result. It said a process is patentable if it results in an artificially created state of affairs, 'belongs to a useful art as distinct from a fine art ... [and] its value to the country is in the field of economic endeavour'.[17]

Despite this broad interpretation, the Patent Commissioner refused applications for computer programs because they were based on logical instructions or algorithms.[18] Attitudes began to change with the development in the USA of the *Freeman–Walter–Abele* test.[19] It said if the claim related to nothing more than a mathematical algorithm, it should be refused, but a patent should not be denied *solely* because it contained a mathematical formula. If the specific use of the algorithm was limited to physical elements or processes within the invention, then it could be patented as a whole.[20] In 1991 the Australian Federal Court affirmed that a mathematical formula applied to produce a commercially useful computer graphics effect could be patented.[21] The court concluded that the specification made sufficient reference to computers as part of the invention to limit the use of the mathematical formula to that environment, and

---

[13] See for example the discussion by the Full Federal Court of the 'historical development of patentable invention' in *Grant v Commissioner of Patents* [2006] FCAFC 120 (18 July 2006), [14]–[24].

[14] See the discussion in Chapter 11.

[15] The *Circuit Layouts Act 1989* (Cth).

[16] *National Research Development Corporation v Commissioner of Patents* [1959] HCA 67; (1959) 102 CLR 252.

[17] At [22]—[25].

[18] See for example *NV Phillips Gloeilampenfabrieken's Application* (1966) 36 AOJP 2392; *British Petroleum Co Ltd's Application* (1968) 38 AOJP 1020; and, for a similar view in the USA, see *Gottchalk v Benson*, 175 USPQ 673 (409 US 63, 972 US).

[19] From the three cases: *Application of Freeman*, 573 F 2d 1237 (CCPA, 1978); *Application of Walter*, 618 F 2d 758 (CCPA, 1980); *In re Abele*, 684 F 2d 902 (CCPA, 1982).

[20] See also *Diamond v Diehr*, 450 US 175 (US, 981).

[21] *Re International Business Machines Corporation* [1990] APO 40 (21 November 1990).

that the altered computer display was an 'artificially created state of affairs' that had economic significance applicable in the industrial or technical arena. It thus satisfied the requirements outlined in NRDC.

There was still doubt about software on its own, or software that did not specify the hardware on which it would run. In 1994 the Full Federal Court considered a method of storing and retrieving Chinese characters on computers.[22] Although the patent was held invalid on other grounds, the court held it was a 'manner of manufacture'. It confirmed the broad NRDC approach, expressing the test as whether the process or method achieved 'an end result which is an artificially created state of affairs of utility in the field of economic endeavour'. Thus, even if it was not limited to specific machines, software was not too broad as long as it was applied, directed or limited to specific outcomes.

Similar developments have occurred with business methods. While a method was not generally considered patentable, in 1998 the US Court of Appeals for the Federal Circuit held that a business method could be patented. It suggested the *Freeman–Walter–Abele* test was unnecessary and misleading—it should not focus on categories of subject matter such as processes, methods or algorithms, and develop individual tests or exclusions for them. The only test for all categories was whether the process, method or algorithm was applied in a practical manner to produce a useful result.[23] The Australia Federal Court confirmed this approach in 2000 when it allowed a business method patent for a system of managing customer loyalty programs on smartcards.[24] There must, however, be a concrete, tangible, physical, or observable effect or phenomenon—a 'pure' business method is still not patentable.[25]

As a result of these developments, numerous successful patent applications have been made for computer programs and e-commerce methods.[26] But the debate is far from over. Several important US e-commerce patents have been criticised for being overly broad or protecting technology that was already in use.[27] Examples include a patent by Priceline.com on reverse auctions,[28] and patents by Amazon.com on 'one-click' online shopping[29] and an 'affiliates program'.[30] Some time after these patents

---

22　*CCOM Pty Ltd v Jiejing Pty Ltd* (1994) 28 IPR 481.
23　*State Street Bank and Trust v Signature Financial Group,* 149 F 3d 1368 (CA Fed (Mass), 1998).
24　*Welcome Real-Time v Catuity Inc* [2000] FCA 445.
25　*Grant v Commissioner of Patents* [2006] FCAFC 120, [47].
26　For a good summary of successful e-commerce patents by 2000, see Swinson J and Middleton G, Chapter 4, 'Patents in cyberspace: electronic commerce and business method patents', in A Fitzgerald et al (eds), *Going Digital 2000*, Prospect Media, Sydney, 2000, pp 74–75.
27　See for example Richard Poynder, 'Internet sparks patenting controversy', November 2000, available at <http://scientific.thomson.com/free/ipmatters/dnsnet/8203655> last accessed 31 July 2007. See also protest websites, such as <Noamazon.com> and <Affiliateforce.com>.
28　US Patent No. 5,794,207, issued 11 August 1998. The patent is for a method by which online purchasers submit prices at which they are prepared to buy. The patent is criticised because transferring a known selling technique to the Web does not constitute a novel invention. Priceline sued for infringement when Microsoft offered reverse auctions of hotel rooms on its Web travel site, but there was an undisclosed out of court settlement.

were issued, the US Patent Office recognised that it needed to be more thorough in comparing software and business method applications with the prior art.[31] The Amazon.com 'one click' patent is worth particular mention, because, in May 2006, the US Patent and Trademark Office ordered a re-examination of the patent, based on a complaint that it was not novel.[32]

During the last decade, debate has also intensified in Europe. The EU prohibits the patenting of computer programs and business methods 'as such'.[33] At first it looked as though the European Patent Office would follow US developments. In 1987, the Technical Board of Appeal (TBA) of the European Patent Office allowed a patent for a 'method and apparatus for improved digital processing' on the basis that it was not the abstract mathematical method 'as such' that was being patented, but a real world technical activity that used a mathematical method.[34] But the Board has not favoured business method patents, holding that they do not satisfy the 'technical nature' requirement.[35]

In 2002 the European Commission initiated a proposal to codify and harmonise the different EU national laws, and to confirm the practice of the EU Patent Office as shaped by the TBA. A strong lobby objected, claiming it was an attempt to make all software patentable, thus favouring the restrictive practices of the large software companies.[36] A struggle developed between the EU Parliament, which was not whole-heartedly in favour of the proposal, and the EU Commission and Council of Ministers,

---

29   US Patent No. 5,960,411, issued 28 September 1999 for an ordering process that enabled users to return to a site and make multiple purchases without having to re-enter credit card and shipping details. The criticism is that it is a simple, logical, and obvious use of the cookie system, not an invention. Amazon's preliminary injunction against competitor Barnes & Noble was overturned in February 2002 and an undisclosed settlement was reached, but not before a boycott of Amazon had been organised by the Free Software Foundation and others.

30   US Patent No. 6,029,141, issued 22 February 2000, which enables 'associates' to market products sold from the Amazon website in return for a commission. This is criticised as being indistinguishable from the customer-referral fees paid in many professional sales environments.

31   Anna Mathews, 'Patent Office to change its tune', *The Wall Street Journal Online*, 28 March 2000, published on ZDNet News.

32   Stephen Hutcheon, 'Kiwi actor v Amazon.com', *The Sydney Morning Herald*, 23 May 2006, available online at <www.smh.com.au/news/technology/kiwi-actor-v-amazoncom/2006/05/23/1148150224714.html> last accessed 31 July 2007.

33   Article 52(2) and (3), *European Patent Convention* (EPC), 1998 (originally enacted 5 Oct 1973) available at <www.epo.org>. When read with the EPC Implementation Regulations, this is taken to mean that a patent must also have a technical nature.

34   *In Re Vicom Sys, Inc* 1987 OJEPO 14 (TBA 1986). See also *Siemens AG v Koch and Sterzel GmbH & Co* 1988 OJEPO 19 (TBA 1987); and *In Re Sohei* 1995 OJEPO 525 (TBA 1994). Cases can be found at <www.epo.org> last accessed 27 April 2007.

35   *In Re Pension Benefit Sys Partnership* 2001 OJEPO 441 (TBA 2000).

36   The proposal was supported by Microsoft, IBM and Hewlett-Packard. A succinct summary of the developments can be found on Wikipedia at <http://en.wikipedia.org> last accessed 27 April 2007.

which supported the proposal. Despite some modifications, the proposed directive was eventually rejected by an overwhelming majority of the EU Parliament in 2005.[37]

So, can you patent computer software or an e-commerce method? The answer appears to be yes, subject to certain qualifications. The claim must not be for ownership of a 'pure' principle or method. It must be for ownership of the process that uses the principle or method to produce some useful, concrete or observable result.

TRADE SECRETS AND CONFIDENTIAL INFORMATION

As highlighted in the introduction to this chapter, the law of confidentiality is not limited to the IP context. For example in *Lennon v Newsgroup Newspapers Ltd*,[38] where the famous former Beatle sought to prevent the publication of intimate details of his marriage, confidentiality was sought to protect privacy on a personal level. Here, however, we focus on confidentiality as a means of protecting trade secrets.

Duty of confidentiality
A duty to keep ideas and other valuable commercial information secret in certain circumstances. Breach of the duty may give rise to a civil action in the law of tort.

Information may be protected by an **obligation (duty) of confidentiality**. There are three elements of an action to restrain a publication of confidential information:

O   The information must be of a confidential nature;

O   The circumstances of the communication must have imposed confidentiality; and

O   There must be an actual (or threat of) unauthorised use of the confidential information.[39]

If all these elements are present, one may be able to rely on an action for breach of confidentiality to protect against the use of the confidential information.

So when is information of a confidential nature? The easiest way to answer this question is to focus on when information is not of a confidential nature. Information is not of a confidential nature where the information is publicly available or can be derived from publicly available information. In other words, to be of a confidential nature, the information must be private in some sense, but need not be an absolute secret known only by the party originally communicating it.

Whether the situation in a particular case is such that the circumstances of the communication impose confidentiality is judged by reference to whether a reasonable

---

[37]   The vote taken on 6 July 2005 was 648 in favour of rejection, 14 against rejection, and 18 abstentions. To some extent the rejection is attributed to indignation over the high-handed actions of the Council of Ministers and Commission in refusing the Parliament's request to restart the process.

[38]   [1978] FSR 573.

[39]   See for example *Commonwealth v John Fairfax & Sons Ltd* (1980) 147 CLR 39.

[40]   *Coco v AN Clark (Engineering) Ltd* [1969] RPC 41, 48.

person, being in the position of the recipient, would have realised that the circumstances of the communication imposed confidentiality.[40] Typically, this test is affected by:

o   the nature of the information; and
o   the nature of the context in which the communication took place.

If the information relates for example to trade secrets or to the personal affairs of the person communicating the information, it may be reasonable to assume the communication imposes confidentiality. Similarly, where information is being communicated between two parties discussing a possible future business venture, it may be reasonable to assume the communication imposes confidentiality. Further, certain types of relationships, such as communications between an employer and an employee, or between a client and a solicitor, automatically attract confidentiality.

The third aspect of an action for breach of confidentiality is unauthorised use of the confidential information, or the threat of such a use. In other words, an action does not lie until the person who communicated the confidential information stands to lose something.

Breach of confidentiality has been an issue in several Internet-related cases. For example some of the copyright cases include substantial arguments about confidential information where an employee has left one employer and later used their knowledge of the employer's computer program.

One illustrative case relates to the admissibility of expert evidence for the purpose of proving a breach of confidentiality in cases where a former employee is alleged to have used the employer's confidential information to develop a competing computer system:

CASE EXAMPLE *ADMAR COMPUTERS PTY LTD V EZY SYSTEMS PTY LTD AND ORS (1997) 853 FCA[41]*

AUSTRALIA, FEDERAL COURT OF AUSTRALIA, 1997

Admar Computers Pty Ltd ('Admar') produced a computer system, called Admar Winery System, used in the wine industry. The dispute arose when former employees and contractors of Admar set up a business producing another computer system, called Ezy Wine Management System, to be used in the wine industry, thereby competing directly with Admar. Admar (as the applicant) alleged that the respondents had infringed its copyright, contravened s 52 of the *Trade Practices Act 1974* (Cth), and breached the obligation of confidentiality it owed to Admar.

The interesting aspect of this case is how the Court dealt with the question of admissibility of expert evidence. Admar had produced expert evidence illustrating the similarities between the two relevant computer systems. This evidence was presented in the form of 'pseudocode'. Pseudocode is:

>>

---

[41]   Available at <www.austlii.edu.au/au/cases/cth/federal_ct/1997/853.html>.

>>   a method of describing the mechanism of a computer program by the use of statements that are written in free english [sic] text, consisting of nouns and verbs (for example `get employee work details'). The statements are linked together either sequentially or by simple controls (for example `if the employee is Claude Smith return to the main menu'). The generation of these statements is usually the final step before a computer program is written in the chosen computer language.

The respondents disputed the admissibility of this evidence.

The Court held the expert evidence provided in the case (the pseudocode analysis) was not admissible in the context of the alleged copyright violation (discussed in Chapter 11), but could nevertheless be admitted for the purpose of proving a breach of confidentiality:

> Pseudocode analysis ... does not constitute or pretend to be a means by which one determines whether the Ezy source code is a substantial reproduction, publication or adaptation of the Admar source code in the *Copyright Act* sense. That is not to say that the pseudocode analysis does not have a function. I am of the opinion that a pseudocode analysis is relevant to the issues which arise in the claim for misuse of confidential information as they bear upon the issue whether the respondents used or had regard to the Admar source code in designing or developing the Ezy source code and used it as a springboard in that development.

PASSING OFF

We have already mentioned passing off in the context of the application of ss 52 and 53 of the *Trade Practices Act 1974* (Cth). So what is passing off? Passing off is a tort typically focused on situations in which one trader is trying to make it appear that there is some connection between it, or its products, and another trader. For example if a manufacturer of soft drink markets its cola-flavoured drink in red and white cans with the text 'Koca Kola' it is likely that a court would find the manufacturer to have committed the tort of passing off.

Cause of action
The legal ground on which a claim is based when going to court.

Quia timet **action**
A type of injunction to restrain wrongful acts which are threatened or imminent but have not yet commenced.

Different texts use different methods for outlining the essential components of the tort. However, the most commonly cited test is that outlined in *Erven Warnink v Townend & Sons (Hull) Ltd*,[42] where Lord Diplock identified five characteristics which must be present in order to create a valid **cause of action** for passing off. These are:

(1) a misrepresentation; (2) made by a trader in the course of trade; (3) to prospective customers of his or ultimate consumers of goods or services supplied by him; (4) which is calculated to injure the business or goodwill of another trader (in the sense that this is a reasonably foreseeable consequence); and (5) which causes actual damage to a business or goodwill of the trader by whom the action is brought or (in a *quia timet* action) will probably do so.[43]

---

42   [1979] AC 731.
43   *Erven Warnink v Townend & Sons (Hull) Ltd* [1979] AC 731, 742.

These five requirements are frequently cited in textbooks and, as noted in *Ward Group Ltd v Brodie & Stone*,[44] they have been adopted as law in Australia.[45] At the same time, the tort of passing off has arguably been expanded to go beyond the classical type of dispute addressed in *Erven Warnink v Townend & Sons (Hull) Ltd*.

Cases such as *Hogan v Koala Dundee Pty Ltd*[46] involve quite a different type of passing off action. In that case, shops in Surfers Paradise and Brisbane were found to be selling 'Dundee Country' merchandise, which featured a koala in the get-up normally associated with Paul Hogan's well-known character from the film *Crocodile Dundee*. The Court held that, as the purpose of the get-up was to initiate a connection in the minds of customers between Paul Hogan's character and the goods being sold, and such a connection did not in fact exist, this amounted to a misappropriation of the image by the retailers. The mere association was enough to enable customers to readily infer a connection between the film and merchandise.

Thus, it could be said that the tort of passing off exists in two different versions: the classic version, exemplified by *Erven Warnink v Townend & Sons (Hull) Ltd*, and the extended version, exemplified by *Hogan v Koala Dundee Pty Ltd*.

The best way to gain an appreciation of how the tort of passing off may be used in the Internet context is to examine cases where that has been done. The tort is often pleaded alongside ss 52 and 53 of the *Trade Practices Act 1974* (Cth), and has been argued in several Internet-related cases:

CASE EXAMPLE *EARTHTECH CONSULTANT (QLD) PTY LTD V EARTH TECH ENGINEERING PTY LTD (2001) QSC 38*[47]

AUSTRALIA, SUPREME COURT OF QUEENSLAND, 2001

In the *Earth Tech* case, two companies had an interest in the same name. The plaintiff (Earthtech Consultant (Qld) Pty Ltd) had been operating in Queensland for more than 10 years and had a substantial reputation there. The defendant (Earth Tech Engineering Pty Ltd) claimed to have a global reputation.

The Court did not follow the five-step test outlined in *Erven Warnink v Townend & Sons (Hull) Ltd*. Instead, it relied on another widely adopted test focusing only on (1) reputation, (2) misrepresentation and (3) damage.

The issue of reputation was not discussed at length as the Court accepted that the plaintiff had a reputation in Queensland.

In relation to the question of misrepresentation, the plaintiff submitted that 'the similarity of the name, the substantial overlap of business activities and the similarity of e-mail   >>

---

44   [2005] FCA 471, paragraph 30.

45   Note, however, that while this test is widely accepted, suggestions have been made that this test alone does not sufficiently clearly describe the relevant law. See for example Dan Svantesson, *Svantesson on the Law of Obligations*, Pearson Education, Sydney, 2007, pp 67–74.

46   (1988) 12 IPR 508.

47   Available at <www.austlii.edu.au/au/cases/qld/QSC/2001/38.html>.

>> addresses all contribute to the misrepresentation and produce the likelihood of confusion'.[48] In addition, the plaintiff pointed to evidence of actual confusion among those with whom it dealt. The Court also noted the similarities between the parties' domain names. The plaintiff's domain name was 'earthtech.com.au', and the defendant's was 'earthtech.com'. Having noted the similarities between the two companies' names as well as the fact that the two companies operated in partly overlapping industries, the Court concluded there was an arguable case that the defendant was guilty of misrepresentation by carrying on business under the disputed name.

The last issue—damages—was easily disposed of after the Court stated that the plaintiff did not need to show that its clients would be likely to choose to do business with the defendant instead; all the plaintiff needed to show was a likelihood that potential clients would not deal with the plaintiff, whomever—if anybody—they chose to deal with instead:

> I accept that it is likely that sooner or later, a person dealing with the defendant and knowing of the existence and characteristics of the plaintiff would work out that he or she is not dealing with the plaintiff. By then, however, it might from the plaintiff's perspective be too late. The client might no longer wish to bother with its original intention. The risk of damage exists so long as there is confusion which may direct a client to the defendant rather than the plaintiff. Moreover, I think the risk of damage also exists in cases where a potential client who is interested in engaging a consulting engineer called Earthtech is aware that there are two engineering firms with similar names. The plaintiff is entitled to all of the benefit of its reputation in Queensland. The defendant has no reputation here. It is not entitled to share that of the plaintiff.[49]

In light of this, the Court granted an injunction restraining the defendant from carrying on business under the name Earth Tech in Queensland.

Another interesting case, *Ward Group Pty Ltd v Brodie & Stone Plc*, illustrates the limitations of the tort of passing off in an international context.

CASE EXAMPLE *WARD GROUP PTY LTD V BRODIE & STONE PLC (2005) FCA 471*[50]

AUSTRALIA, FEDERAL COURT OF AUSTRALIA, 2005

In this case, the plaintiff (Ward Group Pty Ltd) was selling anti-greying hair creams under the name 'Restoria', and had trade mark rights in that name in Australia and some seventy >>

---

[48] *Earthtech Consultant (Qld) Pty Ltd v Earth Tech Engineering Pty Ltd* [2001] QSC 38, paragraph 12.

[49] *Earthtech Consultant (Qld) Pty Ltd v Earth Tech Engineering Pty Ltd* [2001] QSC 38, paragraph 23.

[50] Available at <www.austlii.edu.au/au/cases/cth/federal_ct/2005/471.html>.

>> other countries. The defendant (Brodie & Stone Plc) was selling 'Restoria' in the UK and had the trade mark rights in the name there. The defendant had sold the UK Restoria products to entities or individuals who, in turn, were selling the UK Restoria products on the Internet. This came to the plaintiff's attention, and the plaintiff notified the defendant of this practice. Having reached out of court settlements with those who had sold the UK Restoria product online, Ward Group Pty Ltd took action against Brodie & Stone Plc.

The Court had to decide: (1) whether the advertising and sale of the UK Restoria products on the Internet, by the website proprietors, infringed the Ward Group's Australian trade marks or constituted a passing off of the UK Restoria products as Australian Restoria products, and if so (2) whether Brodie & Stone, as the manufacturer and distributor of the UK Restoria products in the United Kingdom, was jointly liable in respect of the website proprietors' trade mark infringements and passing off.

Interestingly, apart from purchases made by the Ward Group's solicitor there was no evidence of sales of the UK Restoria products in Australia. However, at least one site contained 'Select Shipping Destination' and provided a 'drop down' country box containing a list of various countries, including Australia, for the consumer to select as a shipping destination. Further, on one site the price was listed in British pounds, euros, US dollars and Australian dollars.

The Court concluded that an action of passing off could not succeed. First, it held that as the websites had not targeted Australian consumers, no misrepresentations had been made in Australia. The Court noted:

> If Australian consumers had been targeted by the website proprietors for the marketing and sale of the UK Restoria products under the Restoria name, the fact that the representation, when made *in* the United Kingdom, was accurate would probably not save it from becoming a misrepresentation when the representation was made and received *in* Australia.[51]

Second, the Court noted that the Ward Group had failed to establish actual or probable damages flowing from the alleged passing off:

> [T]he evidence also established that it was most unlikely that anyone else in Australia had searched on the Internet for, and then purchased, the UK Restoria products instead of, or in preference to, the Australian Restoria products. I would add that, as the UK and Australian Restoria products have a common origin and are not materially different in quality or standard, any sale of UK Restoria products in Australia is unlikely to harm the goodwill attaching to the Australian Restoria products.[52]

One very interesting aspect of the *Ward Group* case is its approach to 'targeting'. As is clear from the above, the Court did not find the websites in question had targeted Australian consumers. However, as noted, at least one of the websites listed Australia as a possible shipping destination and prices were listed in Australian dollars among other currencies. In light of this, it could be argued that Australia was targeted to the

---

51   *Ward Group Pty Ltd v Brodie & Stone Plc* [2005] FCA 471, paragraph 32.
52   *Ward Group Pty Ltd v Brodie & Stone Plc* [2005] FCA 471, paragraph 35.

same degree as many other countries, and the fact that Australia is not singled out does not mean it is not targeted.

Against this argument, one could point to the realities of e-commerce website design. It is common for designers of e-commerce websites to include ready-made menus listing countries and currencies. Thus, the fact that a country is listed as a possible delivery destination, or that the currency of a country is listed in the pricing menu, might not necessarily be a clear indication of an intention to sell to that country.

CONCLUDING REMARKS AND FURTHER READING

In this chapter we have discussed three diverse issues; patent law, the law of confidentiality and the tort of passing off. While patents clearly form part of what is commonly referred to as IP law, the other two are only seen as being included when we use the term IP law in a broad sense. All three topics, however, relate to rights in information, ideas or other intangible assets, and, as we have seen, raise issues in the Internet and e-commerce environments.

Further reading on the topic of patent law

Yee Fen Lim, *Cyberspace Law: Commentaries and Materials*, 2nd edn, Oxford University Press, Melbourne, 2007, pp 642–67

On the topic of trade secrets and confidential information

IP Australia, Confidentiality/Trade Secrets <www.ipaustralia.gov.au/ip/confidentiality. shtml>

On the topic of passing off

OzNetLaw, *Fact Sheet: Trade marks, Domain Names and Passing Off* available at <www.oznetlaw.net>

Review questions for this chapter can be found on the book's Online Resource Centre at www.oup.com.au/orc/fordersvantesson.

THE REGULATION OF INTERNET CONTENT

OBJECTIVES // BY THE END OF THIS CHAPTER, YOU WILL:

O Be familiar with federal government legislation regulating online content and interactive gambling services

O Know what content is prohibited under the online content and interactive gambling legislation

O Understand what is meant by co-regulation and how it is implemented regarding online activities in both the Internet and gambling industries

O Be aware of why governments wish to regulate gambling

WHAT THIS CHAPTER IS ABOUT

There are numerous restrictions on what can be published on the Internet. Just as in daily life, one cannot make defamatory statements, incite racial hatred, stalk others or engage in discriminatory conduct. We are not able in this book to deal with all civil and criminal restrictions on free speech and activity. Our focus will be on two areas of legislative intervention aimed directly at the Internet: pornography and **gambling**. In 1999, the Federal Government amended the *Broadcasting Services Act 1992* (Cth) with the aim of censoring, or at least controlling, Internet pornography. And in 2001, the Federal Government passed the *Interactive Gambling Act 2001* (Cth) to control Internet gambling. This chapter outlines the approach taken in each of these Acts.

Gambling
Staking money on uncertain or chance events or on a combination of skill and chance.

Internet content
Information kept on a data storage device and accessed using an Internet carriage service.

Our discussion is restricted to Australian law, but it is worth noting that effective regulation of **Internet content** would require identical laws around the world, together with global enforcement. Worldwide agreement on this scale is unlikely, since nations, like individuals, have different values and beliefs. The only alternative is for a nation to insulate its network from the rest of the Internet, so it can prevent unwanted data from entering the country—but this would make the Internet quite different and far less useful than it is today.

THE REGULATION OF INTERNET PORNOGRAPHY

The prevalence of pornography on the Internet first gained notoriety when *Time* magazine published an article on 'cyberporn' in July 1995.[1] The article provoked continuing media debate, and, by 1999, the Australian Federal Government decided it had to take action. While it accepted that it was impossible to be 100 per cent effective in regulating Internet content, the government's main aim was to do what it could to 'make the Internet safer for children'.[2]

Internet content host (ICH)
An entity that stores Internet content so that it is accessible by others.

Internet service provider (ISP)
An entity that uses a *carrier's* telecommunications facilities, usually in combination with their own servers and other equipment, to provide access to the Internet. See also *Carriage service provider (CSP)*.

Under Australia's system, the Federal Government does not have the constitutional power to control content on local computers belonging to individuals—criminal law is predominantly a state or territory issue. The federal legislation thus makes use of the telecommunications power,[3] and is aimed at those who make the content available on the Internet—both those who host it (**Internet content hosts or ICHs**) and those who provide access to it (**Internet service providers or ISPs**). The Act, however, was only one part of a three-part scheme. The state and territory governments agreed to use their powers to regulate the activity of creators and users of pornographic content, and the Federal Government agreed to allocate resources to monitor content and educate the public.[4]

---

[1]   P Elmer-Dewitt, 'On a screen near you: Cyberporn', *Time Magazine,* 3 July 1995.

[2]   Senator the Hon Richard Alston, then Minister for Communications, IT and the Arts, 'Time for some facts on internet content debate', 27 May 1999, Media Release available at <www.dcita.gov.au> last accessed 18 January 2007.

[3]   Section 51(v) of the Constitution gives the Federal Government power to regulate 'postal, telegraphic, telephonic and other like services'.

[4]   These three parts of the national scheme are spelt out in the legislation itself. See *Broadcasting Services Act 1992* (Cth), Schedule 5, clause 1.

The Online Services Act

The *Online Services Act* was introduced as an amendment to the *Broadcasting Services Act*,[5] and came into force on 1 January 2000. The first step in understanding the Act is the concept of '**prohibited content**'.

Prohibited content

The legislation defines prohibited content by reference to the nationally agreed categories for films and videos under the *Classification (Publications, Films and Computer Games) Act 1995* (Cth). The following three categories[6] are relevant:

Prohibited content
In the context of Internet pornography, the *Broadcasting Services Act 1992* (Cth) prohibits content that is classified as RC, X, or if it is hosted in Australia without a restricted access system, R.

○ RC, which means Refused Classification. Material is likely to be RC if it contains child sexual abuse; detailed instruction in or promotion of crime or violence; high impact depictions of real violence or violent sexual fetishes; the promotion of paedophilia, incest or other abhorrent sexual fetishes; or detailed instruction in or promotion of drug use.

○ X 18+ means sexually explicit material legally restricted to adults 18 years and over. Under this category, actual non-violent sexual intercourse and other activity between consenting adults is allowed, although fetishes such as bondage and body piercing are not.

○ R 18+ means legally restricted to adults 18 years and over. Violence is allowed, but it must not be excessive, gratuitous or exploitative in nature, and sexual violence may only be implied; sexual activity can be realistically simulated, but should not include obvious genital contact; and drug use may be shown but should not be gratuitously detailed or encouraged.

Under the *Online Services Act* material classified RC or X 18+ is prohibited, whether hosted inside or outside Australia. Material rated R 18+ is not prohibited if hosted outside Australia; but if hosted inside Australia, it is only acceptable if subject to an approved restricted access system that excludes users under 18.[7]

One of the difficulties with the scheme is working out how these categories (which were designed for films and videos) might apply to different types of Internet content. The Act defines Internet content as information that (a) is kept on a data storage device; and (b) is accessed, or available for access, using an Internet carriage service.[8] 'Information' includes text, data, speech, music or other sounds, and visual images (animated or otherwise). Two exceptions are not covered by the Act: 'ordinary electronic mail' and information transmitted in the form of a broadcasting service.

---

[5] The *Broadcasting Services Amendment (Online Services) Act 1999* (Cth), which inserted Schedule 5 in the Broadcasting Services Act 1992.

[6] See the National Classification Code, and Film and Computer Games Guidelines, both available at the Office of Film and Literature Classification website <www.oflc.gov.au> last accessed 1 August 2007.

[7] *Broadcasting Services Act 1992* (Cth), Schedule 5, cl 10.

[8] *Broadcasting Services Act 1992* (Cth), Schedule 5, definition in cl 3.

We comment first on the two exceptions.

1   The exclusion of 'ordinary electronic mail' is because the legislation was not aimed at censoring private communications between individuals or groups of individuals. However, e-mail is also used to send messages to bulletin boards and newsgroups, which are publicly available. The definition section takes care of this by making it clear that 'ordinary electronic mail' does not include a posting to a newsgroup. Thus attaching pornographic images to a private e-mail message is not prohibited under the Act,[9] but sending the same images to a publicly available newsgroup would be. Note that, by dealing only with electronic mail, the Act is already showing its age—it does not deal with more recent methods of communication, such as SMS, MMS, video conferencing, public blogs and chat rooms using IRC.

2   The exclusion of broadcasting services is understandable, since the whole broadcasting industry is regulated separately, and has its own code of conduct.

What about material in the form of text or speech—how are the classifications to be applied to them? The Act is unhelpful. It merely provides that if Internet content does not consist of a film or computer game, the Classification Board is to classify it in a corresponding way to the way in which a film would be classified. It is difficult to understand how a piece of licentious text is to be classified as if it were a film. The visual images evoked when reading the text will depend entirely on the subjective interpretation of the reader. The unfortunate use of visual classifications for non-visual material also leads to the criticism that material on the Internet is being treated differently from material in the offline world. The classifications for text-based materials in printed media are arguably far more liberal than for visual images.[10]

The complaints-driven approach

During the debate leading up to the *Online Services Act* one of the concerns commonly expressed was that content hosts and access providers would have to constantly monitor the activities of their customers to determine whether they were dealing with prohibited content. This would have been intrusive, not to mention time-consuming and expensive. Fears were expressed that it would make access to the Internet more expensive in Australia than in other countries, and would change the Internet into a sanitised 'kiddie's playground'.

The legislation addresses this concern by placing the onus on the public to make complaints, rather than requiring ISPs to actively monitor content. When a complaint is received, the Australian Communications and Media Authority (ACMA) has a duty to investigate. Although ACMA also has the power to investigate of its own accord, there is no obligation to do so. ACMA may require unclassified material to be classified, and, for prohibited Australian-hosted content, issue **'take-down'** notices.

---

9   Of course, depending on the content of the image, it might be a criminal offence under other legislation.

10   Details of the classifications scheme for publications can be found at the Office of Film and Literature Classification website at <www.oflc.gov.au> last accessed 1 August 2007.

The approach to non-Australian content effectively depends on encouraging users to install approved filter products. There are two different ways in which this is achieved. The Internet industry is encouraged to develop and actively enforce a suitable code of conduct—a novel approach (at the time it was implemented) known as **co-regulation**. But the Act also includes default provisions in case the industry fails to develop a code or some ISPs refuse to adhere to it. ISPs have generally favoured working with a code of conduct, so the default provisions are seldom used. In the absence of an effective co-regulatory scheme, this is what would happen: Once offshore prohibited content was discovered, ACMA would issue '**access prevention notices**' in writing to all Australian ISPs. The ISPs would then have to take 'reasonable steps' (having regard to technical and commercial feasibility) to prevent end users from accessing that offshore content.[11]

Co-regulation and the codes of conduct

Having set the standard for prohibited content, the Act allows industry organisations to register codes of conduct that effectively implement these or similar standards. Once a code is registered, ACMA may direct ISPs to adhere to it, or, in the absence of a registered code, ACMA has the power to develop industry standards. In either case, an ISP adhering to such a code or standard is taken to have complied with the provisions of the Act. The advantage of this co-regulatory approach is that codes and standards are more flexible than legislation. They can be updated more easily, and they are likely to have a degree of industry support. Another advantage—at least to government—is that some of the burden of developing and implementing codes of conduct is passed on to the industry itself.

The Internet Industry Association has registered three codes of conduct. We provide a summary of their main provisions to give a flavour of what they contain.

Take-down notice
Notice to an Internet content host (ICH) directing it not to host the specified content.

Co-regulation
Regulation of a particular industry through a combination of direct legislative rules and self-regulation through an industry code.

Access prevention notice
Notice to an ISP under the *Broadcasting Services Act 1992* (Cth) or the *Interactive Gambling Act 2001* (Cth) directing the ISP to take reasonable steps to prevent end users from accessing the specified content.

SUMMARY

INTERNET INDUSTRY CODES OF PRACTICE, MAY 2005[12]

Code 1 applies to those who host content within Australia. It includes obligations to:

○ take reasonable steps to ensure that once notified by ACMA, its servers do not accept feeds from newsgroups linked with child pornography and paedophile activity;

>>

---

[11] *Broadcasting Services Act 1992* (Cth), Schedule 5, cl 40(1)(c) and 47(1).
[12] Internet Industry Association, *Codes for Industry Co-regulation in areas of Internet and Mobile Content*, Version 10.4, May 2005, available at <www.iia.net.au> last accessed 27 April 2007.

>>

- take reasonable steps to ensure that restricted content that they host is not provided to minors, for example by requiring end users to provide evidence of their age;
- encourage its customers to use appropriate warnings and labelling on content hosted on its servers;
- take reasonable steps to inform customers that they must not contravene the law in placing content on its servers, and to encourage customers to inform users how to minimise risks;
- have procedures in place for receiving and responding to take-down notices by ACMA.

Code 2 applies to those who provide access to content hosted within Australia. It includes obligations to:

- take reasonable steps to ensure access accounts are not given to minors without the consent of the responsible adult;
- provide online safety information from a button on their home page, including information about family-friendly filters and the complaints procedure to ACMA;
- comply with all reasonable requirements of law enforcement agencies in investigating unlawful content.

Code 2 has a separate section applying to mobile carriers. It provides for example that carriers may only provide restricted content (which, in the case of mobile content, includes MA and MA15+) to end users if they request it, and if reasonable steps have been taken to ascertain they are not minors.

Code 3 applies to those who provide access to content hosted outside Australia. It acknowledges that e-mail notification to ISPs will satisfy the requirement in the Act of a designated notification scheme for prohibited content and that suppliers of family-friendly filters will also be notified. It includes obligations to:

- make family friendly filters available to its end users and;
- at least every four months, advise end users (by notification or on an invoice) about how filters can help manage content.

Non-legislative initiatives

The main initiative has been NetAlert, the government's community education body set up to publicise Internet safety issues and solutions.[13] Apart from distributing guides, brochures, and information on its website, NetAlert has been involved in the government's National Child Protection Initiative. Its main activity has been a two-year training roadshow aimed at parents, teachers and community groups, known as NetAlert Expo.

ACMA is also involved in managing the provision of school activities, a website and other information aimed at children under the 'cybersmart kids' initiative.[14] The federal government has also announced a 'Protecting Australian Families Online'

---

[13]   See the NetAlert website at <www.netalert.org.au> last accessed 13 June 2007.
[14]   See the Cybersmart Kids website at <www.cybersmartkids.com.au> last accessed 13 June 2007.

initiative, which will involve making free Internet content filters available to Australian families and public libraries.[15]

ACMA and the Federal Police cooperate with each other in investigating criminal content, such as paedophilia, and have arrangements to cooperate with equivalent overseas organisations. ACMA staff are also active in international conferences and forums on Internet safety. Details on these and other non-legislative initiatives can be found in the six-monthly reports to Parliament.[16]

States and territories

When the *Online Services Act* was passed, the states and territories agreed to regulate the conduct of those who produced and used pornographic Internet content within their jurisdictions. A draft of model legislation was circulated in 1999,[17] but agreement could not be reached. Three jurisdictions (Victoria, Western Australia and Northern Territory) already had legislation that dealt with Internet content.[18] South Australia subsequently introduced legislation that is substantially similar to the draft model.[19] New South Wales passed similar legislation through both houses of Parliament,[20] but, after an adverse report by a Parliamentary Committee, it was not signed into law. The remaining three jurisdictions (Queensland, Tasmania and the Australian Capital Territory) do not have Internet-specific censorship legislation.

It should be recognised that our focus has been on Internet censorship legislation. There are criminal laws in all states and territories that would cover some of the specific activities of Internet pornographers, such as producing or possessing child pornography or child abuse materials. Some states also have broad criminal provisions which might apply to most Internet pornography, such as possession of 'indecent' or 'obscene' material.[21] Given that it is difficult to investigate these activities unless a complaint is made, it is not surprising that there appears to be little attempt to actively enforce them. You will have gathered that there is little consistency among the states and territories regarding the regulation of producers and users of Internet pornography.

---

[15]   Sen H Coonan, '$116.6 million to Protect Australian Families Online', Media Release 058/06, 21 June 2006, available at <www.minister.dcita.gov.au> last accessed 27 April 2007.

[16]   The reports are available at DCITA's website at <www.dcita.gov.au> last accessed 27 April 2007.

[17]   Electronic Frontiers Australia still has a copy of the draft on their website at <www.efa.org.au/Publish/actdraft1.html> last accessed 27 April 2007.

[18]   *Classification (Publications, Films and Computer Games) (Enforcement) Act 1995* (Vic); *Censorship Act 1996* (WA); and *Classification of Publications, Films and Computer Games Act* (NT) as amended in 1995.

[19]   *Classification (Publications, Films and Computer Games) Act 1995* (SA), as amended by the *Classification (Publications, Films and Computer Games) (Miscellaneous) Amendment Act (No. 2) 2001.*

[20]   *Classification (Publications, Films and Computer Games) Enforcement Amendment Bill 2001* (NSW).

[21]   For example see *Criminal Code 1899* (Qld) s 228 and *Censorship Act 1996* (WA) s 59.

Recent developments and issues

In 2004 a review of the operation of the scheme took place.[22] One of the topics was filtering technology. The review found that user-level filtering had not developed to the extent that it could filter R-rated overseas content, and, while filtering at the ISP level was feasible, cost and efficiency concerns made it unjustifiable. NetAlert and the Federal Government commissioned another report on server-based filtering in 2006,[23] but it reached similar conclusions.

A second important topic addressed in the review was whether audio-visual content made available over mobile phones, media players, online game machines and similar devices (known as convergent devices) required regulation. The review recommended further study, and **DCITA** commissioned a more focused report. In the meantime, interim rules were introduced[24] and the IIA inserted the clause in Code 2 (mentioned earlier) regarding mobile carriers. In April 2006 DCITA's report[25] concluded that a co-regulatory framework for content delivered over convergent devices needed to be developed. Among a number of other recommendations, it suggested that where carriage service providers have some control over the content offered on their service, they ought to have some obligation to pre-assess its content.

DCITA
The Federal Government's Department of Communications, Information Technology and the Arts.

THE REGULATION OF INTERNET GAMBLING

As indicated above, Internet gambling is regulated by the *Interactive Gambling Act 2001* (Cth). In addition, state-based legislation, such as the *Interactive Gambling (Player Protection) Act 1998* (Qld), also regulates aspects of Internet gambling. We will, however, focus exclusively on the federal Act.

Regulatory options and motives

There are three approaches to Internet gambling. Some countries leave it unregulated; others prohibit it altogether. The third approach allows Internet gambling, but regulates it to some degree. Each approach has advantages and disadvantages. The choice depends on which of the reasons for regulation are considered to be most important.

---

[22] DCITA, *Review of the Operation of Schedule 5 to the Broadcasting Services Act 1992*, available at <www.dcita.gov.au> last accessed 27 April 2007

[23] NetAlert, *A Study on Server Based Internet Filters: Accuracy, Broadband Performance Degradation and some Effects on the User Experience*, May 2006, available at <www.netalert.net.au>.

[24] *Telecommunications Service Provider (Mobile Premium Services) Determination (No. 1) 2005* (Cth).

[25] DCITA, *Review of the Regulation of Content Delivered over Convergent Devices*, April 2006, available at <www.dcita.gov.au/__data/assets/pdf_file/39890/Final_Convergent_Devices_Report.pdf> last accessed 27 April 2007.

There are several reasons why governments are keen to regulate Internet gambling. One is that gambling, like drugs, can be addictive. Bearing in mind that Internet gambling can be accessed 24 hours a day, 7 days a week, from the comfort of one's own home, it is particularly seductive to people with addictive personalities. Regulation seeks to limit the social harm.

Another reason is consumer protection. The providers of online gambling facilities such as computerised poker, slot machines and roulette are technically able to program their games so as to minimise the players' chances of winning. It is difficult for a player to identify programmed cheating. Regulation is an important ingredient in protecting the consumer, but it is a two-edged sword. Encouraging trust in gambling facilities encourages more gambling and potentially more social harm.

On the other hand, governments are reluctant to ban Internet gambling, despite the social harm it causes. Like any other popular leisure activity, banning it would inconvenience too many voters; in addition, there is potential for substantial revenue from the taxation of Internet gambling.

The Australian approach to Internet gambling

The *Interactive Gambling Act 2001* (Cth) does four main things:

O   It prohibits interactive gambling services from being provided to customers who are physically in Australia.[26]

O   It encourages the development of an industry code.[27]

O   It establishes a complaints system to deal with the prohibited services.[28]

O   It prohibits the advertising of interactive gambling services.[29]

Co-regulation has been discussed above, and a similar approach is taken in relation to gambling. We will focus on how the *Interactive Gambling Act 2001* (Cth) prohibits interactive gambling services from being provided to customers in Australia and some other specifically designated countries.

The prohibition

The key provision is s 15(1), which states:

A person is guilty of an offence if:

(a) the person intentionally provides an interactive gambling service; and

(b) the service has an Australian-customer link ...

An 'interactive gambling service' is a gambling service provided by a business to customers using the Internet or other similar services.[30] While this definition is rather wide, a number of forms of interactive gambling, such as traditional telephone

---

26   *Interactive Gambling Act 2001* (Cth) Part 2.
27   *Interactive Gambling Act 2001* (Cth) Part 4.
28   *Interactive Gambling Act 2001* (Cth) Parts 3–7.
29   *Interactive Gambling Act 2001* (Cth) Part 7A.
30   *Interactive Gambling Act 2001* (Cth) s 5(1). The Act uses technical terms defined in other Acts, such as a listed carriage service, and broadcasting, datacasting and content services.

Gaming and wagering

The *Interactive Gambling Act 2001* (Cth) distinguishes between two forms of gambling: gaming (casinos, gaming machines, keno, lotteries) and wagering (betting on races and sporting events).

Online wagering

Use of the Internet or other similar service to bet on sporting events or races—a permitted form of gambling under the *Interactive Gambling Act 2001* (Cth). See also *Gaming and wagering.*

betting, are excluded.[31] After successful lobbying by some sections of the gambling industry, there are three other major exclusions.

o   Online wagering (betting on horse and dog races, sports, and other similar events) is allowed, as long as bets are not accepted after the event has started.[32] There can be no real-time, 'ball by ball' betting.

o   Gaming in a public place—this exclusion allows linked poker machines to be played in bars and social clubs.[33]

o   Online lotteries are generally allowed, although electronic instant and scratch lotteries are still prohibited.[34]

The requirement of an Australian-customer link is fulfilled 'if, and only if, any or all of the customers of the service are physically present in Australia'.[35]

Where a person did not know and could not, with reasonable diligence, have known that the service had Australian customers, they have not committed an offence. The following factors are taken into account in assessing whether there has been reasonable diligence:[36]

(a) whether prospective customers were informed that Australian law prohibits the provision of the service to customers who are physically present in Australia;

(b) whether customers were required to enter into contracts that were subject to an express condition that the customer was not to use the service if the customer was physically present in Australia;

(c) whether the person required customers to provide personal details and, if so, whether those details suggested that the customer was not physically present in Australia;

(d) whether the person has network data that indicates that customers were physically present outside Australia:
   (i) when the relevant customer account was opened; and
   (ii) throughout the period when the service was provided to the customer;

(e) any other relevant matters.

The Act does not prohibit an Australian business from providing interactive gambling services to people outside Australia. Interestingly, though, the Minister has power to designate other countries with which Australia has cooperative arrangements.

---

31   *Interactive Gambling Act 2001* (Cth) s 5(3).
32   *Interactive Gambling Act 2001* (Cth) ss 5(3)(aa), 8A.
33   *Interactive Gambling Act 2001* (Cth) ss 5(3)(ab), 8B.
34   *Interactive Gambling Act 2001* (Cth) ss 5(3)(ae), 8D.
35   *Interactive Gambling Act 2001* (Cth) s 8.
36   *Interactive Gambling Act 2001* (Cth) s 15(3) and (4).

Once designated, it *is* an offence to provide a service based in Australia to people in that country.[37] No countries had been designated by the end of 2006.

Industry codes and standards

The Internet Industry Association has registered a code of conduct as required by the Act.[38] Compliance with the code is voluntary, although ACMA can direct an ISP to comply with it. ACMA also has power to develop industry standards if the industry code is unsatisfactory.

The code deals with content hosted overseas. It requires ISPs to provide their customers with one of the approved filters listed in the schedule to the code.

The complaints system

Like the online content provisions, the complaints system is administered by ACMA. If ACMA receives a complaint about content hosted in Australia, it may issue directions or formal warnings to comply with industry codes or standards, or refer the matter to the Federal Police. Complaints about content hosted outside Australia are investigated and, if found to be prohibited, ACMA notifies suppliers of filter software so they can update their filters.

Advertising

It is an offence to publish or broadcast in Australia an advertisement for an interactive gambling service, although there are numerous exceptions.[39] The prohibition covers a number of media, including the Internet, print media and broadcast services.[40] The advertising ban does not extend to the wagering, public place and lottery exclusions, nor to media published overseas or websites that are aimed at non-Australian audiences.

The review

The Act required that its operation be reviewed by July 2003.[41] The report of the review was published in July 2004.[42] We summarise some of its main findings.

Impact of the Act

The review found there had been some growth in interactive gambling, but mainly for legal wagering on racing and sporting events. A large proportion of this growth was due to movement away from offline methods because of the convenience of Internet wagering. It found no evidence suggesting that prohibited online gaming services

---

37 *Interactive Gambling Act 2001* (Cth) s 15A.

38 Internet Industry Association, *Interactive Gambling Industry Code*, Version 1.0, December 2001, available at <www.iia.net.au/index.php?option=com_content&task=section&id=3&Itemid=33> last accessed 27 April 2007.

39 *Interactive Gambling Act 2001* (Cth) s 61EA and other provisions of Part 7A.

40 *Interactive Gambling Act 2001* (Cth) ss 61CA, 61DA.

41 *Interactive Gambling Act 2001* (Cth) s 68.

42 DCITA, *Review of the Operation of the* Interactive Gambling Act 2001, Report, July 2004, available at <www.dcita.gov.au> last accessed 27 April 2007.

had grown, and concluded that 'the overwhelming majority of Australian Internet gambling consumers use services permitted under the [Act]. The [Act] has, therefore, broadly achieved its overall objective, which is to minimise the potential expansion of interactive gambling that may exacerbate problem gambling in Australia.'[43]

Technological developments

The review found that filtering technology had not advanced to a point where it was suitable for mandatory blocking at the ISP level—filtering at the personal computer level was still the most appropriate method. While geo-location technologies (which determine the location of Internet users—see our discussion in Chapter 3) were becoming commercially available, the Report concluded there were still issues with their accuracy. It also noted that 'geolocation is only one of a number of factors that are to be taken into account in determining whether an IGSP [interactive gambling service provider] had used reasonable diligence to ascertain whether their service had an Australian-customer link'.[44]

Financial regulation

The review was specifically asked to investigate whether the Minister should exercise powers under the Act[45] to regulate financial agreements (and thus payments) for illegal gambling. This strategy has been used in the USA—credit card companies have been prohibited from honouring illegal online gambling debts—and this has severely curtailed the provision of online gambling services to US gamblers. The Report concluded that similar provisions in Australia would be unlikely to achieve their objective, since:

o   Australian card-issuing institutions would probably respond by blocking use of their cards for all gambling-related transactions, including those permitted under the Act; and

o   the provisions would be easy to circumvent by gambling merchants or payment providers failing to correctly code their transactions, and the use of other payment systems.

CONCLUDING REMARKS AND FURTHER READING

The last decade has seen an interesting attempt by the Australian Federal Government to regulate what the Internet is used for. Cynics suggest that both the *Online Services Act* and the *Interactive Gambling Act* achieve little, cost money which could be better spent elsewhere, and really amount to a political approach designed to appeal to conservative voters. On the other hand, as a result of the pressure to co-regulate, industry players have had to develop codes of conduct and take a much more active and responsible role.

---

43   Ibid, Executive summary, p vi.
44   Ibid, p 73.
45   *Interactive Gambling Act 2001* (Cth) s 69A.

One of the remarkable aspects of both the pornography and gambling regimes is the emphasis on user education and international cooperation. In many ways, it is the rather contentious attempt to regulate extraterritorial activities affecting Australians that makes the Acts interesting.

As for further reading on this topic, we recommend the following:

DCITA, *Review of the Operation of Schedule 5 to the Broadcasting Services Act 1992,* available at <www.dcita.gov.au>

Yee Fen Lim, Ch 8, 'Internet Content Regulation', in *Cyberspace Law: Commentaries and Materials,* 2nd edn, Oxford University Press, Melbourne, 2007

Gavin R Skene, 'A new role as regulator: Australian financial institutions and the Interactive Gambling Regulations (Cth)' (2004) 15 *JBFL & P* 41

Review questions for this chapter can be found on the book's Online Resource Centre at www.oup.com.au/orc/fordersvantesson.

16

CRIME

- O Appreciate how crime has moved to the Internet context

- O Understand the basic difficulties of prosecuting cybercrime

- O Have a solid understanding of how Australia deals with cybercrime

- O Be aware of some international regulation of cybercrime

WHAT THIS CHAPTER IS ABOUT

The Internet is nothing but a reflection of our real-world society. Consequently, both the goods and the evils of our real world have spread to the Internet. In light of this, it is only natural that criminal behaviour has found a new home in cyberspace, and this chapter provides an introduction to such cybercrime.

WHAT IS CYBERCRIME?

While most people would have an instinctive idea of what cybercrime is, it is not easy to define it in absolute terms. Often criminal acts may be partly cyber-based and partly taking place in the real world. A useful starting point is to examine what functions technology can play in criminal activities. It is useful to distinguish between three such functions:

1   Computers can be incidental to criminal activities. That would for example be the case where detailed plans to blow up a building are found on a suspected terrorist's laptop.
2   Computers can be the tool used to commit traditional forms of criminal acts. For example computers are used to commit online fraud, to sell illegal products and to stalk people.
3   Computers may be the target for illegal activities. For example where a hacker accessed another person's server in order to shut it down, the target of the crime is a computer.

While the first function is interesting mainly from the perspective of electronic evidence, the other two are discussed in more detail below.

How does society deal with crime?

Before we discuss cybercrime in more detail, it is useful to first say a few words about crime on a general level, because societies approach criminal acts quite differently from those acts giving rise to civil liabilities.

The police relatively rarely detect crime. Instead, crime is typically reported to the police by the public. The police will then investigate the alleged crime and decide whether or not to charge the person alleged to be responsible for the act. Where the person responsible for the crime is charged, the matter is then handed over to the prosecution.

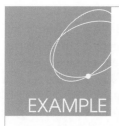

EXAMPLE

Imagine a car accident where due to the fault of one of the drivers, two cars have collided. In such a situation, the innocent driver is likely to seek to recover damages from the driver who caused the accident. That would typically be done under the tort of negligence—a civil action.

At the same time, the driver who caused the accident may be prosecuted for committing a crime—a criminal action. For example if the accident was caused due to the driver in the wrong having been intoxicated, he may receive a fine or a jail sentence.

In the first of these actions, the civil action, the dispute is between the two drivers—that is, between two civil parties. In contrast, the second dispute, the criminal action, involves the state on the one hand and an individual on the other hand. In other words, the same event (here the car accident) can give rise to both civil actions and criminal actions. Thus for example where a person instigates >>

Denial of service (DoS) attack
An attempt to make a computer resource unavailable to intended users by flooding the system with superfluous requests.

>> a **denial of service** attack on a server (see below), the owner of the affected server may take both civil action against the perpetrator seeking damages, and report the matter to the police in the hope that it will lead to a criminal prosecution.

Standard of proof
The degree of evidence which a party must present in a trial in order to succeed.

One of the key differences between civil disputes and criminal disputes is how the courts approach the **standard of proof**. In criminal actions the prosecutor must show that the accused is guilty beyond reasonable doubt. Civil disputes involve a much lower standard. The claimant need only prove 'on the balance of probabilities' that he or she is entitled to the remedy sought. Thus, there are situations where a civil action would succeed and a criminal action would fail in relation to one set of circumstances.

The international nature of cybercrime

Jurisdictional borders
Geographical or other limits, outside of which the court or other entity holds no power.

The international nature of cybercrime has at least two consequences. First, cyber criminals can operate from virtually anywhere in the world—unlike most traditional criminals they need not even be in the proximity of the scene of the crime. Second, both the investigation and prosecution of cybercrime is hampered by **jurisdictional borders**. The following example is illustrative.

EXAMPLE

Imagine that a person located in Malaysia unlawfully accesses the computer system of a bank located in Australia and transfers money to an account held in a Singaporean bank. Technically, neither distance nor geographical borders affect the cyber criminal's ability to carry out the crime. However, where authorities in Australia seek to prosecute the Malaysian criminal both distance and borders constitute obstacles.

First, the Australian government cannot simply send people to Malaysia and Singapore to collect evidence. Instead assistance must be gained from the Malaysian and Singaporean governments.

Second, the Australian government cannot simply send people to Malaysia to collect the suspected criminal, and it would perhaps be unlikely that she would come to Australia voluntarily. The Australian government would need to seek to have the suspected criminal extradited to Australia.

The matter may be complicated even further where the criminal has used computers in a range of other countries to cover her trail. If, in our example above, the criminal had accessed the Australian bank's computer system by going via servers in Finland, Brazil and Japan, the Australian government may need to cooperate with the authorities in those countries as well, in order to gather sufficient evidence.

Due to Australia's federal structure, problems of jurisdiction may also arise within Australia. Generally, the location of the computer that the offender has used to commit the offence determines which state's law enforcement agency should investigate the matter.[1]

Further, extradition in the context of cybercrime is sometimes complicated, or even rendered impossible, by the requirement of **dual criminality**. While this may be a sensible requirement, it means that where a country has been slow to enact suitable legislation criminalising certain undesirable online activities, other countries will find it difficult to have offenders extradited from that country.

> **Dual criminality**
> A requirement for extradition—the act in question must be criminal in both the country seeking extradition and the country from which the alleged criminal is to be extradited.

FORMS OF CYBERCRIME

As there are many different forms of cybercrime, we focus here on some of the more important types of crimes, where computers are used as tools to commit traditional crimes and where crimes are targeted at computers.

Computers as tools to commit traditional crimes

Computers are versatile tools that can be used for a variety of aims, including committing crimes.

Fraud

As a large number of spam messages are sent for the purpose of committing fraud, it could perhaps be said that online fraud, or rather attempted online fraud, is the type of cybercrime that most people come into contact with. For example many Internet users would have received e-mails appearing to be notifications of a lottery win, stating that all the receivers need to do to get the large amount they have won is to send a small amount of money to cover administration costs. Of course, if the administration costs are paid, the fraudster knows they have the victim on the hook, and will start asking for more and more money. Needless to say, the 'lucky' lottery winner never receives any money.

Another typical form of online fraud is so-called phishing. The likeness with the word 'fishing' gives an indication of the purpose of the activity. Typically, the victim receives an e-mail looking as if it has come from a financial institution (such as a

---

[1] See for example Queensland Police Services, Jurisdiction, 11 May 2007 available at: <www.police.qld.gov.au/programs/crimePrevention/eCrime/jurisdiction.htm>.

bank), an e-trader (such as eBay), or an ISP (like AOL). In the e-mail the victim is asked to go to the website (using a hyperlink in the e-mail) of a legitimate organisation (the financial institution, e-trader or ISP). Normally, the phisher urges the victim to go to the relevant website to re-enter their password, username or credit card details due to some security issue, or to confirm a purchase.

A victim who follows the link is taken to a website set up by the phisher. This website will typically be a copy of the relevant legitimate organisation's website and the URL will look authentic at first glance. When the victim has entered the password, username, credit card details or other account details on the phisher's website, the phisher records this information.

The damage flowing from phishing ranges from loss of e-mail accounts to significant financial loss and **identity theft**.

Identity theft
Fraudulent use of another person's personal information to take on their identity.

Harassment, threats and stalking

Harassment and stalking can take place online. Indeed, with the offender feeling a sense of anonymity, the features of the online environment may be particularly inviting for such behaviour.

Harassment can take many forms, and we have already dealt with one form of harassment in Chapter 10, involving spam. Where harassment is of a commercial nature, trade practices law such as s 60 of the *Trade Practices Act 1974* (Cth) may be of relevance:

> A corporation shall not use physical force or undue harassment or coercion in connection with the supply or possible supply of goods or services to a consumer or the payment for goods or services by a consumer.

This provision may prove highly useful, but has so far been underutilised.

More commonly, however, the harassment is of an even more sinister kind and may be aimed at threatening the victim for personal rather than commercial reasons. Stalking is a major issue online as exemplified in the following case.

CASE EXAMPLE *DPP V SUTCLIFFE* (2001) VSC 43[2]

AUSTRALIA, SUPREME COURT OF VICTORIA, 2001

The respondent in this case (one Brian Sutcliffe) had allegedly been stalking a Canadian former actress named Sara Ballingall (better known as Melanie in the television series 'Degrassi Junior High' and later 'Degrassi High'). A Magistrates' Court had found it could not hear the matter, as it lacked jurisdiction over the alleged offence:

>>

---

[2]   Available at <www.austlii.edu.au/au/cases/vic/VSC/2001/43.html>.

>> It is an essential element of the offence that any course of conduct engaged in, by the defendant, actually did have the effect of arousing apprehension or fear in the victim for her personal safety. This can only have occurred in Canada. In the absence of any express provision in the legislation that is in the Crimes Act, this charge cannot proceed in this court.[3]

Thus, despite the fact that Mr Sutcliffe had performed all his actions in Australia, such as sending parcels and e-mails and operating a website, the Magistrates' Court did not consider itself competent to decide the matter in light of the jurisdictional issue flowing from the transborder nature of the crime. This decision was appealed, leading to the Supreme Court case discussed here.

The Supreme Court took a better approach and stated:

While the argument below described the issue as one of jurisdiction, strictly it is not. The respondent resides in this State, is present in the State, the proscribed acts of the respondent took place in this State and the Magistrates' Court in this State had jurisdiction to hear a charge brought under s 21A of the Act [the provision of the *Crimes Act 1958* (Vic) dealing with stalking]. The court does have jurisdiction to hear the charge against the respondent.

Whether or not the respondent could be guilty of the offence in circumstances where an essential ingredient of the offence took place outside the territorial limits of Victoria is a question of construction of s 21A.[4]

Having noted that s 21A did not expressly state that it may have extraterritorial application, the Court examined the policy reasons for making stalking a crime:

Stalking could occur by use of the telephone, Internet, e-mail and computer and in circumstances where the victim and offender could be many thousands of kilometres apart. Parliament in 1994 was well aware that with the advent of new technologies stalking could take many forms including through mediums of e-mail, Internet and computer.

Given that knowledge, given the purpose of the legislation and the fact that the proscribed conduct is 'a course of conduct', in order for the legislation to operate effectively it is necessary that it should have extraterritorial operation and effect. It would have been apparent to all members of Parliament that some of the conduct which constituted the stalking could occur within this State and some outside this State and that the effect upon the victim could occur partly within this State and partly without. To pass a law which confined all the ingredients constituting the offence to occur in this State would rob the provision of much of its effect.[5]

---

3   *DPP v Sutcliffe* [2001] VSC 43, paragraph 16.
4   *DPP v Sutcliffe* [2001] VSC 43, paragraphs 29–30.
5   *DPP v Sutcliffe* [2001] VSC 43, paragraphs 87–88.

In light of this, the Court set aside the Magistrates' Court's judgment and ordered that the charge be remitted to the Magistrates' Court for determination.

This case is interesting both as an example of the prosecution of online stalking and as an illustration of the fact that courts have become aware of the impact of new technologies. It is very pleasing to see the Court acknowledge the impact of technology:

> But in the past 100 years crimes have ceased to be confined to single locations.
>
> Criminals are not respecters of borders. State and international boundaries do not concern them. They commit their evil acts anywhere and without thought to location.
>
> Movement between countries is much greater now than in the past and subject to less [sic] restrictions. Technology has reached the point where communications can be made around the world in less than a second. The Internet provides a speedy, relatively inexpensive means of communication between persons who have access to a computer and a telephone line. Access is not confined to ownership of a computer and businesses have sprung up offering access to the Internet for a small charge.
>
> The law must move with these changes.[6]

Piracy

People engaged in unlawful copying or distributing of copyright protected materials are often referred to as pirates. This is arguably a somewhat misguided or even defamatory description, bearing in mind the violent acts committed by those classed as pirates in the more traditional sense.

Either way, while the civil implications of copying or distributing of copyright protected materials were discussed in earlier chapters, such activities may also be classed as criminal acts subject to severe penalties.

Pornography

We have already discussed how the law places restrictions on the types of content that can be provided online (see Chapter 15). In addition, the distribution and even possession of certain forms of pornography are regarded as so serious as to amount to crimes. Most importantly, the distribution and possession of child pornography are serious crimes.

Other crimes

It is not difficult to think of other traditional crimes that may be committed using computers. For example crimes such as blackmail, forgery and unlawful threats may very well be committed using computers. However, those crimes will not be discussed any further here.

---

6   *DPP v Sutcliffe* [2001] VSC 43, paragraphs 60–63.

Computers as targets for crimes

There are a range of crimes aimed directly at computers. We will focus on hacking, unauthorised modifications, unauthorised copying, computer viruses and denial of service attacks.

Hacking

Most people have heard stories of people using only a computer connected to the Internet and their skills to 'hack' their way into heavily guarded computer systems. The skill displayed by such individuals is often admired. Indeed, some hackers simply seek to illustrate, and bring attention to, the weakness of our interconnected society. Thus, it would be wrong to view all hacking as undesirable.

The problem is that it may be difficult to know in advance the intentions of a hacker. Hackers can cause substantial damage and loss to society. Therefore, hacking—the unauthorised entering into a data system—is a crime.

Once the security protecting a data system have been penetrated, the hacker can do a variety of things that, in themselves, are unlawful. For example the hacker can modify, copy, or delete data. The less malicious hacker may, however, choose simply to leave a message demonstrating that they did indeed manage to enter the system in question.

Unauthorised modification

Once hackers have gained access to data, they can do several things with it—one of which is to modify it. When we talk about modification in this part of the chapter, we refer to any form of alteration of the original data collection, including the deletion of data.

There are many reasons why somebody would want to modify the data in a particular collection. For example if one were to gain access to a bank's data system, one could delete one's mortgage and increase the amount held in one's account. In other words, modifications are sometimes made for commercial gain. However, there are many other reasons, such as a desire to cause problems for the operator of the data collection.

Naturally, unauthorised modification of data is unlawful.

Unauthorised copying

Just as with unauthorised modification, there is a wide range of reasons why somebody would wish to engage in unauthorised copying of data, such as industrial espionage and privacy invasions. There are also many instances where unauthorised copying of data has taken place, with the consequence that new songs and movies are made available online before they are supposed to be publicly available.

This clearly overlaps with piracy, and apart from being contrary to copyright laws, such copying may also constitute a criminal offence.

Computer viruses

There are many different forms of computer viruses, and more are created daily. A computer virus is software that attaches itself to a host file, and is able to spread with the host file or to other host files without the knowledge or permission of the hardware operator. The term virus is also used in a broad sense to mean all malicious or unwanted software that spreads onto hardware without the knowledge or permission of the user. Examples include worms, trojans, spyware and adware. While the modern term 'malware' is gaining acceptance in describing all malicious software, we continue to use virus in its broad sense because it is well-understood.

Before the widespread use of the Internet, viruses typically spread when a floppy disk or CD with an infected file was inserted into an uninfected computer. However, with more computers being connected through networks, viruses can now spread much more easily.

Some viruses are benign, and do nothing harmful. Others are intended to cause damage to the computers they infect—for example by deleting files or reformatting the hard disk. While benign viruses may be annoying, malicious viruses can be very costly. For example one of the most well-known viruses, the 'I Love You' virus, entailed a worldwide economic cost counted in billions of dollars.

Denial of service attacks

A denial of service attack (DoS attack) is an attempt to render a computer resource inaccessible. Typically, the instigator of the attack will seek to flood the computer resource with communications, making it impossible for the resource to communicate with its intended contacts. An analogy is useful to describe how this works.

Imagine a situation where all the students in a class speak at the same time. In such a situation, the lecturer has little chance to hear what any individual student is saying. Similarly, when a web server receives several authentication requests at once, it gets tied up trying to address those requests and is unable to receive any legitimate requests.

Several high-profile websites have been the victims of denial of service attacks, and sometimes threats of such attacks have been used for extortion purposes.

AUSTRALIAN LAW ON CYBERCRIME

Having identified the various forms of cybercrime, we can now examine how Australian law seeks to address these crimes. While many Australian laws, such as those relating to copyright, spam and trade practices may affect criminal behaviour, we will here focus on purely criminal law.

---

[7] *Criminal Code Act 1995* (Cth).

The regulatory framework is complicated by the fact that Australia is a federation. As a result, we find criminal law both at the Commonwealth level,[7] and at the state and territory level.[8] In examining Australian cybercrime law, we must take both into account. Having said that, the criminal law has been harmonised in several Australian jurisdictions. An important step towards such harmonisation was taken when the Standing Committee of Attorneys-General presented a National Model Criminal Code. This Model Code, which adopts a terminology consistent with that of the Council of Europe's *Convention on Cybercrime* (see below), contains provisions specifically aimed at cybercrime. It is now the foundation for the criminal laws in New South Wales, Victoria, South Australia, the Australian Capital Territory, and the Northern Territory, as well as for the Commonwealth legislation. In contrast, Queensland, Western Australia and Tasmania have yet to implement the Model Code.

Most importantly for our purposes, the Model Code led to the creation of the *Cybercrime Act 2001* (Cth), which replaced a part of the *Crimes Act 1914* (Cth) and inserted Part 10.7 of the *Criminal Code Act 1995* (Cth). As far as the approach taken in the Model Code is concerned, we will focus on the federal legislation.

Looking at the *Criminal Code Act 1995* (Cth), the two most relevant parts are Part 10.6, dealing with telecommunications services, and Part 10.7, dealing with computer offences. Other parts of the Act are also relevant, such as Part 7.3, dealing with fraudulent conduct. However, we will only focus on Parts 10.6 and 10.7.

The offences outlined in Part 10.6 are mainly traditional offences committed via telecommunications services. Thus for example Part 10.6 makes it an offence to do any of the following using telecommunications services:

o   Make an unlawful threat;[9]
o   Menace, harass or cause offence;[10]
o   Access, transmit, publish, possess, control, produce, supply or obtain child pornography,[11] or child abusive material;[12]
o   Procure, encourage, entice, recruit or induce a person under 16 years of age to engage in sexual activity;[13] or
o   Access, transmit, publish, possess, control, produce, supply or obtain suicide-related material.[14]

---

8   *Criminal Code Act 1899* (Qld) s 408D, *Crimes Act* 1900 (NSW) ss 308–308I, *Crimes Act* 1958 (Vic) ss 247A–247I, *Summary Offences Act 1953* (SA) ss 44–44A, *Criminal Code* (WA) s 440A, *Criminal Code Act 1924* (Tas) ss 257A–257F, *Criminal Code 2002* (ACT) ss 412–421, and *Criminal Code Act* (NT) ss 222, 276–276F.
9   *Criminal Code Act 1995* (Cth), Schedule, ss 474.15 and 474.16.
10   *Criminal Code Act 1995* (Cth), Schedule, s 474.17.
11   *Criminal Code Act 1995* (Cth), Schedule, ss 474.19 and 474.20.
12   *Criminal Code Act 1995* (Cth), Schedule, ss 474.22 and 474.23.
13   *Criminal Code Act 1995* (Cth), Schedule, ss 474.26 and 474.27.
14   *Criminal Code Act 1995* (Cth), Schedule, ss 474.29A and 474.29B.

Similarly to the *Broadcasting Services (Online Services) Act 1992* (Cth), Part 10.6 also places obligations on Internet service providers and Internet content hosts. For example s 474.25 states:

A person commits an offence if the person:

(a) is an Internet service provider or an Internet content host; and
(b) is aware that the service provided by the person can be used to access particular material that the person has reasonable grounds to believe is:
   (i) child pornography material; or
   (ii) child abuse material; and
(c) does not refer details of the material to the Australian Federal Police within a reasonable time after becoming aware of the existence of the material.

Part 10.7, dealing with computer offences, is the main regulation for the crimes described above as targeted at computers. A distinction is drawn between serious computer offences on the one hand and other computer offences on the other hand. A *serious offence* is 'an offence that is punishable by imprisonment for life or a period of 5 or more years'.[15]

The key part of s 477.1 reads as follows:

A person is guilty of an offence if:

(a) the person causes:
   (i) any unauthorised access to data held in a computer; or
   (ii) any unauthorised modification of data held in a computer; or
   (iii) any unauthorised impairment of electronic communication to or from a computer; and
(b) the unauthorised access, modification or impairment is caused by means of a carriage service; and
(c) the person knows the access, modification or impairment is unauthorised; and
(d) the person intends to commit, or facilitate the commission of, a serious offence against a law of the Commonwealth, a State or a Territory (whether by that person or another person) by the access, modification or impairment.

Interestingly, subsection 3 goes on to state that '[i]n a prosecution for an offence against subsection (1), it is not necessary to prove that the defendant knew that the offence was an offence against a law of the Commonwealth, a State or a Territory, or a serious offence'. Furthermore, subsection 7 states that '[a] person may be found guilty of an offence against this section even if committing the serious offence is impossible'.

In outlining other serious offences, s 477 mentions unauthorised modification of data to cause impairment,[16] and unauthorised impairment of electronic communication.[17]

The *other computer offences* are outlined in s 478 and include:

○   'Unauthorised access to, or modification of, restricted data';[18]

---

[15]   *Criminal Code Act 1995* (Cth), Schedule, s 477.1.
[16]   *Criminal Code Act 1995* (Cth), Schedule, s 477.2.
[17]   *Criminal Code Act 1995* (Cth), Schedule, s 477.3.
[18]   *Criminal Code Act 1995* (Cth), Schedule, s 478.1.

○   'Unauthorised impairment of data held on a computer disk etc.';[19]

○   'Possession or control of data with intent to commit a computer offence';[20] and

○   'Producing, supplying or obtaining data with intent to commit a computer offence'.[21]

Of the states not following the Model Code, we will focus on Queensland. However, the relevant law of Queensland bears strong similarities with that of Western Australia. In contrast, the law in Tasmania merely features provisions similar to the old *Crimes Act 1914* (Cth).

Computer offences are regulated in s 408E of the *Criminal Code Act 1899* (Qld). That provision outlines three different levels of offences:

(1) A person who uses a restricted computer without the consent of the computer's controller commits an offence. Maximum penalty—2 years imprisonment.

(2) If the person causes or intends to cause detriment or damage, or gains or intends to gain a benefit, the person commits a crime and is liable to imprisonment for 5 years.

(3) If the person causes a detriment or damage or obtains a benefit for any person to the value of more than $5000, or intends to commit an indictable offence, the person commits a crime and is liable to imprisonment for 10 years.

Further, subsection 4 makes clear that 'it is a defence to a charge under this section to prove that the use of the restricted computer was authorised, justified or excused by law'.

The application of s 408E is exemplified in the following case (in which the selection is referred to by its former number, s 408D).

CASE EXAMPLE *R V BODEN* (2002) QCA 164[22]

AUSTRALIA, SUPREME COURT OF QUEENSLAND—COURT OF APPEAL, 2002

This case involved a violation of *Criminal Code Act 1899* (Qld) s 408D. The applicant (Mr Vitek Boden, who was appealing his sentence handed down by the District Court) was a former employee of Hunter Watertech. While Mr Boden worked at Hunter Watertech he had been part of a team installing a computerised system controlling the Maroochy Shire Council's sewerage system.

He later sought employment with the Council but was refused. Following that refusal, Mr Boden repeatedly hacked into the sewerage computer system. On at least one occasion that intrusion caused severe environmental damage.

Mr Boden was caught possessing hardware belonging to Hunter Watertech as well as other hardware and software used for the hacking.

>>

---

19   *Criminal Code Act 1995* (Cth), Schedule, s 478.2.

20   *Criminal Code Act 1995* (Cth), Schedule, s 478.3.

21   *Criminal Code Act 1995* (Cth), Schedule, s 478.4.

22   Available at <www.austlii.edu.au/au/cases/qld/QCA/2002/164.html>.

>>   In the District Court of Maroochydore, Mr Boden was found guilty of violating the
Criminal Code Act 1899 (Qld) s 408D. The Court of Appeal largely upheld the District
Court's judgment and made the following observations:

> The appellant's conduct was engaged in over a period of some weeks. It was deliberate
> and the appellant, when engaging in it, misused confidential information and made
> use of stolen property. He must have been aware that his acts would cause the Council
> and his former employer considerable disruption, inconvenience and expense. The
> cost to the Council alone was many thousands of dollars. Indeed, it may be inferred
> that the conduct was calculated to cause disruption. As the trial judge pointed out,
> the appellant, being aware of the risk of sewerage spills, was prepared to take that risk
> to gain his own ends.
>
> It is implicit in the jury's verdicts that an intent to cause damage was established in
> each case. The sewerage spill was significant. It polluted over 500 metres of open drain
> in a residential area and flowed into a tidal canal. Cleaning up the spill and its effects
> took days and required the deployment of considerable resources. The appellant was
> ordered to pay $13 110.77 to the Council by way of compensation for the loss and
> damage cause to it by the spill. That is a relevant consideration.[23]

Like the *Criminal Code Act 1995* (Cth), the *Criminal Code Act 1899* (Qld) contains
other parts relevant to cybercrime. One example is Chapter 33A, dealing with stalking.
However, those parts will not be discussed here.

THE *CONVENTION ON CYBERCRIME*

At the international level, the most important instruments are without a doubt the
many bilateral and multilateral agreements in place between various states. However,
in addition to those geographically limited agreements, one major international
agreement has been concluded specifically to address cybercrime—the Council of
Europe's Cybercrime Treaty.

The Council of Europe is an international organisation founded in 1949, mainly
focused on human rights. In 2001, it drafted the *Convention on Cybercrime*, which
came into force in 2004. To date, the convention has been signed by 43 states and
ratified by 21 of them.

This international instrument is significant, though Australia has not become
a signatory. First, while the convention was drafted by the Council of Europe, non-
European states including the USA, Canada and Japan acted as observers in the drafting
process and the USA has now ratified the convention. Thus, it is not just a European
instrument. Second, while not free from criticism, the convention represents the
largest step taken so far towards international cooperation against the international
problem of cybercrime.

---

[23]   *R v Boden* [2002] QCA 164, paragraphs 53–54.

Looking at the convention in more detail, it has three main objectives:

1   It outlines a list of acts that member states must criminalise.
2   It outlines a list of powers for gathering of evidence that member states must afford to its law enforcement authorities.
3   It outlines a range of rules aimed at increasing the level, and efficiency, of international cooperation against cybercrime.

Article 2 of the convention deals with hacking and reads as follows:

> Each Party shall adopt such legislative and other measures as may be necessary to establish as criminal offences under its domestic law, when committed intentionally, the access to the whole or any part of a computer system without right. A Party may require that the offence be committed by infringing security measures, with the intent of obtaining computer data or other dishonest intent, or in relation to a computer system that is connected to another computer system.

Similar provisions regulate:

o   'the interception without right, made by technical means, of non-public transmissions of computer data to, from or within a computer system, including electromagnetic emissions from a computer system carrying such computer data';[24]

o   'the damaging, deletion, deterioration, alteration or suppression of computer data without right';[25]

o   'the serious hindering without right of the functioning of a computer system by inputting, transmitting, damaging, deleting, deteriorating, altering or suppressing computer data';[26]

o   'the input, alteration, deletion, or suppression of computer data, resulting in inauthentic data with the intent that it be considered or acted upon for legal purposes as if it were authentic, regardless whether or not the data is directly readable and intelligible';[27]

o   'the causing of a loss of property to another person by: (a) any input, alteration, deletion or suppression of computer data, (b) any interference with the functioning of a computer system, with fraudulent or dishonest intent of procuring, without right, an economic benefit for oneself or for another person';[28]

o   'the production for distribution, offering or making available, distribution or transmission, procurement, or possession of child pornography'[29]; and

o   certain copyright-related actions.[30]

---

[24]   Council of Europe, *Convention on Cybercrime* (Budapest, 23.XI.2001), article 3.
[25]   Council of Europe, *Convention on Cybercrime* (Budapest, 23.XI.2001), article 4.
[26]   Council of Europe,*Convention on Cybercrime* (Budapest, 23.XI.2001), article 5.
[27]   Council of Europe, *Convention on Cybercrime* (Budapest, 23.XI.2001), article 7.
[28]   Council of Europe, *Convention on Cybercrime* (Budapest, 23.XI.2001), article 8.
[29]   Council of Europe, *Convention on Cybercrime* (Budapest, 23.XI.2001), article 9.
[30]   Council of Europe, *Convention on Cybercrime* (Budapest, 23.XI.2001), article 10.

Article 11 regulates attempts made at committing any of the offences listed above, as well as the aiding and abetting of such offences. Further, article 6 provides rules regarding 'the production, sale, procurement for use, import, distribution or otherwise making available of'[31] a wide range of technical tools and devices used for committing the mentioned offences.

The articles dealing with powers for gathering evidence that member states must afford to their law enforcement authorities include things such as the interception, search, seizure and preservation of various types of computer data.

The measures of cooperation prescribed in the convention include things such as mutual assistance and extradition.

In 2003 the Council of Europe presented the *Additional Protocol to the Convention on Cybercrime, Concerning the Criminalisation of Acts of a Racist and Xenophobic Nature Committed Through Computer Systems*. The aim of this Additional Protocol is to treat certain acts of a racist and xenophobic nature in the same manner as the crimes listed in the Convention on Cybercrime. So far thirty-one states have signed the Additional Protocol, which came into force in 2006. However, to date, only eleven of the signatories have ratified it.

CONCLUDING REMARKS AND FURTHER READING

This chapter has illustrated how criminal activities have found a new home in cyberspace, giving rise to what we refer to as cybercrime. It has been made clear that many types of cybercrime are merely electronic versions of criminal activities that have taken place offline for many years. However, other types of cybercrime are unique to the Internet context.

On the topic of criminal law, the Internet and e-commerce, we recommend the following further reading:

AusCERT Computer Crime and Security Survey <www.auscert.org.au>

Australian High Tech Crime Centre <www.ahtcc.gov.au>

Australian Institute of Criminology <www.aic.gov.au>

Computer Crime Research Center <www.crime-research.org>

Cybercrime Law <www.cybercrimelaw.net>

Yee Fen Lim, *Cyberspace Law: Commentaries and Materials,* 2nd edn, Oxford University Press, Melbourne, 2007

Greg Taylor, 'The Council of Europe Cybercrime Convention: A Civil Liberties Perspective' (2001) PLPR 35

United States Department of Justice, Computer Crime and Intellectual Property Section (CCIPS) <www.cybercrime.gov>

Review questions for this chapter can be found on the book's Online Resource Centre at www.oup.com.au/orc/fordersvantesson.

---

[31] Council of Europe, *Convention on Cybercrime* (Budapest, 23.XI.2001), article 6(1)(a).

GLOSSARY

ACCC
Australian Competition and Consumer Commission, responsible for administering the *Trade Practices Act 1974* (Cth).

ACMA
Australian Communications and Media Authority, the Federal Government regulator of broadcasting and the Internet. It superseded the Australian Broadcasting Authority (ABA).

Acceptance
The final, unqualified agreement with the terms of an offer that completes the formation of a contract.

Access prevention notice
Notice to an ISP under the *Broadcasting Services Act 1992* (Cth) or the *Interactive Gambling Act 2001* (Cth) directing the ISP to take reasonable steps to prevent end users from accessing the specified content.

Admissible evidence
Evidence that is admissible in court—it is required to be relevant, not overly prejudicial, and reliable.

Algorithm
A list of steps or instructions for accomplishing a task.

Anonymiser
An application designed to allow web users to visit websites anonymously, disguising their IP addresses.

Arbitration
An out-of-court process by which the parties to a dispute submit their differences to the judgment of an impartial person or group appointed by mutual consent or statutory provision.

ARPANET
Advanced Research Projects Agency Network (see also *DARPA*). In 1969 DARPA launched the wide-area network from which the Internet evolved.

Authentication
A process by which you verify whether someone or something is genuine or valid.

Authorised deposit-taking institution (ADI)
A financial institution that is authorised to conduct banking business under the *Banking Act 1959* (Cth).

Automated teller machine (ATM)
A networked terminal that enables cash withdrawals from an account with a financial institution; it may also provide account-related information or permit funds to be transferred between accounts.

Bait advertising
An appealing but insincere advertisement for a product or service where the main purpose is not to sell at the advertised price, but to lure consumers so there is an opportunity to sell a different or more expensive product.

Banking business	Defined under the *Banking Act 1959* (Cth) to involve both the taking of money on deposit and the making of advances.
Biometrics	The use of unique personal characteristics (such as fingerprints) to identify a person or authenticate their identity.
Bit tax	A tax on every binary digit of information transmitted across the Internet.
Breach	A contravention of a legal duty, often one contained in a statute, contract or other legal document.
Browsewrap	A method of attempting to incorporate terms into an online contract which relies on the customer voluntarily following a link and reading the terms. See also *clickwrap*; *shrinkwrap*.
Burden of proof	A party bears the burden of proof in a court case if it is their responsibility to adduce sufficient evidence to prove the fact alleged.
Carriage service provider (CSP)	An entity that uses a *carrier's* facilities to supply telecommunications services to the public. An *Internet service provider* (ISP) is a type of CSP.
Carrier	An entity (like Telstra) that owns telecommunications facilities, and uses them to supply telecommunications services to other entities or the public. Carriers must be licensed by the Australian Communications and Media Authority (ACMA).
Case law	The body of law made by judges whose decisions are, according to the doctrine of precedent, binding on other courts.
Cause of action	The legal ground on which a claim is based when going to court.
Certification authority	In cryptography, a trusted third party who issues a digital certificate that attests to the authenticity of a public key, thus validating the person, organisation, or server noted in the certificate.
Cheque	An unconditional order in writing addressed by a person to a financial institution, signed by the person giving it, requiring the institution to pay a sum of money on demand.
Civil action	Litigation brought by one or more parties protecting their own interests (as opposed to a criminal action, in which someone is prosecuted on behalf of the state).

Civil law	In the context of court cases, the law that applies when one party sues others for damages or other redress (as compared with criminal law); in the context of a legal system, refers to a system based primarily on the interpretation of statutory codes (like the legal systems of much of Europe) as opposed to systems based on the doctrine of precedent (like the English common law system).
Clearing organisation	An organisation that gathers payment instructions from collecting banks, and transmits them to paying banks, seeking confirmation that the payment instruction will be honoured.
Clickwrap	A method of incorporating terms into an online contract which requires the customer to indicate their assent by clicking on a button or other object before the agreement can be concluded. See also *shrinkwrap*; *browsewrap*.
Common law	When compared with statute law, refers to judge-made law; when used in the context of a legal system, refers to a system strongly based on the doctrine of precedent (like the English system), as opposed to systems based on the interpretation of statutory codes (like the civil law systems of Europe).
Computer virus	Used in a broad sense to mean all malicious or unwanted software that spreads onto hardware without the knowledge or permission of the user.
Conflict of laws	Also known as 'private international law', the area of law concerned with jurisdiction, choice of law, declining jurisdiction, and recognition and enforcement of foreign judgments.
Consideration	The giving of (or the promise to give) something of legal value in return for a promise, which is a requirement for a valid contract in most common law systems.
Consumer	For the purposes of the *Trade Practices Act* in Commonwealth law and Fair Trading legislation in state law, someone who purchases goods or services for personal, domestic or household use, or costing less than $40 000.
Consumer protection	The law that protects the interests of consumers, notably the *Trade Practices Act 1974* (Cth) and similar state legislation such as the various Fair Trading Acts.
Contravention	See *Breach*.
Convention	See *Treaty*.

Co-regulation	Regulation of a particular industry through a combination of direct legislative rules and self-regulation through an industry code.
Country code top level domain (ccTLD)	See *Top level domain (TLD)*.
Criminal action	A court case brought on behalf of the state to determine guilt and punish someone for wrongful conduct (as opposed to a civil action).
Criminal law	The branch of law that relates to wrongful actions that are prosecuted and punished by the state.
Cryptography	The study of methods of keeping information secret by transforming the information into something unintelligible except to a person who knows the secret method of decoding it.
Cybercrime	Crimes facilitated or aided by computing devices or the Internet, or committed where a computer or network is a target.
Cybersquatting	Registering a domain name without intending to use it in the long term, but with the intention of making a profit, for example, by selling it to someone who already has an interest in using that name but who failed to register it themselves.
DARPA	Defense Advanced Research Projects Agency (originally ARPA, renamed twice, now DARPA again), a research body set up by the US Department of Defense in 1957. See also *ARPANET*.
Database	A structured collection of records or data, stored in a way that makes it easy to access the information.
DCITA	The Federal Government's Department of Communications, Information Technology and the Arts.
Defamation	A cause of action in torts law, which involves publication of material that unfairly impugns the reputation of another.
Denial of service (DoS) attack	An attempt to make a computer resource unavailable to intended users by flooding the system with superfluous requests.
Digital cash	Digital data representing value that can be transferred as the equivalent of money.

Digital signature	Narrow meaning: a digital method of authenticating a person using public key cryptography. Broad meaning: a digital method of authenticating a person who creates a document or sends a message. See also *electronic signature*.
Direct entry payments	A payment system enabling the transfer of funds by entering the transaction directly in the accounts of the paying and receiving institutions so that it has immediate effect. A direct credit is where the paying party initiates the transaction; a direct debit is where the receiving party initiates the transaction.
Directive of the European Union (EU)	A legislative instrument of the European Parliament that compels member states to enact legislation of similar effect.
Domain name	A unique name corresponding to one or more IP addresses, used as an Internet address (for example www.svantesson.org).
Domicile	The place of a person's permanent residence for legal purposes.
Double actionability test	A two-stage test used in determining the choice of law question in tort actions in some common law jurisdictions. First, the wrong alleged must be actionable if it were to be committed within Australia. Second, the act must not have been justifiable by the law of the place where it was done.
Dual criminality	A requirement for extradition—the act in question must be criminal in both the country seeking extradition and the country from which the alleged criminal is to be extradited.
Duty of confidentiality	A duty to keep ideas and other valuable commercial information secret in certain circumstances. Breach of the duty may give rise to a civil action in the law of tort.
Electronic banking	Electronic provision of banking products and services, including use of electronic terminals, the Internet, telephone and wireless networks.
Electronic funds transfer (EFT)	A transfer of funds effected through a computerised banking system.
Electronic funds transfer at point of sale (EFTPOS)	Electronic transfer of funds effected by using a plastic card at a card-reader terminal typically located in the merchant's premises.
Electronic purse	See *stored value card*.

Electronic rights management information (ERMI)	Electronic information attached to copyright material disclosing the name of the copyright owner and the terms under which the material can be used.
Electronic signature	A method of electronically authenticating the identity of a person who sends a message.
Encryption	The process of transforming information into something unintelligible except to a person who knows the secret method of decoding (decrypting) it.
European Union	An international organisation of European countries formed in 1993 to reduce trade barriers and increase cooperation among its members.
Evidentiary burden	See *Burden of proof*.
Forum non conveniens	Literally, an 'inconvenient forum'. Refers to the discretionary power courts have to decline the exercise of jurisdiction in a particular matter.
Gambling	Staking money on uncertain or chance events or on a combination of skill and chance.
Gaming and wagering	The *Interactive Gambling Act 2001* (Cth) distinguishes between two forms of gambling: gaming (casinos, gaming machines, keno, lotteries) and wagering (betting on races and sporting events).
Generic top level domain (gTLD)	See *Top level domain (TLD)*.
Geo-identification	The ascertaining of the geographical location of Internet users.
Goods and services tax (GST)	A value-added tax of 10% on most goods and services sold in Australia.
HTML	Hyper Text Markup Language. HTML is the authoring language most commonly used to create Web documents.
Hyperlink	An electronic reference to another document or web page that can be activated by clicking on it with a pointing device such as a mouse.
IANA	Internet Assigned Numbers Authority, the first body established to allocate IP numbers to registrants on the Internet.

ICANN	Internet Corporation for Assigned Names and Numbers. An international, non-profit organisation established in 1998 to organise the domain name and IP number systems (including the accreditation of domain name registrars).
Identity theft	Fraudulent use of another person's personal information to take on their identity.
Immovable property	Legal term referring to land and/or any permanent feature or structure above or below the surface.
Imposed terms	Certain conditions and warranties imposed on contracts by the law.
Income tax	A personal tax levied on annual income.
Infringer	In the context of intellectual property (IP), a person who makes unauthorised use of copyright, a patent, trade mark or other IP right.
Injunction	A court order whereby a party is required to do, or to refrain from doing, an act.
Intangibles	Rights that have legal value but are not necessarily related to a physical object; examples include a debt owed, copyright in computer software, and the supply of services rather than goods.
Intellectual property rights	A collective term used to describe a number of concepts involving rights closely connected with information, ideas, or other intangibles. Examples include copyright, patents, and trade marks.
Internet	A global network of interconnected computer systems using the suite of protocols known as TCP/IP.
Internet banking	A type of electronic banking in which access to products and services is provided via the Internet.
Internet content	Information kept on a data storage device and accessed using an Internet carriage service.
Internet content host (ICH)	An entity that stores Internet content so that it is accessible by others.
Internet Protocol (IP)	The protocol that ensures that packets of data arrive at the correct network destination.
IP number	The address used by the Internet protocol to identify a computer or other network destination.

Internet service provider (ISP)	An entity that uses a *carrier's* telecommunications facilities, usually in combination with their own servers and other equipment, to provide access to the Internet. See also *Carriage service provider (CSP)*.
Jurisdiction	1. The power granted to a formally constituted legal body to administer justice within a defined area of responsibility; 2. A geographical area within which certain laws operate (for example a country).
Jurisdictional borders	Geographical or other limits, outside of which the court or other entity holds no power.
ISOC	The Internet Society, formed in 1992 by Internet experts and enthusiasts to oversee administration of the Internet.
Key	In cryptography, a secret method used to protect data.
Law of confidentiality	The law relating to breaches of confidentiality having regard to the nature of the sensitive information and any subsequent communication of that information.
Lex loci delicti	Literally, 'the law of the place where the delict [tort] was committed'; a rule used in Australian courts to determine the applicable law in tort cases.
Message integrity	The status of a message that can be proved not to have been altered during transmission.
Micropayments	Payments involving fractions of the normal units of value, such as ½ cent—useful in e-commerce, for example to pay per page viewed in a document.
Misleading or deceptive conduct	Any conduct in trade or commerce which misleads or deceives or is likely to do so.
Misrepresentation	A false statement of fact; to be actionable in tort law, it must be made intentionally or negligently and must induce a person to act on it to their detriment.
Model code	A 'best practice' model typically suggested by an international organisation, aimed at harmonising and reforming an area of law.
Negligence	A cause of action in *torts* law where one party who owes a 'duty of care' to another breaches that duty by failing to meet the standard of care expected of a reasonable person, resulting in material damage.

Negotiable instrument	A written and signed document that entitles the holder to receive a payment, and which can be transferred in such a way as to give the new holder an unconditional right to payment, even if the transferor did not have such a right. Examples include cheques and promissory notes.
Network money	See *digital cash*.
NSFNET	A network established in 1986 by the US National Science Foundation (NSF) that replaced ARPANET as the foundation of the Internet.
NSI	Network Solutions Inc, a private organisation originally licensed by the US Department of Commerce to administer the .com, .org and .net generic top level domain names. This function was eventually handed over to ICANN, and NSI now operates as a registrar of domain names.
Nuisance	A cause of action in torts law that involves unlawful interference with an owner's or occupier's use or enjoyment of land.
Object code	A set of machine-readable instructions usually generated by compiling or assembling source code.
Offer	The stated contractual terms on which the offeror promises to be bound if the other party (the offeree) accepts them. See also *Acceptance*.
Online wagering	Use of the Internet or other similar service to bet on sporting events or races—a permitted form of gambling under the *Interactive Gambling Act 2001* (Cth). See also *Gaming and wagering*.
Organisation for Economic Co-operation and Development (OECD)	An organisation formed by 30 economically developed nations, which meet regularly to agree on policies for economic cooperation and development.
Packet switching	A communication system that divides messages into packets of data and sends each packet separately, to be reassembled at their destination.
Passing off	A cause of action in torts law that involves misrepresenting goods or services as being those of another, or holding out goods or services as having some association or connection with another.

Patent	A form of monopoly granted by legislation that gives the owner of the patent the exclusive right to exploit a device, substance, method or process which is new, inventive and useful.
Permanent establishment	A fixed place from which a business is wholly or partially conducted, making its profits taxable in that place.
Personal Identification Number (PIN)	An alphanumeric string of digits used to identify an individual.
Piracy	In the Internet context, the unlawful copying or distributing of copyright protected material.
Private international law	Also known as 'conflict of laws', the area of law concerned with jurisdiction, choice of law, declining jurisdiction and recognition and enforcement of foreign judgments.
Procedural law	Law that tells you how to enforce your rights (as opposed to substantive law, which tells you what your rights and duties are).
Prohibited content	In the context of Internet pornography, the *Broadcasting Services Act 1992* (Cth) prohibits content that is classified as RC, X, or if it is hosted in Australia without a restricted access system, R.
Protocol	A standard or agreed way of doing something.
Pseudocode	A high-level description of a computer program. The description generally uses natural language explanations (e.g. English) of the steps to be taken but does not contain actual program code.
Public key (asymmetric) system	A cryptographic system in which two different but related keys are used to encrypt and decrypt a message. One key is made public, the other is kept private, and the private key cannot easily be derived from the public key. See also *Single key (secret key or symmetric) system*.
***Quia timet* action**	A type of injunction to restrain wrongful acts which are threatened or imminent but have not yet commenced.
Root server system management	An important function carried out by the Internet governing body, ICANN, to update and maintain the primary Domain Name Servers, which are essential to the Internet's lookup functionality.
Safe words	A list of ordinary words, injected by spammers into e-mails, meant to trick spam filters into identifying the message as legitimate.

Shrinkwrap	Where contractual terms are sealed inside the packaging of a product, so they are unavailable before the product is purchased. See also *clickwrap*; *browsewrap*.
Single key (secret key or symmetric) system	A cryptographic system in which the same key, known to both sender and receiver, is used to encrypt and decrypt a message. See also *Public key (asymmetric) system*.
Situs	The place where an event happened or where property is located, which can be reasons for a court to exercise jurisdiction.
Source code	A set of computer instructions expressed in a high-level programming language, which can be read and amended by humans. See also *Object code*.
Spam	Unsolicited e-mail, often sent in bulk.
Standard of proof	The degree of evidence which a party must present in a trial in order to succeed.
Statute	A law passed by Parliament, also known as an Act of Parliament or legislation.
Stored value card (SVC)	A card that permits the electronic storage and use of prepaid value; also known as an electronic purse or wallet.
Substantive law	Law that tells you what your rights and duties are, as opposed to procedural law, which tells you how to enforce these rights.
Sui generis	Literally 'of its own kind', a term used to indicate a legal classification that, because of its uniqueness, should be seen to exist independently of other categorisations.
Take-down notice	Notice to an Internet content host (ICH) directing it not to host the specified content.
Tax havens	Countries that offer very low tax rates.
TCP/IP protocol	Technically a suite of protocols that implement a packet switched network and have become the standard for data transmissions over the Internet. The main protocols are the Transmission Control Protocol (TCP) and the Internet Protocol (IP).
Top level domain (TLD)	The last or right-most part of a domain name. It may be a country code top level domain (ccTLD), arranged by a two-letter country code, such as .au; or a generic top level domain (gTLD) arranged by type of organisation, such as .com or .edu.

Torts	A collective name used to describe civil actions that provide remedies where wrongful conduct causes harm. Common tortious causes of action include *negligence, nuisance,* and *defamation*.
Trade mark	A sign or mark used to distinguish one's goods or services from those of another, usually registered under the *Trade Marks Act 1995* (Cth), although the laws of passing off and the *Trade Practices Act 1974* (Cth) may provide some protection for the use of an unregistered mark.
Transfer pricing	The practice of reducing the overall tax placed on a company group by strategically distributing profits and deductions among the members of the group.
Transactional anonymity	Where the purchaser of goods or services remains unidentified and anonymous.
Treaty	An agreement formed under international law by states and/or international organisations.
Trespass to chattels	A cause of action in torts law that involves intentional or negligent interference with another person's possession of movable property (chattels).
Trespass to land	A cause of action in torts law that involves unlawful interference with land which is in the possession of another.
UNCITRAL	The United Nations Commission on International Trade Law.
Unconscionable conduct	Unfair or unreasonable conduct in business transactions that goes against good conscience.
URL	A uniform resource locator identifies an Internet resource and provides a method of locating it; often also used in the sense of a web address.
Value-added tax (VAT)	A tax levied on the difference between a commodity's price before taxes and its cost of production.
Web crawler	An automated computer program which navigates the Internet indexing its content, usually for search engines. Also known as web spiders or robots.
White list words	See *Safe words*
Withholding tax	A tax that is paid directly to the taxation authorities by a third party on behalf of a taxpayer. The best example is the PAYG system in which employers deduct tax from an employee's wages and pay it directly to the tax office.

Works and secondary works

In the context of copyright law, original literary, dramatic, musical and artistic creations are known collectively as works; sound recordings, films, television and sound broadcasts, and published editions of works are also protected—we refer to these as 'secondary works'.

World Intellectual Property Organization (WIPO)

A specialised agency of the United Nations with headquarters in Geneva, established in 1967 to promote the protection of intellectual property throughout the world.

World Wide Web

A system of making documents and other multimedia resources available to others over the Internet, based on a protocol that supports clickable links between the documents.

INDEX